Merleau-Ponty

Key Concepts

Key Concepts

Published

Theodore Adorno: Key Concepts
Edited by Deborah Cook

Gilles Deleuze: Key Concepts
Edited by Charles J. Stivale

Merleau-Ponty: Key Concepts
Edited by Rosalyn Diprose and
Jack Reynolds

Forthcoming

Pierre Bourdieu: Key Concepts
Edited by Michael Grenfell

Michel Foucault: Key Concepts
Edited by Dianna Taylor

Martin Heidegger: Key Concepts
Edited by Bret Davis

Wittgenstein: Key Concepts
Edited by Kelly Dean Jolley

Merleau-Ponty

Key Concepts

Edited by
Rosalyn Diprose and Jack Reynolds

ACUMEN

First published in 2008 by Acumen

Acumen Publishing Limited
Stocksfield Hall
Stocksfield
NE43 7TN
www.acumenpublishing.co.uk

ISBN: 978-1-84465-115-3 (hardcover)
ISBN: 978-1-84465-116-0 (paperback)

British Library Cataloguing-in-Publication Data
A catalogue record for this book is available
from the British Library.

Typeset by Graphicraft Limited, Hong Kong
Printed and bound by Biddles Limited, King's Lynn

Contents

Contributors

Rosalyn Diprose is Associate Professor of Philosophy at the University of New South Wales. She is the author of *Corporeal Generosity: On Giving with Nietzsche, Merleau-Ponty, and Levinas* (2002), *The Bodies of Women: Ethics, Embodiment and Sexual Difference* (1994), many chapters and journal articles, and co-editor of *Cartographies: Poststructuralism and the Mapping of Bodies and Spaces* (1991).

Jack Reynolds is Lecturer in Philosophy at La Trobe University. He is the author of *Merleau-Ponty and Derrida: Intertwining Embodiment and Alterity* (2004), *Understanding Existentialism* (Acumen, 2005), and multiple journal articles on the relation between Merleau-Ponty and philosophers including Levinas, Derrida and Deleuze.

Harry Adams is Assistant Professor of Philosophy at Prairie View A & M University. He is a moral and political philosopher and an emerging Merleau-Ponty scholar whose publications include "Merleau-Ponty and the Advent of Meaning: From Consummate Reciprocity to Ambiguous Reversibility", in *Continental Philosophy Review* (2001).

Thomas Busch is Professor of Philosophy at Villanova University. He is a leading scholar in Merleau-Ponty studies and existentialism. His books include: *Circulating Being: From Embodiment to Incorporation* (1999), *The Power of Consciousness and the Force of Circumstances in Sartre's Philosophy* (1990), and *Merleau-Ponty, Hermeneutics and Postmodernism* (co-editor, 1992).

Taylor Carman is Professor of Philosophy at Barnard College, Columbia University. He has published numerous articles on topics in phenomenology, including Merleau-Ponty's philosophy. He is author of *Heidegger's Analytic: Interpretation, Discourse, and Authenticity in "Being And Time"* (2003), *Merleau-Ponty* (2008) and co-editor of *The Cambridge Companion to Merleau-Ponty* (2004).

Suzanne L. Cataldi is Professor of Philosophy at Southern Illinois University. She has published numerous papers utilizing Merleau-Ponty's philosophy and is well known for her detailed study of emotion and affectivity in *Emotion, Depth, and Flesh: A Study of Sensitive Space: Reflections on Merleau-Ponty's Philosophy of Embodiment* (1993). She is also co-editor of *Merleau-Ponty and Environmental Philosophy* (2007).

David R. Cerbone is Associate Professor of Philosophy at West Virginia University. He is the author of *Understanding Phenomenology* (Acumen, 2006) and multiple journal articles on Heidegger, Merleau-Ponty, perception, and Daniel Dennett.

Scott Churchill is Professor of Psychology at the University of Dallas. He is the author of numerous articles on phenomenology, gestural communication, sexuality and second-person perspectivity, often drawing on the philosophy of Merleau-Ponty. He is editor of *The Humanistic Psychologist* and studies interspecies communications with bonobos at the Fort Worth Zoo.

Diana Coole is Professor of Political and Social Theory at Birkbeck College, University of London. She has extensive publications in the fields of modern political and social theory and continental political philosophy, which include several essays on Merleau-Ponty's political philosophy. Her books include *Negativity and Politics: Dionysus and Dialectics from Kant to Poststructuralism* (2000) and *Merleau-Ponty and Modern Politics after Anti-Humanism* (2007).

Nick Crossley is Professor of Sociology at the University of Manchester. He has been at the forefront of bringing Merleau-Ponty's philosophy to bear on sociology and critical social theory. His books include: *The Social Body: Habit, Identity and Desire* (2001), which draws on the work of Gilbert Ryle and Merleau-Ponty, *Intersubjectivity: The Fabric of Social Becoming* (1996), *The Politics of Subjectivity: Between Foucault and Merleau-Ponty* (1994) and *Reflexions in the Flesh: The Body in Late Modernity* (forthcoming).

Fred Evans is Professor of Philosophy at Duquesne University. He has numerous publications on Merleau-Ponty's philosophy, which are unique in the way they intersect with philosophy of psychology, language and technology. He has chapters on Merleau-Ponty in his books, *Psychology and Nihilism: A Genealogical Critique of the Computational Model of Mind* (1993) and *The Multi-Voiced Body: Society, Communication, and the Age of Diversity* (forthcoming), and is co-editor of *Chiasms: Merleau-Ponty's Notion of Flesh* (2000).

Shaun Gallagher is Professor of Philosophy at the University of Central Florida and Research Professor of Philosophy and Cognitive Science at the University of Hertfordshire. He has led the way in bringing Merleau-Ponty's concepts to philosophy of mind, psychology and cognitive neuroscience. His most recent book, *How the Body Shapes the Mind* (2005), is a detailed study of this topic. He is also author of *The Inordinance of Time* (1998), co-author of *The Phenomenological Mind* (forthcoming) and co-editor of *Ipseity and Alterity: Interdisciplinary Approaches to Intersubjectivity* (2004), and *Merleau-Ponty, Hermeneutics, and Postmodernism* (1992).

Sonia Kruks is Danforth Professor of Politcs at Oberlin College. She is a leading scholar in twentieth-century European political thought and contemporary feminist political theory. Her engagement with Merleau-Ponty's philosophy includes the following books: *Retrieving Experience: Subjectivity and Recognition in Feminist Politics* (2001), which draws on de Beauvoir, Fanon, Merleau-Ponty and Sartre, *The Political Philosophy of Merleau-Ponty* (1981), and *Situation and Human Existence: Freedom, Subjectivity, and Society* (1990).

David Morris is Associate Professor of Philosophy at Concordia University, Montreal. He has published important research on notions of embodiment in phenomenology and existentialism. Alongside several published papers on Merleau-Ponty, he is author of *The Sense of Space* (2004), a study of Merleau-Ponty and Bergson's ideas of embodiment.

Ann Murphy is Assistant Professor of Philosophy at Fordham University. She is currently writing a book on violence, vulnerability and embodiment. Her publications on Merleau-Ponty include articles in *Feminist Interpretations of Merleau-Ponty* (2006) and in *Chiasmi*.

Philipa Rothfield is Senior Lecturer in Philosophy at La Trobe University. She specializes in contemporary European philosophy, philosophy of the body, and the work of Merleau-Ponty, having published papers applying his work to bioethics and the philosophy of dance in *Ethics of the Body* (2005) and *Topoi* (2005).

Michael Sanders is Assistant Professor of Philosophy at Cazenovia College. He is the author of several articles on Merleau-Ponty's philosophy, including a key essay comparing Merleau-Ponty with Levinas on the issue of alterity and intersubjectivity in *Philosophy Today* (2000).

Hugh J. Silverman is Professor of Philosophy and Comparative Literary and Cultural Studies at Stony Brook University. He has translated Merleau-Ponty's *Consciousness and the Acquisition of Language* (1973), co-edited *Texts and Dialogues* (1992), and written two monographs that substantially engage with Merleau-Ponty's work: *Inscriptions* (1987) and *Textualities* (1994).

Beata Stawarska is Assistant Professor of Philosophy at the University of Oregon. She has published numerous essays engaging with Merleau-Ponty's thought, often in relation to developmental psychology and psychoanalysis, including articles in *Philosophy Today, Continental Philosophy Review, Chiasmi* and *Journal of the British Society of Phenomenology*, and chapters in *Feminist Interpretations of Merleau-Ponty* (2006), *Ipseity and Alterity: Interdisciplinary Approaches to Intersubjectivity* (2004) and *Merleau-Ponty: Critical Assessments* (2007).

Ted Toadvine is Assistant Professor of Philosophy and Environmental Studies at the University of Oregon. He has published numerous articles on Merleau-Ponty's relation to phenomenology and on the applicability of his concepts to environmental studies. He is co-editor of *The Merleau-Ponty Reader* (2007), *Merleau-Ponty's Reading of Husserl* (2002), and editor of *Merleau-Ponty: Critical Assessments* (2007).

Gail Weiss is Professor of Philosophy and Human Sciences at George Washington University. She has published widely on philosophy of the body and the work of Merleau-Ponty. She is the author *of Body Images: Embodiment as Intercorporeality* (1999), and co-editor of *Thinking the Limits of the Body* (2003), *Perspectives on Embodiment* (1999) and *Feminist Interpretations of Maurice Merleau-Ponty* (2006). She is editor of *Intertwinings: Interdisciplinary Conversations with Merleau-Ponty* (forthcoming) and has completed a new book, *Refiguring the Ordinary* (forthcoming).

Acknowledgements

The editors would like to thank the contributors for their timely and important reflections on Merleau-Ponty's work, as well as Tristan Palmer, Steven Gerrard and the entire editorial team at Acumen, including Sue Hadden, Elizabeth Teague and the helpful reviewers of the manuscript. In addition, we are grateful to Jacqueline Hamrit and Marion Tapper for providing some obscure information pertaining to Merleau-Ponty's life, David Morris for thorough advice, Joanne Shiells for her fine efforts in subediting and standardizing the manuscript, and to Anne Gearside for her assistance with the initial literature review.

Translations and abbreviations

Reference throughout is made to English translations of Merleau-Ponty's work. The publication details of the English editions are listed below, as are the details of the original French publications, together with the abbreviations that we employ throughout the book.

In some cases the same translated work has been published in more than one form, with a change in pagination between the different editions. This applies in particular to *Phenomenology of Perception*, where the 2002 edition has different page numbers to the 1962 edition, even though the translation is the same. To avoid any confusion we refer to the page numbers of the 1962 edition as there are more copies of that in circulation. Readers who have access only to the 2002 edition can work out the equivalent page numbers by using a helpful conversion program available on-line at David Morris's website at Concordia University, which also allows one to find the corresponding pagination for the French paperback edition. There is a link to this program at: http://www.iep.utm.edu/m/merleau.htm.

Likewise, the same translation of *Themes from the Lectures at the Collège de France* (TL) is also published as *In Praise of Philosophy and Other Essays*, comprising the "Other Essays" in that volume (EP). Both books are cited in *Merleau-Ponty: Key Concepts*. Finally, the two essays referred to in this book as "Indirect Language and the Voices of Silence" (in *Signs*) and "Eye and Mind" (in *The Primacy of Perception*) are also available, in a different translation, in *The Merleau-Ponty Aesthetics Reader* edited by Galen Johnson, as well as in *The Merleau-Ponty Reader* edited by Len Lawlor and Ted Toadvine.

AD   *Adventures of the Dialectic*, Joseph Bien (trans.). Evanston, IL: Northwestern University Press, 1973 (*Les Aventures de la dialectique*. Paris: Gallimard, 1955).

CAL *Consciousness and the Acquisition of Language*, Hugh J. Silverman (trans.). Evanston, IL: Northwestern University Press, 1973 ("La Conscience et l'acquisition du langage". In *Merleau-Ponty à la Sorbonne: Résumés de ses cours établi par des étudiants et approuvé par lui-même*. Special issue of *Bulletin de Psychologie*, n. 236, tome 18 (November 1964, 226–59).

EP   *In Praise of Philosophy and Other Essays*, J. Wild & J. M. Edie (trans.). Evanston, IL: Northwestern University Press, 1988 (*Éloge de la Philosophie*. Paris: Gallimard, 1953 and *Résumés de cours, Collège de France 1952–1960*. Paris: Gallimard, 1968).

HT   *Humanism and Terror*, John O'Neill (trans.). Boston, MA: Beacon Press, 1969 (*Humanisme et terreur, essai sur le problème communiste*. Paris: Gallimard, 1947).

N   *Nature: Course Notes from the Collège de France*, Robert Vallier (trans.). Evanston, IL: Northwestern University Press, 2003 (*La Nature, Notes, Cours du Collège de France*, Dominique Séglard (ed.). Paris: Seuil, 1995).

PhF   "Phenomenology and Psychoanalysis: Preface to Hesnard's *L'Oeuvre de Freud*", A. Fisher (trans.). In *Merleau-Ponty and Psychology*, K. Hoeller (ed.). Atlantic Highlands, NJ: Humanities Press, 1993.

PP   *Phenomenology of Perception*, Colin Smith (trans.). London: Routledge & Kegan Paul/New York: Humanities Press, 1962 (*Phénoménologie de la perception*. Paris: Gallimard, 1945).

PrP   *The Primacy of Perception and Other Essays on Phenomenological Psychology, the Philosophy of Art, History and Politics*, J. M. Edie (ed.). Evanston, IL: Northwestern University Press, 1964.

PW   *The Prose of the World*, John O'Neill (trans.). Evanston, IL: Northwestern University Press, 1973 (*La Prose du monde*. Paris: Gallimard, 1969).

RNAG "Reading Notes and Comments on Aron Gurwitsch's *The Field of Consciousness*", E. Locey & T. Toadvine (trans.). In *Husserl Studies* **17** (2001), 173–93.

S   *Signs*, Richard McCleary (trans.). Evanston, IL: North-western University Press, 1964/London: Methuen, 1965 (*Signes*. Paris: Gallimard, 1960).

SB *The Structure of Behavior*, A. L. Fisher (trans.). Boston, MA: Beacon Press, 1963 (*La Structure du comportement*. Paris: Presses Universitaires de France, 1942).

SNS *Sense and Non-Sense*, Hubert Dreyfus & Patricia Allen Dreyfus (trans.). Evanston, IL: Northwestern University Press, 1964 (*Sens et non-sens*. Paris: Nagel, 1948).

TD *Texts and Dialogues*, H. J. Silverman & J. Barry Jr (eds), M. B. Smith *et al.* (trans.). Atlantic Highlands, NJ: Humanities Press, 1992.

TL *Themes from the Lectures at the Collège de France 1952–60*, J. O'Neill (trans.). Evanston, IL: Northwestern University Press (*Résumés de cours, Collège de France 1952–1960*. Paris: Gallimard, 1968).

VI *The Visible and the Invisible*, Alphonso Lingis (trans.). Evanston, IL: Northwestern University Press, 1968 (*Le Visible et l'invisible, suivi de notes de travail*, Claude Lefort (ed.). Paris: Gallimard, 1964).

WP *The World of Perception*, Oliver Davis (trans.). London: Routledge, 2004 (*Causeries 1948*. Paris: Seuil, 2002).

PART I

Introduction

ONE

Maurice Merleau-Ponty: life and works

Jack Reynolds

In many respects Merleau-Ponty is the unknown man of the twentieth century's major European philosophers. This is not to deny that he has been widely read and influential – in fact, there is good reason to agree with Paul Ricoeur that he was the greatest of the French phenomenologists – but simply to observe that his life and personality have not been examined, some might say fetishized, in the manner that might be expected for a French academic philosopher of significant public repute. Certainly, he did not initially receive the same amount of attention as his contemporaries and sometimes friends, Jean-Paul Sartre and Simone de Beauvoir. He has not had biographies written about him as they have, nor had photographic diaries and movies devoted to him, as have Michel Foucault, Gilles Deleuze and Jacques Derrida, and he never courted the media in the manner of, say, Sartre, and more recently, Bernard-Henri Lévy. In fact, the life of Merleau-Ponty and the force of his personality remain something of a mystery. He seems to personify what Heidegger is reputed to have said of Aristotle: that he lived, he worked, and he died, and that was all that needed to be said about the relation between a philosopher and their biography. On the other hand, perhaps this mystery and this anonymity that surround Merleau-Ponty partly reveal his personality. At least according to Sartre's remarkable, heartfelt eulogy, "Merleau-Ponty Vivant" (Stewart 1998), one never felt wholly familiar with Merleau-Ponty. According to both Sartre and de Beauvoir's reflections, he had a reserve, a certain aloofness, although this should not be taken to indicate a lack of charm or charisma.

There are, of course, certain basic facts about his life that we can quickly and easily delineate. He was born on 14 March 1908 in Rochefort-sur-Mer, Charente-Maritime. As for many others of his generation, his "father" (not his biological father, as we shall see) was killed in the First World War, when Maurice was three. All accounts suggest, however, that he had a very happy childhood, living with his mother and sister in the country before moving with them to Paris. He apparently confided to Sartre that he never got over the incomparable contentment of his childhood, something that Sartre later vividly recounted in "Merleau-Ponty Vivant" in the process of implying that Merleau-Ponty's theoretical work was always nostalgically desiring a return to such a pre-reflective state of happiness and innocence – Emmanuel Levinas and Jacques Derrida were also to make similar criticisms of Merleau-Ponty's work at later dates, albeit without the *ad hominem* aspect.

Merleau-Ponty was educated at the Lycée Louis-le-Grand, and he began his *agrégation* in philosophy at the École Normale Supérieure in 1926, studying with Sartre, de Beauvoir, Simone Weil and other luminaries. Sartre recounts one interesting story about Merleau-Ponty's student days. Merleau-Ponty apparently hated obscene songs and tasteless jokes, along with brutality of any kind, and tended to see good and evil in all, albeit to varying degrees. When a group of ENS students were singing some crude anti-military songs, Merleau-Ponty and Maurice de Gandillac hissed and interrupted them, only to be physically set upon, before Sartre intervened to diplomatically salvage the situation and begin a friendship that would last for about twenty-five years (Cohen-Solal 2005; Francis & Gontier 1988). It was a curious encounter between these two great French philosophers, perhaps the inversion of their more common relation to both one another (thereafter) and the world.

Early on at the ENS, Merleau-Ponty and de Beauvoir were also very close friends (Francis & Gontier 1988: 64). Within a year or so, however, their friendship was somewhat tempered due to a tragic relationship that Merleau-Ponty had with de Beauvoir's best friend at the time, Elisabeth Le Coin (Zaza), which had a profound impact on all three of them. Zaza and Merleau-Ponty met as students and secretly agreed to marry after Merleau-Ponty passed his *agrégation* and completed his military service (*ibid.*: 83). According to de Beauvoir's (early) account of events, however, Zaza's parents had already arranged for their daughter's marriage to another man and demanded that Zaza not see either Merleau-Ponty or de Beauvoir again, deeming both to be corrupting influences. For de Beauvoir, Merleau-Ponty vacillated regarding his commitment to marry Zaza for fear of what it would do to his mother, who was ill. Zaza died of encephalitis soon after in 1929 and it seems that de Beauvoir partly blamed Merleau-Ponty for the distress he caused Zaza at this time. De Beauvoir did not find out for thirty years that things were more complicated than she had thought. Various sources confirm that Zaza's parents had been quite keen on the prospect of their daughter's marriage with Merleau-Ponty, but when they found out that Merleau-Ponty's father was an adulterous professor rather than his mother's husband – something that Merleau-Ponty himself did not know until Zaza's father told him – they would not allow their daughter to marry him (*ibid.*: 83–8).

Despite this tragedy, Merleau-Ponty completed his *agrégation* in 1930, and began teaching philosophy at *lycées* in Beauvais, Chartres and, after 1935, as a junior member of the ENS. In the meantime he worked on the Catholic journal, *Esprit*, and struggled with his Catholicism, which he was soon to renounce. During the Second World War, Merleau-Ponty served in the infantry in the rank of second lieutenant, unlike Sartre who took it as a badge of honour that he was but a run-of-the-mill soldier. During the Nazi Occupation, Merleau-Ponty was active in the Resistance and returned to his teaching. When the Liberation came in 1945, he joined the University of Lyon and became founding co-editor of *Les Temps modernes* from October 1945 without ever putting his name to it in that capacity. While he repeatedly refused to be explicitly named as an editor alongside Sartre, he was at least as important behind the scenes. Officially he was political editor for the influential political, literary and philosophical magazine.

Around this time, Merleau-Ponty was married to a physician and psychiatrist in Paris, Suzon, and they had one child, a daughter, Marianne. By most accounts it was a happy marriage, although that is not to say it was monogamous. For a time, Merleau-Ponty had an affair with Sonia Brownell (soon to be Sonia Orwell). His eventual breaking off of the relationship clearly devastated Sonia, who declared Merleau-Ponty the love of her life and wrote that the fact that "a lover" and "un amour" are not an exact translation of each other has caused more confusion between the English and the French than most of the wars of politics and religion. Although one could never reconstruct the reasons for her marriage to George Orwell, who was a bed-ridden invalid at the time (the marriage lasted for fourteen weeks), the break in her and Merleau-Ponty's prior relationship seems to have been a factor in her acceptance of Orwell's second marriage proposal (Spurling 2003).

With the completion of his *docteur des lettres* based on two dissertations, *The Structure of Behavior* (1942) and *Phenomenology of Perception* (1945), Merleau-Ponty rather rapidly became one of the foremost French philosophers of the period immediately following the Second World War. He was made Professor at the University of Lyon in 1948, Chair of Child Psychology and Pedagogy at Sorbonne from 1949–52, and was the youngest ever Chair of Philosophy at the Collège de France when he was awarded this position in 1952. He continued to fulfil this role until his untimely death on 44 May 1961 of a stroke from coronary thrombosis, apparently while preparing a lecture on Descartes.

In the period from 1948 until 1953, Merleau-Ponty was one of the first philosophers to bring structuralism and the linguistic emphasis of thinkers such as Ferdinand de Saussure into a relationship with phenomenology and existentialism. In the 1960s his structuralist friend Claude Lévi-Strauss devoted arguably his major work, *The Savage Mind*, to Merleau-Ponty's memory. Throughout his career an abiding cross-disciplinarity was a feature of his work, and his various essays on politics, history, aesthetics, psychology and so on are collated in several collections of enduring importance, including *Humanism and Terror* (1947), *Sense and Non-Sense* (1948), *Adventures of the Dialectic* (1955) and *Signs* (1960).

Merleau-Ponty was initially more Marxist than Sartre, but it was the latter's continuing support for the Soviet Union that forced a break in their friendship in December 1952. As a result Merleau-Ponty quit *Les Temps modernes* and eventually published his book, *Adventures of the Dialectic*. The fallout between them was rather acrimonious, although not as vicious as the earlier confrontation between Camus and Sartre. With his political ambitions somewhat attenuated by these historical and personal events, Merleau-Ponty returned to ontological considerations and began work on his final, unfinished opus, *The Visible and the Invisible* (posthumously published in 1964), which continues to stimulate much philosophical interest. Various different collections of Merleau-Ponty's course notes (or those collated by students and checked by him) have also been published recently, perhaps most significantly *Nature* (2003). His work remains highly influential in contemporary "continental" philosophy as it is practised both on the European continent and beyond, but it is also increasingly significant to those aspects of the analytic tradition that are concerned with the relation between mind and body, perception, developmental psychology and the interdisciplinary "discipline" of cognitive science.

TWO

A guide to *Merleau-Ponty: Key Concepts*

Rosalyn Diprose

Merleau-Ponty: Key Concepts introduces the reader to the fundamental ideas that have emerged from these intertwinings, outlined
in Chapter 1, of Merleau-Ponty's philosophical heritage, cross-
disciplinary interests, and his personal and political life. His own
reflections on the philosophical enterprise indicate how he may have
understood the relationship between "life" and "work", and they
also provide the best guide to how we might approach his philosophy,
as well as to how to approach the essays in this book.

In the Preface to *Phenomenology of Perception*, Merleau-Ponty
concludes his rendition of phenomenology and existentialism with
the suggestion that philosophy "is not the reflection of a pre-existing
truth, but, like art, the act of bringing truth into being" and "[t]rue
philosophy consists in relearning to look at the world" (PP: xx). He
later made a similar point in his inaugural lecture at the Collège de
France in 1952 (published as *In Praise of Philosophy* in 1953): "the
philosopher, in order to experience more fully the ties of truth which
bind him to the world and history, finds neither the depth of himself
nor absolute knowledge, but a renewed image of the world and of
himself placed within it among others" (EP: 63). These definitions
of philosophy in part reflect Merleau-Ponty's ontological commitments, in particular the idea that the self and world are inextricably
entwined: to express oneself is to express a world that is already
both a historical and natural event of meaning, but is no less real for
that; and expression, whether philosophical, historical or scientific,
is fundamentally creative. The idea that philosophy is creative in its
attempt "to complete and conceive" an "unfinished world" (PP: xx)

presents the reader of Merleau-Ponty's philosophy with a particular challenge. Not only does this mean that Merleau-Ponty transforms the philosophical and other traditions with which he engages in decidedly creative and innovative ways, but also it means that it is often difficult to work out where tradition ends and Merleau-Ponty's own philosophy begins. While more often than not he presents his ideas in the context of expositions of the concepts of others, in a mark of his own philosophical generosity Merleau-Ponty rarely indicates exactly where he departs from his interlocutors, and never in a confrontational way. Even Descartes, whose philosophy of the *cogito* provides the most obvious contrast to Merleau-Ponty's idea that the body is the ground of experience, is treated less as an adversary than a resource for ideas that merely need extra development. Hence, in *The Visible and the Invisible* Merleau-Ponty applauds Descartes's attempt (in his *Meditations*) to restore perceptual faith in a world, suggesting also that "Cartesianism, whether it intended to do so or not, did inspire a science of the human body" in an analysis that requires rectifying rather than abandoning (VI: 26).

Given the complexities of Merleau-Ponty's own conviction that philosophy is creative, his readers would be advised to approach his texts in the same way that he characterizes the phenomenological project: with "the same kind of attentiveness and wonder, the same demand for awareness, the same will to seize the meaning of the world or of history as that meaning comes into being" (PP: xxi). *Merleau-Ponty: Key Concepts* aims to assist in this process of better understanding and appreciating Merleau-Ponty's "renewed image of the world".

The volume is divided into four parts (Part I consists of two introductory chapters): the essays in "Part II: Interventions" situate Merleau-Ponty's work with regard to the key philosophical influences and debates with which he was concerned; the essays in "Part III: Inventions" explain and discuss the main conceptual innovations of his philosophy; and the chapters in "Part IV: Extensions" focus on how his work has been taken up in other fields, outside philosophy, in the last two decades. The authors of these essays include some of the most significant established and exciting new anglophone scholars of Merleau-Ponty's philosophy. As such, they approach his work with the same passion for philosophy's creative dimension. The essays guide the reader through Merleau-Ponty's ideas, noticing how these ideas develop and the different ways they might be understood. They aim to inspire further reading of his *oeuvre* rather than claiming to be the final word on what it means. That task, like the taking up and renewing of a world that Merleau-Ponty describes, is "unfinished".

The two philosophical traditions with which Merleau-Ponty is most associated are phenomenology and existentialism. The first two chapters of Part II situate Merleau-Ponty as an interlocutor in these traditions. As Ted Toadvine suggests in Chapter 3, while Merleau-Ponty drew "on a range of disciplines and intellectual traditions in crafting his own unique philosophical style, including psychology, psychoanalysis, linguistics, anthropology, literature and biology" (p. 17), it was phenomenology that provided him with the basis not only for his philosophical method, but also for his account of perceptual experience as an alternative to realist and idealist doctrines. While particularly interested in Husserl's phenomenology, Merleau-Ponty revised it in novel ways, most notably by departing from Husserl's focus on consciousness as the seat of experience of the world and paying more attention to the latent content of experience that marks the limits of the phenomenological method. Toadvine guides us through this revision, including Merleau-Ponty's later call for a "hyper-reflection" that measures the incompleteness of consciousness and, hence, of phenomenology. Merleau-Ponty's unique take on phenomenology would not have been what it is without the influence of existentialism on his thought. In *Phenomenology of Perception* he describes his understanding of the relation between the two as follows: while phenomenology "is the study of essences", including "the essence of perception, or the essence of consciousness", phenomenology also "puts essences back into existence, and does not expect to arrive at an understanding of man and the world from any starting point other than that of their 'facticity'" (PP: vii). Along with existentialism, Merleau-Ponty puts existence before essence where "'existence' is the movement through which man is in the world and involves himself in a physical and social situation which then becomes his point of view on the world" (SNS: 72). As with phenomenology, though, Merleau-Ponty leaves his unique stamp on this tradition. In Chapter 4, Thomas Busch takes us through Merleau-Ponty's debts to, and departures from, Sartre's existentialism, paying particular attention to the advances Merleau-Ponty makes in terms of four aspects of human existence: embodiment, the advent of meaning, the relation to "otherness", and freedom. While together phenomenology and existentialism provide Merleau-Ponty with his starting point for developing an account of human existence between realism and idealism, he characterizes realist and idealist doctrines in his own unique way, usually preferring the labels

10

"empiricism" and "intellectualism". Taylor Carman outlines in Chapter 5 what Merleau-Ponty means by "empiricism" and "intellectualism", noting how his critiques of these traditions are crucial to the development of his account of the bodily basis of perception.

Unlike other phenomenologists and existentialists, Merleau-Ponty was sympathetic to many aspects of the account of human existence emerging from psychoanalytic theory in France in the first half of the twentieth century. While not adopting Freud's notion of the unconscious as such, nor psychoanalysis as a cure for our ills, Merleau-Ponty does appreciate, in ways outlined by Beata Stawarska in Chapter 6, how "psychoanalysis helps to thicken and deepen the meaning of human existence by transcending the classical subject–act–object structure of pure consciousness" (p. 58). Stawarska maps Merleau-Ponty's engagement with psychoanalysis in several of his works, noting in particular how this is the most likely source of Merleau-Ponty's conviction that sexuality (understood in terms of affective or erotic perception rather than a predisposition toward particular kinds of sex acts, aims and objects) pervades human existence without either being reducible to the other (PP: 166). It is also evident from "The Child's Relations with Others" (PrP) that Merleau-Ponty, like Lacan, draws from Henri Wallon's 1949 account of the "mirror stage" of childhood development in refining his own model of the "corporeal schema" as the basis of perception.

More pervasive in Merleau-Ponty's works is a particular notion of temporality that informs the way he understands "how individually situated and intersubjective selves are instantiated, shaped, and shape themselves in time" (p. 70), as Sonia Kruks puts it in Chapter 7. Kruks's focus, however, is on how Merleau-Ponty's understanding of temporality and meaning informs his philosophy of "institution" and "public history". By tracing his engagement with Hegel's and Marx's philosophies of history and his critique of liberal humanist conceptions of history, Kruks shows how, for Merleau-Ponty, history is neither random nor predetermined. By forging a path between relativism and determinism, Kruks argues, Merleau-Ponty points to our responsibility to act to influence the course of events even if we do not have the freedom or power to alter the future completely. Merleau-Ponty's philosophy of history not only informs his account of human existence; it also influences his approach to politics and the political, the topic of Diana Coole's discussion in Chapter 8. While Merleau-Ponty does not provide a political theory in the conventional sense, Coole argues that his philosophy is "political in the widest sense of pursuing a transformation of modern experience. But it is also political in a narrower sense of trying to show those who do engage with this risky political realm how they might negotiate its ambiguities and sheer complexity" (p. 83) in ways that do not exhibit the violence of many modern political regimes. Coole unfolds this project by outlining Merleau-Ponty's own political experience, his political critiques in texts such as *Humanism and Terror* (1947) and *Adventures of the Dialectic* (1955), and his challenges to the main "prejudice" underlying the usual approaches to the political – "Cartesian (and Kantian) rationalism, with its ontological presuppositions concerning mind/ body dualism and the subject/object opposition" (p. 85). In contrast to the latter, Merleau-Ponty's political ontology, Coole argues, is based on the interworld of intercorporeal relations, communications and expressions of meaning. Understanding this as the domain of the political, she suggests, provides the means for avoiding violence in political practice, an idea that explains why there is renewed interest among political philosophers in Merleau-Ponty's work. In Chapter 9 Hugh Silverman performs a similarly important task in delineating Merleau-Ponty's aesthetics, showing the manner in which an engagement with art, particularly painting, was vital to his philosophical practice throughout.

These seven essays in the second part of *Merleau-Ponty: Key Concepts*, provide comprehensive background to the specific concepts for which Merleau-Ponty is most famous. While mentioned in Part II, these are outlined and discussed in detail in Part III. Merleau-Ponty is perhaps best known for his unique account of the bodily basis of perception. So, in Chapter 10, David Morris addresses the privilege that Merleau-Ponty's philosophy accords to the body, paying particular attention to his accounts of "motor intentionality" and the "corporeal schema" or "postural schema" in his earlier work. Perception and its corporeal basis are explored in further detail by David Cerbone in Chapter 11. Cerbone explains Merleau-Ponty's critiques of "empiricist" and "intellectualist" accounts of perception, as well as illuminates his alternative model. Together, Chapters 10 and 11 reveal what Merleau-Ponty means by perception: the pre-reflective openness on to the world that for Merleau-Ponty is the fundamental feature of human existence and the expression of meaning. The idea that perception takes place in this corporeal "interworld" leads Merleau-Ponty to characterize human existence in terms of ambiguity. In Chapter 12 Gail Weiss discusses how this idea of ambiguity is a response to the dualisms that haunt philosophical conceptions of the subject. While explaining several kinds of ambiguity in Merleau-Ponty's work, Weiss also includes comparison with de Beauvoir's philosophy of ambiguity. Michael Sanders examines the innovative dimensions of Merleau-Ponty's concept of intersubjectivity in Chapter 13, paying particular attention to whether it allows for genuine alterity or otherness. This is a point of some debate following criticisms of Merleau-Ponty's ontology posed by Emmanuel Levinas and Jacques Derrida. Sanders's discussion is hence important in tacitly posing the question of Merleau-Ponty's relation to his post-structuralist successors on the French philosophical scene.

With the corporeal, worldly and intersubjective foundations of Merleau-Ponty's ontology of perception elaborated, Harry Adams, in Chapter 14, shows how emerging from this ontology is a unique concept of "expression". Adams explains "expression" with regard to meaning and language but also how, for Merleau-Ponty, the body actualizes expression and why expression is fundamentally creative and ambiguous. In Chapter 15, Suzanne Cataldi focuses upon the themes of affect and sensibility. As she suggests, while Merleau-Ponty did not provide a systematic account of the emotions, "affectivity is so intertwined with sense-perception in the living experience" for Merleau-Ponty that there is an account there to be found. In reconstructing such an account, Cataldi makes Merleau-Ponty's work available for the current resurgence of interest in theories of affect. Similarly, there is renewed interest in Merleau-Ponty's philosophy of nature since the recent publication in English of previously unavailable course notes on this theme. Scott Churchill examines Merleau-Ponty's approach to nature and animality in Chapter 16. In the final chapter of this section Fred Evans considers Merleau-Ponty's concept of "flesh", a very important, if somewhat complex and dense, idea found in his final unfinished work, *The Visible and the Invisible*. In exploring this and associated ideas such as "reversibility" and the "chiasm", Evans's chapter allows for consideration of changes in Merleau-Ponty's ontology, particularly in regard to his move from the "body-subject", which dominates his early work, to an account of an arguably more dispersed relation between corporeality, intersubjectivity and meaning.

In the final section of the book, "Part IV: Extensions", the chapters examine the manner in which Merleau-Ponty's key concepts have been borrowed and extended in fields outside philosophy. In Chapter 18 Ann Murphy explores applications in feminism and race theory; Shaun Gallagher explores intersections between Merleau-Ponty's ontology and cognitive science in Chapter 19; the extension of Merleau-Ponty's rethinking of the body to questions of living well and health is the topic of Philipa Rothfield's discussion in Chapter 20; and

Nick Crossley focuses on the turn to the body in sociology in the final chapter of the book. We let these essays speak for themselves. They are fascinating studies of some of the sometimes surprising directions in which such a creative philosophy as Merleau-Ponty's can take the reader. They are also testimony to how not only is the reading of Merleau-Ponty's philosophy "unfinished", so is its application.

PART II

Interventions

THREE

Phenomenology and "hyper-reflection"

Ted Toadvine

Like many of the thinkers who inspired him, such as Henri Bergson and Max Scheler, Merleau-Ponty drew liberally on a range of disciplines and intellectual traditions in crafting his own unique philosophical style, including psychology, psychoanalysis, linguistics, anthropology, literature, biology and others. Even so, it was the phenomenological tradition of philosophy that most consistently inspired and guided his thinking, and it is with this tradition that he is most often associated today. Although Merleau-Ponty had little exposure to phenomenology as part of his formal studies, at a time when the neo-Kantianism of Léon Brunschvicg and the legacy of Bergsonism dominated the philosophical scene in France, phenomenology began to play a decisive role at the very beginning of his career and continued to occupy his attention throughout the twenty years in which he completed his major works.

Merleau-Ponty read and commented on a number of phenomenological thinkers, including Heidegger, Sartre and Scheler, but it was to the work of Edmund Husserl, founder of the modern phenomenological movement, that he returned most often in developing his own interpretation of the phenomenological project. Merleau-Ponty was the first outside visitor to consult Husserl's unpublished writings at the Louvain Husserl Archives in 1939, he assisted in the establishment of a Husserl archive in Paris, and he continued to lecture on and write about Husserl until his death in 1961 (Toadvine 2002).

Early in his career, especially in his main thesis, *Phenomenology of Perception*, Merleau-Ponty identifies his method as phenomenological and even equates philosophy itself, in its most developed form,

17

with phenomenological reflection. Whether Merleau-Ponty maintained this identification with phenomenology up to the end of his career is a matter of debate among scholars, since his final and incomplete manuscript, *The Visible and the Invisible*, suggests a newly critical perspective on his earlier subjectivism. It is clear, nonetheless, that Merleau-Ponty understood his work as the continuation of the efforts begun by Husserl, even if these efforts required articulating the unthought elements of Husserl's work, and phenomenology more generally, in unexpected ways.

To understand what phenomenology means in Merleau-Ponty's thinking and how he appropriates its methodology in a unique and creative way, I shall begin with his early study of the problem of perception, where phenomenology provides an alternative to the debate between realist and idealist accounts of perceptual experience. Already in this early concern with perception in the narrow sense, we can discern the lineaments of Merleau-Ponty's later enthusiasm about a phenomenology of the perceived world in its entirety, including the social, historical, aesthetic, political and scientific aspects of human experience. In his first two major works, *The Structure of Behavior* and *Phenomenology of Perception*, phenomenology becomes a general method for understanding the paradoxical link of the "objective" and the "subjective" dimensions of the perceived world, thereby reconciling the empirical facts of the sciences with the historical and cultural emergence of meaning. It therefore culminates in a philosophy of radical reflection, that is, of a rationality that recognizes its own contingency and dependence on the given existence of the world. The preface to *Phenomenology of Perception* is a key text for our elucidation of this understanding of phenomenology, since in it Merleau-Ponty offers a rare systematic overview of his interpretation of its method. Lastly, I shall briefly consider Merleau-Ponty's later reservations about certain aspects of the phenomenological project. Since phenomenology, as Merleau-Ponty practises it, is an inherently self-critical enterprise, his critical remarks might be read not as a break with phenomenology, but instead as evidence of his continued commitment to its larger horizon, namely, the development of a reflective account of experience that strives to remain cognizant of its own inherent limits. In this sense, what Merleau-Ponty will later call "philosophical interrogation" or "hyperdialectic" (VI: 94) can be seen as continuous with the phenomenological enterprise.

Phenomenology and perception

One of the first indications of Merleau-Ponty's budding interest in phenomenology is found in his 1934 application for a grant to study "The Nature of Perception" (TD: 74–84). In this study, Merleau-Ponty's goal is to provide an account of perception that avoids reducing it either to the causal mechanisms described by scientific naturalism or to an activity of consciousness, as it was understood by critical idealism in the tradition of Brunschvicg. In this context, he identifies Husserl's phenomenology as "doubly interesting", since it is a "new philosophy" distinct from both empirical psychology and critical thought and is therefore promising for the effort to move beyond the opposition of realism and idealism (TD: 77).

This understanding of phenomenology as an alternative to realism and idealism is the guiding thesis of *The Structure of Behavior* (1942), which combines the insights of Gestalt psychology with phenomenology to provide a new understanding of the relation between consciousness and nature. While critical thought reduces nature to an object of consciousness, naturalistic psychology and the sciences treat consciousness and nature as two juxtaposed realities to be explained by causal interaction (SB: 3–4). Merleau-Ponty develops an alternative account of the consciousness–nature relation starting with the example of "behaviour", that is, the relation between an organism and its environment, arguing that the structures manifest in organic behaviour are irreducible to causal interactions. Instead, behaviour forms a "Gestalt", a holistic structure unified through a common signification. As a significative whole or structure, behaviour is properly situated neither in the external world nor in an inner life of consciousness; it therefore calls realism in general into question (SB: 182). Starting from this new concept of Gestalt structure, Merleau-Ponty offers a reformulation of the traditional problem of the relation between soul and body, and here the decisive influence of phenomenology becomes apparent. On the one hand, the critique of naturalistic explanations of meaningful structures seems to point to the need for a transcendental turn, that is, a return to consciousness as the constitutive source of the meanings of these structures. But an idealist return to consciousness would ultimately deny that these meanings are meanings of the structures themselves, meanings that are perceptually encountered in the world rather than given ready-made to a consciousness. If the perceiving body is not to be reduced either to a causal mechanism or to an object for consciousness, if it is to have a significative structure in its own right, then an alternative philosophical approach is required. Such a philosophy must be transcendental, Merleau-Ponty argues, but in an entirely different sense from that of the transcendental idealism of critical thought (SB: 206). Phenomenology provides this alternative philosophy by countering our habitual tendency to transform our perceptual experiences into a world of fully constituted things, either the "real" things of the naturalistic sciences or the mental givens of idealism. The "phenomenological reduction" or shift to the "transcendental attitude" is a rediscovery, then, of the meaningful, structural relations formed between the perceiving subject and the perceived world, relations of "intentionality" rather than causality (SB: 220). Although Merleau-Ponty explicitly discusses phenomenology at only a few points in *The Structure of Behavior*, these points are decisive for understanding the project of this work, which is ultimately to reconcile the legitimate truths of naturalism and critical idealism and thereby to "define transcendental philosophy anew in such a way as to integrate it with the very phenomenon of the real" (SB: 224). For Merleau-Ponty, phenomenology promises precisely this integration of transcendental philosophy with the real. Nevertheless, this task remains incomplete at the end of this first work, which reveals the need for a deeper investigation of the relationship between "perceptual" consciousness – the embodied subjectivity engaged with the perceived world – and "intellectual" consciousness, the subject of philosophical reflection (*ibid.*: 176, 210, 224).

When Merleau-Ponty returns to the analysis of perceptual consciousness in his sequel, *Phenomenology of Perception*, it is with the resources gained by study of Husserl's unpublished manuscripts at Louvain and an increasing command of the phenomenological literature. Here Merleau-Ponty describes the "expressive unity" that characterizes the human body and the extension of this expressive structure to the perceived world in its entirety, including its social and historical dimensions (PP: 206). The "perceived world" therefore expands to become Merleau-Ponty's equivalent of Husserl's *Lebenswelt* or "lifeworld", the concrete world of our practical involvements (*ibid.*: 365n). As the purview of the perceived world expands, so does Merleau-Ponty's conception of phenomenology, which in this text becomes a general method for understanding the inherently paradoxical nature of the perceived: a reality is perceived only in so far as it is experienced, and it is therefore always "for me". But the perceived thing, to be real, must also present itself as "in itself", that is, as preceding and exceeding my experience of it. This paradox of immanence and transcendence defines the experience of the perceived as such, and Merleau-Ponty rediscovers it in all the dimensions of our lives that take root in the perceptual world, including the experience of time, others, nature, the body and ideality (PP: 363–5; PrP: 16, 26). While idealism privileges immanence and realism privileges transcendence, only phenomenology manages to think their paradoxical interconnection, but it does so precisely by faithfully describing the contradiction rather than aiming to explain or resolve it. Thus we find that phenomenology's own methodological principles instantiate a contradictory tension that is not their failing but precisely their power for articulating the paradox of every sensible. Merleau-Ponty expresses this tension within phenomenology in his descriptions of it as "radical reflection", a reflection that recognizes its own contingency and dependence on the pre-reflective givenness of the world (PP: 61–3).

The phenomenological method

Merleau-Ponty develops this complex account of phenomenology's internal tensions in the preface to *Phenomenology of Perception*, which is his most detailed and systematic exposition of the meaning of phenomenology and its method. The preface examines four key themes of the phenomenological method: the privileging of phenomenological description over scientific explanation and idealist reconstruction; the phenomenological reduction; the eidetic reduction; and intentionality. But Merleau-Ponty does not simply adopt these methodological elements from Husserl or other phenomenological writers. As the preface explains, phenomenology existed as "a manner or style of thinking" before "arriving at complete awareness of itself as a philosophy", and consequently, a creative appropriation of its meaning and methods is required: "We shall find in ourselves, and nowhere else, the unity and true meaning of phenomenology" (PP: viii). In fact, this unfinished character of phenomenology, the requirement that it be taken up and completed by the thinker who practises it, turns out to be an essential aspect of its efforts to "reveal the mystery of the world and of reason" (*ibid.*: xxi). Although Merleau-Ponty lays out here a preliminary definition and method for phenomenology, it also remains for him a "manner or style of thinking" that can be understood only through its living practice. Let us try to evoke the philosophical style of Merleau-Ponty's phenomenology by taking each of the four key aspects of its method in turn.

First, phenomenology is a matter of description rather than of explanation, which differentiates it immediately from the approach of the empirical sciences. While the sciences offer an account of perception, thought, culture or history in terms of causal relations between already-determinate entities, phenomenology seeks to disclose the original experience of the world that such explanations take for granted. All forms of reflection, including science and philosophy, assume the existence of the world as it is perceived and the embodied subject that perceives it. But just as a perceiver has the tendency to forget her own role in the disclosure of a perceptual object – for instance that the appearance of the object as at a certain distance or from a certain angle refers to the position from which she perceives – so reflection has a tendency to forget its own role as the experiencing correlate of what it reflects on. Scientists (and most philosophers) are thereby led to replace the objects of perception, which are inherently experiential and indeterminate, with the reified abstractions of naturalistic explanation. Initially, then, phenomenology must set aside all scientific explanations of perception and the perceived in order to investigate the pre-scientific experience that such explanation take for granted.

However, phenomenology does not, in the end, reject scientific explanation or the idealized objects that it posits. It only insists that the world as experienced is directly or indirectly the foundation for all legitimate scientific claims. For instance, all scientific explanations and theoretical objects take for granted the existence of time, but the unity of time, Merleau-Ponty argues, is founded on perceptual experience, and consequently, "all consciousness is perceptual" (PrP: 13). Once this reliance of scientific explanation on the direct experience of the world is recognized, then science may be understood as a useful rationale or explanation of the world, like a map in relation to the landscape (PP: ix).

Since phenomenology strives to describe the world as given to experience, it must equally avoid engaging in a reconstruction of that experience in terms of its conditions of possibility, and this differentiates phenomenology from critical idealism. The experience of the world precedes our reflection on it, yet the tradition of reflective philosophy from Descartes to Kant traces this experience back to its conditions in the activity of consciousness; the self-certainty or self-experience of consciousness thereby becomes the ground from which the world is reconstructed. But this move detaches the subject from the world that it experiences, juxtaposes it with the world as a distinct region of being, and grants it a priority over the world. Phenomenology, however, reverses this priority by recognizing that the world exists prior to any analysis or act of consciousness. Reflective analysis is therefore a naive or incomplete form of reflection, precisely because it forgets the pre-reflective experience of the world from which it sets out:

> When I begin to reflect my reflection bears upon an unreflective experience; moreover my reflection cannot be unaware of itself as an event, and so it appears to itself in the light of a truly creative act, of a changed structure of consciousness, and yet it has to recognize, as having priority over its own operations, the world which is given to the subject because the subject is given to himself. (PP: x)

Perception, as our pre-reflective openness on to the world, is not the result of a conscious act but the background against which such acts appear. On Merleau-Ponty's interpretation, Husserl's "noematic" analysis, that is, the description of objects of experience as experienced, provides an access to this perceptual level of experience without retreating into subjectivity (*ibid.*).

Yet phenomenology is not a denial of the necessity of reflection or an attempt to return to a pre-reflective immersion in the world, and this brings us to the second aspect of its method: the phenomenological reduction. As Merleau-Ponty notes, Husserl himself presents the reduction as a means of attaining the pure givenness of consciousness, definitively distinguishing the transcendental consciousness that is the concern of phenomenology from the natural, empirical life of the human being (Bernet *et al.* 1993: 58–77). But to be consistent, according to Merleau-Ponty, such a transcendental idealism must completely transform the world into a meaning for consciousness and eliminate any determinable difference between self and other, since both would share in the one pre-personal transcendental consciousness in its grasp of universal truths (PP: xi–xii). That this is not the whole story, Merleau-Ponty suggests, is clear from Husserl's recognition of the paradoxical character of our experience of the world and of others, which is that our openness on to the world involves us in a perspective and a situation that are necessarily embodied and visible from the outside. Reflection reveals not only a presence to oneself, then, but also an inherence in the world, an "incarnation in some nature", that exposes the self to the gaze of the other and introduces a kind of "internal weakness" into reflection's efforts to achieve pure self-consciousness (*ibid*.: xii–xiii).

In Merleau-Ponty's philosophy, then, the phenomenological reduction is not to be understood as the purification of consciousness of all empirical involvement, but rather as the reflective effort to disclose our pre-reflective engagement in the world. As Merleau-Ponty notes in 1948, "the world of perception is, to a great extent, unknown territory as long as we remain in the practical or utilitarian attitude" (WP: 39). The role of the reduction is to suspend our practical involvements in order to bring them to light and, along with them, the perceptual world that is their correlate. The natural attitude, our common-sense certainty about the world, is not to be rejected, therefore, but only put "out of play" in order to better bring into view its intentional character, the manner of relating to the world that it entails. It is in this context that Merleau-Ponty approvingly quotes Eugen Fink's characterization of the reduction as "'wonder' in the face of the world" (PP: xiii).

By suspending our practical engagement in the world, we are able to bring to light the correlation between our intentions and the world as the meaning towards which those "intendings" aim. More than this, we also catch a glimpse of the "unmotivated upsurge of the world", the manner in which it exceeds all of our meaning-giving acts and presents itself as always already there before reflection begins (PP: xiv/viii). Furthermore, through the process of the reduction, we discover the inherence of the one who reflects in the world that is reflected on, and consequently, the essentially incomplete character of every act of reflection. This is what Merleau-Ponty means by stating that the "most important lesson that the reduction teaches us is the impossibility of a complete reduction" (*ibid*.: xiv). It is at this point that phenomenology becomes a second-order or "radical" reflection, since it must interrogate its own possibility as a reflective enterprise. Philosophy therefore becomes an "ever-renewed experiment in making its own beginnings", a perennial investigation of the emergence of reflection from a pre-reflective life that conditions it and makes it possible (*ibid*.). Consequently, the phenomenological reduction is not an idealistic method but an existential one, according to Merleau-Ponty, since it recognizes that involvement of the questioner in what is questioned (*ibid*.: xiv, xx–xxi). Phenomenology as Merleau-Ponty describes it in *Phenomenology of Perception* shares all four of the characteristics that he attributes to existential thought: a concern with incarnation, philosophy as mystery, the other and history (TD: 132–4).

Merleau-Ponty suggests a similar recuperation of the "eidetic reduction" – Husserl's intuition of essential relations within the flux of conscious experience – which Merleau-Ponty identifies as the third key feature of phenomenology's method. A turn towards essences is necessary if phenomenology is to make any descriptive claims that go beyond the brute facts of a particular experience. To apply the term "red" to an object or to describe the characteristics of perception in general is already to shift from the fact of experience to its essential features. But this delineation of essential features is in the service of better reflecting on the fact of the world's existence; it is not, as Merleau-Ponty interprets the logical positivists, an attempt to solve philosophical problems by recourse to linguistic analysis. Such an approach forgets that the meanings of words are a function of perceptual experience, not vice versa. Against logical positivism, therefore, Merleau-Ponty proposes a "phenomenological positivism", according to which perception is "not presumed true, but defined as access to the truth": "We must not, therefore, wonder whether we really perceive a world, we must instead say: the world is what we perceive" (PP: xvi). The description of essential features of experience should not be understood, then, as founding the actual existence of the world on essential conditions that are separable from it; rather, "the eidetic method is the method of a phenomenological positivism which bases the possible on the real" (*ibid.*: xvii; cf. PrP: 50).

The fourth and final feature of the phenomenological method is intentionality, the recognition that all consciousness is consciousness *of* something. But Merleau-Ponty finds this emphasis on consciousness misleading, since the unity of the world is first "lived as ready-made or already there", not produced as a conscious judgement (PP: xvii). Following Husserl, he distinguishes between two kinds of intentionality: the "act intentionality" of explicit conscious judgements, and the "operative intentionality" that "produces the natural and antepredicative unity of the world and our life" (*ibid.*: xviii; cf. *ibid.*: 418). The latter, broader conception of intentionality redefines the task of philosophy as the effort to take in the "total intention" of a perceived thing, a historical event or a philosophical theory, which will be its "unique mode of existing" or its "existential structure" (*ibid.*: xviii–xix):

Should the starting-point for the understanding of history be ideology, or politics, or religion, or economics? Should we try to understand a doctrine from its overt content, or from the psychological make-up of its author? We must seek an understanding from all these angles simultaneously, everything has meaning, and we shall find this same structure of being underlying all relationships. (PP: xix)

Reflection must gather together all the intentional relations that converge in the unique existence of what it reflects on. In so doing, it discloses a rational significance within what may first appear to be contingent, chance circumstances. Thus a historian can speak about the "spirit" of an age, or we can pursue the unthought dimensions of a certain philosopher's style. Through the broad notion of intentionality, then, phenomenology becomes a means of expressing the emergence of reason in a contingent world, a reason that has no guarantees or inevitability, but that exists precisely to the extent that "perspectives blend, perceptions confirm each other, a meaning emerges" (*ibid*.: xix). The only foundation for this reason is the "pre-existent Logos [of] the world itself" (*ibid*.: xx).

This presentation of phenomenology allows Merleau-Ponty to interpret its inherent tensions and unfinished character in a positive light: "The unfinished nature of phenomenology and the inchoative atmosphere which has surrounded it are not to be taken as a sign of failure, they were inevitable because phenomenology's task was to reveal the mystery of the world and of reason" (*ibid*.: xxi). Like the artist or the political activist, the phenomenologist must, through the expressive act of reflection, bring a truth into being without any guarantees or foundation in a pre-existing order. To reflect is to take up the unfinished world "in an effort to complete and conceive it", and it is therefore a "violent act which is validated by being performed" (*ibid*.: xxxv). Because reflection has no pre-existing guides or foundations, it must ceaselessly interrogate its own possibility, especially its relationship with the pre-reflective world that it aims to express. Philosophy as such is therefore called to the task of "radical" or self-referential reflection on its own possibilities; it becomes an "infinite mediation" that is true to its intentions only by "never knowing where it is going" (*ibid*.: xxi). That phenomenology provides the methodological resources for such a radical reflection is precisely what opens it to the "mystery" of the world and of reason, granting it a privileged role in contemporary philosophy, and revealing its deep affinity with modern literary and artistic movements (*ibid*.: xxi).

Elsewhere, Merleau-Ponty develops in greater depth the comparison of philosophical reflection with the expressive creations of literature and the arts, and his description of reflection as a "violent act" involving a "decision on which we stake our life" also implies a political philosophy. These themes are dealt with in later chapters of this volume, but it is worth noting that Merleau-Ponty's later accounts of the Socratic irony that prescribes for the philosopher a singular form of action (EP: 38–41, 60–64) and of the new humanism that acknowledges contingency (S: 239–43) rely on the conditional and finite conception of rationality that Merleau-Ponty attributes to phenomenology.

The limits of phenomenology

Our exposition of Merleau-Ponty's interpretation of phenomenology has concentrated on his earlier writings, where he is most enthusiastic about its promise as a new philosophical approach. But Merleau-Ponty adopts a critical stance towards this earlier interpretation of the phenomenological method and subjects it to ongoing scrutiny in his later writings. For instance, his criticisms, in *The Visible and the Invisible*, of his earlier reliance on the notion of consciousness in *Phenomenology of Perception* have often been taken as evidence of a parting of ways with phenomenology, in so far as it remains a philosophy of consciousness (VI: 183, 200). Merleau-Ponty also comes to reject the eidetic reduction, which he holds responsible for the strains of intellectualism in Husserl's thought (RNAG: 173–93).

In the "Reflection and Interrogation" chapter of *The Visible and the Invisible*, Merleau-Ponty argues that the translation of the world into its essential character leads inevitably to a pure correlation between consciousness and the world and to a retrospective reconstruction of the world in terms of its signification. But the experience of a transcendence, for instance, is not the pure consciousness of an essence of transcendence; rather, it is an openness or incompleteness of consciousness itself. Merleau-Ponty is therefore led to reject his earlier commitment to a "phenomenological positivism": "All consciousness is consciousness of something or of the world, but this *something*, this *world*, is no longer, as 'phenomenological positivism' appeared to teach, an object that is what it is, exactly adjusted to acts of consciousness" (PhF: 70).

Increasingly, Merleau-Ponty turns his interest toward those residues or remainders that are not "exactly adjusted" to consciousness, and that are revealed less through the application of the phenomenological method than through its *limits*, its "latent content" or its "unconscious" (PhF: 71). This is clear in Merleau-Ponty's final (1959) essay on Husserl, "The Philosopher and his Shadow" (S: 159–81), where "the ultimate task of phenomenology as philosophy of consciousness is to understand its relationship to non-phenomenology":

> What resists phenomenology within us – natural being, the "barbarous" source Schelling spoke of – cannot remain outside phenomenology and should have its place within it. The philosopher must bear his shadow, which is not simply the factual absence of future light. (S: 178; cf. N: 38)

But to insist that phenomenology "bear its shadow", that it recognize a relationship with what necessarily exceeds its grasp, is still to develop a line of thought present in Merleau-Ponty's writings on phenomenology from the beginning, namely, that phenomenology discloses, albeit indirectly, a contradiction of transcendence and immanence that cannot ultimately be resolved. When, in *The Visible and the Invisible*, Merleau-Ponty calls for a "hyper-reflection" that would measure the distance between reflection and the pre-reflective situation that it aims to express (VI: 38, 46), we should recognize the same structure of radical, second-order reflection that Merleau-Ponty had already described in *Phenomenology of Perception*. Something similar may also be said concerning phenomenology's commitment to consciousness, as Merleau-Ponty notes in a late essay on "Phenomenology and Psychoanalysis": "When Doctor Lacan writes that the phenomenology of hallucination, to the extent that it attempts to be rigorous, goes beyond the limits of a philosophy of consciousness, he is retracing the steps of a phenomenology which is deepening itself" (PhF: 71). Rather than a rejection of phenomenology, then, these remarks may be taken as a testament to its ongoing relevance for Merleau-Ponty, precisely as the best means that we have for "unveiling a back side of things that we have not constituted" (S: 180).

Despite his ongoing critical examinations, Merleau-Ponty presents phenomenology in a positive light throughout his later writings, and the manuscript of *The Visible and the Invisible*, including its working notes, is steeped in themes and language drawn from close study of Husserl, including the reversibility of touch and even the concept of "flesh". The reversibility of touch is introduced, with reference to Husserl, already in *Phenomenology of Perception* (93), while the concept of "flesh" may be traced to the discussions of Husserl in the lectures on nature (N: 73) and "The Philosopher and his Shadow" (S: 167).

This is not to deny that Merleau-Ponty recognizes, and increasingly accentuates, certain paradoxical tensions of the phenomenological method. But these tensions inevitably point us back to the contradictory intertwining of immanence and transcendence that is the perceived world. In the end, phenomenology confronts us with an insoluble bond between our openness to a world that remains resolutely other and our reflective return to ourselves. It is this equivalence between "leaving oneself" and "retiring into oneself" that Merleau-Ponty calls "true philosophy" (VI: 49, 199).

Further reading

Barbaras, R. 2004. *The Being of the Phenomenon: Merleau-Ponty's Ontology*, T. Toadvine & L. Lawlor (trans.). Bloomington, IN: Indiana University Press.
Dillon, M. C. 1997. *Merleau-Ponty's Ontology*, 2nd edn. Evanston, IL: Northwestern University Press.
Madison, G. B. 1981. *The Phenomenology of Merleau-Ponty: A Search for the Limits of Consciousness*. Athens, OH: Ohio University Press.

FOUR

Existentialism:
the "new philosophy"

Thomas Busch

In 1948 Maurice Merleau-Ponty published *Sense and Non-Sense*, a collection of essays on art, philosophy and politics. Two of these essays, "The Battle Over Existentialism" and "A Scandalous Author", involve a vigorous defence of Jean-Paul Sartre, whom critics were attacking as a "corrupter of youth", a "demoniacal novelist", a "voice of filth, immorality, and spinelessness". Merleau-Ponty responded to this sort of name-calling, inviting instead a serious study of Sartre's work: "If it is true that many young people are welcoming the new philosophy with open arms, it will take more than these peevish criticisms, which deliberately avoid the question raised by Sartre's work, to convince them to reject it" (SNS: 71). Sartre, he continued, is challenging "classical views" of our relation to our natural and social surroundings. "The merit of the new philosophy", Merleau-Ponty tells us,

> is precisely that it tries, in the notion of existence, to find a way of thinking about our condition. In the modern sense of the word, "existence" is the movement through which man is in the world and involves himself in a physical and social situation which then becomes his point of view on the world.
>
> (*Ibid.*: 72)

The classical primacy of cognitional relationship between subject and object is now to be replaced by an actional and involved relationship. This has apparently confused Sartre's Catholic critics who accuse him of materialism, as well as his Marxist critics who accuse him of idealism. As Merleau-Ponty defends many of the key notions of this new philosophy – subjectivity, finitude, contingency, freedom and responsibility – it is important to note the criticisms of Sartre's views that Merleau-Ponty also politely suggests, similar to those criticisms of *Being and Nothingness* (hereafter BN) that he suggested in *Phenomenology of Perception* published in 1945. These two key works established the new philosophy in France and, in addition, a philosophical influence that continues to this day. As time passed, the criticisms sharpened on both sides, as Sartre went on to articulate his views on social and political life, culminating in a break in the relationship of these two friends. Merleau-Ponty's criticisms of Sartre offer a valuable place to mark his own imprint on the development of the notions of subjectivity, rationality and meaning, alterity, and freedom, central issues in the new existential philosophy.

Embodied subjectivity

Wary of philosophies of subjectivity based upon consciousness and reflection, but equally critical of the modern project of explaining behaviour in terms of the mechanical relationships of stimulus–organism–response, Merleau-Ponty negotiates between a realism that would reduce plurality of meaning and an idealism of meaning that would "reabsorb" or free itself from the real. It is precisely the latter that Merleau-Ponty finds problematic in Sartre's philosophy of the subject, as its primary focus is on subjectivity as consciousness. Repeatedly Merleau-Ponty refuses the stark binary option proposed by Sartre of either being a self-conscious subject (being-for-itself) or a thing (being-in-itself). Subjectivity, for Merleau-Ponty, is "existence", a notion that includes consciousness as well as the physical, physiological and biological in an integrated process.

> At the very moment when I live in the world, when I am given over to my plans, my occupations, my friends, my memories, I can close my eyes, lie down, listen to the blood pulsating in my ears, lose myself in some pleasure or pain, and shut myself up in this anonymous existence which subtends my personal one. But precisely because my body can shut itself off from the world, it is also what opens me out upon the world and places me in a situation there. The momentum of existence towards others, towards the future, towards the world can be restored as a river unfreezes. (PP: 164–5)

In this process of "existence" there is continual bleeding into one another of the "physical" and the "conscious", so that no behaviour is merely one or the other. Sartre had famously proclaimed that "Existence precedes essence", and Merleau-Ponty in the chapter on sexuality similarly proclaims that "Man is a historical idea and not a natural species" (PP: 170). Both reject essentialism, but Merleau-Ponty nuances his position from that of Sartre:

> Since . . . all human "functions", from sexuality to motility to intelligence, are rigorously unified in one synthesis, it is impossible to distinguish in the total being of man a bodily organization to be treated as a contingent fact, and other attributes necessarily entering into his make-up. Everything in man is a necessity . . . On the other hand, everything in man is a contingency in the sense that this human manner of existence is not guaranteed to every child through some essence acquired at birth, and in the sense that it must be constantly reforged in him through the hazards encountered by the objective body.
>
> (*Ibid.*: 170)

In other words, all transcendence is a "taking up" that conditions that transcendence. We are sexual beings as, in a footnote, he reminds us that we are economic beings, and have no choice about that, but how we take up these given situations and work out our sexuality or our economy is not determined by those givens: "All that we are, we are on the basis of a *de facto* situation which we appropriate to ourselves and which we ceaselessly transform by a sort of *escape* which is never an unconditioned freedom" (*ibid.*: 170–71). Sartre had used the expression "*ex nihilo*" in depicting free acts and Merleau-Ponty's use of "transform" is significant in understanding their respective views not only on freedom, but also on the issue of meaning.

Meaning

In *Being and Nothingness* Sartre often attributes the constitution of meaning to subjectivity itself: in anguish, for example, we are thought to apprehend ourselves as totally free and as not being able to derive the meaning of the world except as coming from ourselves. In contrast, Merleau-Ponty asserts in his preface to *Phenomenology of Perception* that "because we are in the world, we are *condemned to meaning*" (PP: xix). There is meaning, for Merleau-Ponty, in the body's encounter with its situation, in the very fact that perception presents one with a figure on a background. Such a perceptual given is meaningful because something stands out instead of being mere flux. There is a sensible organization, there is a "perceptual 'something' [which] is always in the middle of something else, [and] always forms part of a 'field' . . . Each part arouses the expectation of more than it contains, and this elementary perception is therefore already charged with *meaning*" (*ibid.*: 4). The perceiving body, whose senses act together as one perceiving organ, is the noetic correlate of the origin of perceptual meaning by its attentional focus bringing the indeterminate to determinate figuration. There is never complete determination since a determinate figure always stands out on an indeterminate background that runs off in various directions. Perceptual meaning is contingent and finite, embedded always in point of view. "[W]hat we see is always in some respects not seen: there must be hidden sides of things, and things 'behind us,' if there is to be a 'front' of things, and things 'in front of' us, in short perception" (*ibid.*: 277). Thought itself cannot evade this perceptual finitude: "All consciousness is, in some measure, perceptual consciousness", so that what is "evident" to thought is "irresistible" on the basis of a background of conditions, "a certain acquisition of experience, a certain field of thought, and precisely for this reason it appears to me as self-evident for a certain thinking nature" (*ibid.*: 396). For Merleau-Ponty, meaning happens. In this sense, he differs from thinkers of the absurd such as Sartre. Sartre holds that factical existence itself is absurd. This absurdist view, for Merleau-Ponty, is completely opposite to the rationalist view that proclaims that everything has meaning, and he rejects both: "[I]t is impossible to say that *everything has significance*, or that *everything is nonsense*, but only that *there is significance*" (*ibid.*: 296). Both the absurdist and the rationalist assume metaphysical positions about meaning while overlooking the "actual life of consciousness". The actual life of consciousness in perception reveals that the perceiving body is always involved in an organized experience, even though all organization is subject to reversals, surprises and readjustments. Again, this is true for all cognitive life inasmuch as we conceptually, meaningfully, organize our experience based upon past experience and learning, and expect to understand our future experience in those terms. These cognitive categories themselves seep into perception, enlarging it from its mere sensible dimension. In this enlarged sense we see how the contingencies of life-experience constantly challenge our perception of life, compelling us to redefine our perceptual categories or adopt forms of denial. In this give and take there is always a background of meaning, and that background has its underpinning in the always-present sensible organization of experience.

While experience is always organized, Merleau-Ponty insists that the body itself is not the sole player in bringing about meaningful organization. To be sure, the body is a condition of possibility in the organizing process, but the body is motivated in its meaning-giving activity. "The relations between things or aspects of things having always our body as their vehicle, the whole of nature is the setting of our own life, or our interlocutor in a sort of dialogue" (PP: 373). Merleau-Ponty gingerly tries to step between realism's penchant to speak of a coincidence of knower and known, and idealism's tendency to reduce the known to the knower. For him the knower both belongs to the world and knows the world from its place in the world. Our sense of "reality" must come from our lived experience of reality, that is, from the body's involvement in and transactional dealings with reality. This dialogical model of the creation of meaning is in contrast to Sartre's early view of imagination as a negation of reality (an act of disengagement from it), which led Sartre to define existence in terms of a distantiation that burdened the subject with being the sole creator of meaning. For Merleau-Ponty, at the same time as my body brings its sensible fields to bear, it is moved to do so, so as to bring about an articulately perceived thing. Since a thing's intelligibility depends on its identity, its determinateness, Merleau-Ponty phenomenologically places this intelligibility in the relation of phenomena to one's body. A thing's "true" or "objective" size, weight and colour, for example, are defined in relation to the body's grip (*prise*) on a thing. A "thing" itself is defined as the "correlate" of the synthetic sensible fields and activity of the perceiving subject (e.g. PP: 318).

For Merleau-Ponty the perceiving subject is not a mind taking note of sense data or representations, but a body at grips with phenomena. The body is, so to speak, always running ahead of conscious mind, and is again, so to speak, "pre-personal". The pre-personal level of perception does not exist in itself, outside of it being taken up into personal categories of organizing experiences, but is always present as enabling background condition. The lived body, then, is a momentum towards the world, such that the subject can never coincide with itself, never be an immanently closed existence. As opposed to the traditional understanding of the *cogito* as pure immanence, he speaks of a "*new cogito*", or an "existential *cogito*".

If we keep, for the *cogito*, the meaning of "existential experience" and if it reveals to me, not the absolute transparency of thought wholly in possession of itself, but the blind act by which I take up my destiny as a thinking nature and follow it out, then we are introducing another philosophy, which does not take us out *of time*. (PP: 374)

A consciousness that perfectly coincided with itself would be sealed off from the world and would be, for Merleau-Ponty, "no longer a finite self" (*ibid.*: 373). Reflection, existentially considered, takes up an unreflected life, one always already there, situationally embedded so that reflection always bears the traces of the unreflective. Thoughts, feelings and emotions in this sense always bear a relation to one's dealings with the world and are not merely private states, but an orientation of one's existence (see Chapter 15). This means that self-knowledge is mediated through the self's situation and its ambiguity. The certainty sought by followers of Descartes's methodology must give way to the risk of existing, of committing oneself to one's projects and living them out.

It is true neither that my existence is in full possession of itself, nor that it is entirely estranged from itself, because it is action or doing, and because action is, by definition, the violent transition from what I am to what I intend to be. I can effect the *cogito* and be assured of genuinely willing, loving or believing, provided that in the first place I actually do will, love or believe, and thus fulfil my own existence. (*Ibid.*: 382)

Without exaggeration it is possible to say that this inseparability of thought and action is the heart of the "new" philosophy. Whatever differences there are between Sartre and Merleau-Ponty, and there are important ones, the philosophers are in strong agreement in identifying human existence with action in the world and in situating knowledge within that ongoing context. Reflection and the unreflected are related as founded to founding, where the former, while rooted in the latter, never absorbs it. Existence runs ahead of reflection in action so that reflection feeds off existence, which, while never reabsorbed by reflection, is nevertheless "experienced". Existence is not an objective state, as it were closed in upon itself and totally mute – a thing. "We do not mean that the primordial *I* completely overlooks itself. If it did it would be a thing, and nothing

35

could cause it subsequently to become conscious" (PP: 404). Rather, Merleau-Ponty, following Sartre on this issue, holds that the existing self is "tacitly" aware of itself. It is "myself experienced by myself", not in knowledge, but where "a glimpse" of oneself is revealed. Tacit or "lived" experience is the "silence" that precedes speech and, in coming to meaning in speech from an "inarticulate grasp upon the world", "conditions" speech. Language, for Merleau-Ponty, is a form of mediation and, as such, is founded in the tacit experience of existence in a process of bringing existence to meaning, a dimension in which existence can encounter itself critically.

Language and expression

The mediated character of our knowledge of existence was apparent in Merleau-Ponty's position on language when he claimed that "thought is no 'internal' thing, and does not exist independently of the world and of words" (PP: 183). Words are not, for him, sounds or graphic markings external to the speaker's "mental" meanings. He likens speech to expression in the arts, such as music and theatre where one can see that the sonata's meaning and the character's personality are the performances themselves. What creates the "illusion of an inner life" (*ibid*.) is the presence in the speaker of sedimented words that form a silent background to the figure of an act of expression, operative even when one thinks to oneself. Expression emerges for Merleau-Ponty from "a certain void of consciousness . . . a momentary desire" (*ibid*.) that gropes for available means to express itself, thereby bringing itself to meaning. What is seductively dangerous about language is that it is here, as among no other expressive media, that meaning can appear to break away from its incarnation and take on a life of its own. How he thinks this mistake takes place can be seen in his distinction between original and sedimented speech. Original speech is a form of language use that, while dependent upon given meanings, past uses of language, nevertheless manages to say something new or different. Such a speech-act can take up speech that has been used to fit former contexts and bend it appropriately to new contexts. In turn, the new speech-act becomes a public deposit.

> Speech is, therefore, that paradoxical operation through which, by using words of a given sense, and already available meanings, we try to follow up an intention which necessarily outstrips, modifies, and itself, in the last analysis, stabilizes the meanings of the words which translate it.   (*Ibid.*: 389)

Language "in us" takes the form of a sedimented expressive capacity that, like our limbs in the form of actional capacities, is always already there for us in a non-objective way. One thinks through and by means of language, through language (*ibid*.). In this way, language is on the "inside" of the subject, and when the subject speaks he or she creates new expressions, which are public and "outside". "Inside and outside are inseparable. The world is wholly inside and I am wholly outside myself" (*ibid*.: 407). For Merleau-Ponty, meaning is in the expression to the point that they are inseparable. Meaning, thus, never escapes space and time. Ideality has its unique form of time, as can be seen in the history of ideas, where a book's influence is traceable, in terms of the commentaries upon it, in the ideas that it inspires. But the book's "life" is inseparable from its inscriptions.

Merleau-Ponty's claim that ideality is inseparable from its inscriptions is at the heart of his version of the "new philosophy's" recognition of the significance of finitude: "Every truth of fact is a truth of reason, and vice versa" (PP: 394). His contribution to the new philosophy is primarily in his focus on the body-subject and its inescapable belonging to, in terms of "living", space and time (*ibid*.: 388). "Our body . . . is the condition of possibility . . . of all expressive operations and all acquired views which constitute the cultural world" (*ibid*.). This tethering of ideality and culture to perception and the body has led to unfortunate misreading of Merleau-Ponty's view as a reductionism of ideality and cultural meaning in general. It is important to remember that in his understanding of the founding–founded relation the "originator [founding] is not primary in the empiricist sense and the originated is not simply derived . . ." (*ibid*.: 394). The founding term, thus, is considered to be a necessary but not sufficient condition for the founded. Realms of ideality (art, mathematics, cultural institutions) are really transformations of our bodily rootedness in a natural world and have their own unique meanings.

Merleau-Ponty's approach to expression, and language in particular, differs subtly, but quite significantly, from that of Sartre. Sartre's stress is on the speaker's freedom to create meaning. "Since the verbal unity", he tells us, "is the meaningful sentence, the latter is a constructive act which is conceived only by a transcendence which surpasses and nihilates the given toward an end" (Sartre 1993: 515). By nihilation, Sartre means a clean and total break from any given and apparently constraining situation. Language in a given state cannot constrain the speaker. "Each for-itself, in fact, is a for-itself only by choosing . . . the designation beyond the syntax and morphemes. This 'beyond' is enough to ensure its total independence in relation to the structures which it surpasses . . ." (*ibid.*: 520). Merleau-Ponty does not eliminate subjectivity from his account of speaking, for he employs the vocabulary of intentionality: "The new sense-giving intention knows itself only by donning already available meanings, the outcome of previous acts of expression" (PP: 183). He does, however, diffuse the autonomy of the speaker by emphasizing the dependence (in contrast to Sartre's "total independence") of the speaker on givenness, on the available categories of expression and their possibilities for expression. There is present in his account a dialectic typical of his general approach to issues, a give and take between the subject and what is given, an exchange that Sartre's stress on transcendence as nihilation of the given would appear to preclude.

Others; intersubjectivity

Because of the new philosophy's stress on subjectivity, the issue of alterity (of the otherness of the world and other people) is a sensitive and even controversial one for it. For Merleau-Ponty, in his version of the new philosophy featuring the subject as body-subject, this is no less the case. He did say, after all, that the body is the ultimate "condition of possibility" of all phenomena, marking them as always having the sense of being "for me". Emmanuel Levinas, in many ways an admirer of Merleau-Ponty's work, finds it seriously flawed with regard to giving alterity its due (see Chapter 13). Nonetheless, Merleau-Ponty devotes a chapter in *Phenomenology of Perception* to the existence of others, human existents, and one key feature of this chapter is to critique Sartre's more conflictual understanding of our relation with others. At the centre of Merleau-Ponty's version of human relationships is "the body of the other person as the vehicle of a form of behavior" (PP: 348). Considered this way, the body is neither totally subjective nor objective, but is "a third genus of being" (*ibid.*: 350), which cuts across those categories. Our encounter with others is not a matter of mind and reasoning to find an other "behind" behaviour, but is a matter of one body recognizing another.

> A baby of fifteen months opens its mouth if I playfully take one of its fingers between my teeth and pretend to bite it. And yet it has scarcely looked at its face in a glass, and its teeth are not in any case like mine. The fact is that its own mouth and teeth as it feels them from the inside, are immediately for it, capable of the same intentions. "Biting" has for it an intersubjective

significance. It perceives its intentions in its body, and my body with its own, and thereby my intentions in its own body.

(PP: 352)

The body is structured for action and it is this structuration that lends itself to overlap, just as if, he tells us, "my body and the other person's are one whole, two sides of one and the same phenomenon" (ibid.: 354). It is true that one's own lived experience is precisely, as lived, one's own, and so there is a truth to solipsism, but one's consciousness adheres to one's body, and in action and communication is revealed. Bodies exist in an "interworld" of mediations, at the basis of which are body and language. The latter allows personal communication across life perspectives. A dialogue is a "shared operation", a "dual being", where those involved are "collaborators in a consummate reciprocity". There is "reciprocity" because in the experience of dialogue "the other is for me no longer a bit of behavior in my transcendental field, nor I in his" (ibid.). Both the other and I, in a dialogical experience, are revealed as in an I–thou relationship of address and response.

Merleau-Ponty's dedication to the mediated nature of relations with the other separates him from Sartre's position on relationships with the other as they are presented in Being and Nothingness, dichotomized as they are into the binary relation of subject and object. Recall that for Sartre there is no option other than to be in a subjective mode of being (being-for-itself) or in an objective mode (being-in-itself). From the perspective of one's own subjectivity, others are objects by definition. When one is looked at by the other, one experiences oneself in the mode of object and in a state of alienation. For Sartre, objectification is inevitable in any human relationship, and in Being and Nothingness this is the basis for conflict: "Conflict is the original meaning of being-for-others" (Sartre 1993: 364). The human relationships depicted in Being and Nothingness are indeed conflictual, psychological variations of Hegel's master/slave relation. Although Sartre thought that authentic, non-conflictual relationships were possible and promised to address them in a later work, Merleau-Ponty challenges the premise that human relationships are originally alienated.

With the cogito begins that struggle between consciousnesses, each one of which, as Hegel says, seeks the death of the other. For the struggle ever to begin, and for each consciousness to be capable of suspecting the alien presences which it negates, all must necessarily have some common ground and be mindful of their peaceful coexistence in the world of childhood. (PP: 355)

Given the mediation of bodies and their mutual recognition, "the intersubjective world" is always already there prior to consciousness ever assuming a position with regard to it. Merleau-Ponty situates Sartre's objectifying look as possible only due to an act of psychological withdrawal from mediated relations and their shared comprehension towards that ever-present, but always incomplete truth of solipsism in our lived experience. But, as we have observed, complete withdrawal is impossible.

> But even then, the objectification of each by the other's gaze is felt as unbearable only because it takes the place of possible communication. A dog's gaze directed towards me causes me no embarrassment. The refusal to communicate, however, is still a form of communication. (*Ibid.*: 361)

One of the consequences of their differences over this issue was that Merleau-Ponty was quick to realize the political dimension of human relationships by virtue of mediating structures, while Sartre, adhering to his binary ontology, focused on issues of psychological alienation. One can now understand the critical comments about *Being and Nothingness* that Merleau-Ponty made, even when defending Sartre, in *Sense and Non-Sense*:

> We must analyze involvement, the moment when the subjective and objective conditions of history become bound together, how class exists before coming aware of itself – in short, the status of the social and the phenomenon of coexistence. *L'Être et le néant* does not yet offer this social theory . . . . (SNS: 81)

It was Merleau-Ponty who would gradually lead Sartre in the direction of commitment to political activism.

Freedom

It is not surprising that mediating structures play a central role in Merleau-Ponty's understanding of freedom and that he is sharply critical of Sartre on this key issue in the new philosophy. Sartre's ontology of freedom centres on the structure of consciousness itself,

40

on the negation that splits self-consciousness from coinciding with itself and at the same time splits it off from all objects that it confronts. Freedom is, for Sartre, based upon differentiation, a perpetual distancing of the conscious self from lapsing into the self-coincidence that defines a thing.

> [T]he subject without relation to himself would be condensed into the identity of the in-itself . . . The *self* therefore represents an ideal distance within the immanence of the subject in relation to himself, a way of *not being* his own coincidence, of escaping identity . . .　　　　　　　　　　　　　　(Sartre 1993: 76–7)

Not having a fixed identity or essence that would ground activity, the human existent's very being escapes this ground in a groundless freedom. Existence precedes essence. While freedom is always, Sartre insists, situated, no situation or given state of affairs can act upon or limit freedom. This is because the ontological distancing, or negation (*néant*), constitutive of the being of subjectivity (being-for-itself), leaves no room for passivity. The ontology of negation was intended to ensure the autonomy of the subject. As constituted by continuous negation/separation, the subject is pure action, immune to being acted upon: "it is impossible to act upon consciousness" (Sartre 1993: 422). Sartre's free subject is in a continuous process of surpassing the given towards future possibilities chosen by itself alone.

> If the given cannot explain the intention, it is necessary that the intention by its upsurge realize a rupture with the given . . . It would be in vain to imagine that consciousness can exist without a given . . . but if consciousness exists in terms of the given, this does not mean that the given conditions consciousness; consciousness is a pure and simple negation of this given.
> 　　　　　　　　　　　　　　　　　　　　(*Ibid.*: 478)

Merleau-Ponty objects that this ontological version of freedom is too abstract. It claims too much, for if freedom is located in the structure of consciousness itself, then all conscious acts are guaranteed to be free. Concrete freedom, for Merleau-Ponty, as can be expected, is to be found in the exchange between the subject and its situation, in mediated action. Freedom "must have a *field*, which means that there must be for it special possibilities, or realities which tend to cling to being" (PP: 438). In deflecting focus from consciousness to action, one must bring into consideration situational possibilities, "open situations requiring a certain completion and capable of constituting a background to either a confirmatory or transformatory decision . . ." (*ibid*.: 438). There can be degrees of concrete freedom, for the enablements and limitations of one's situation must factor into an appreciation of how free one is. Additionally, for Merleau-Ponty, during the course of the subject's transactions with the situations of its life, traces of its choices leave sedimentation in the subject. One's life gains thereby a certain "momentum" so that certain "probabilities" arise in the face of future action. He rejects essentialism, as Sartre did, but maintains a thicker sense of subjectivity than Sartre did because of his emphasis upon the body. It is here that one can see, in full clarity, how existentialism was developed differently by these two advocates. They both promoted a new philosophy, opposing traditional philosophy with a shared stance against essentialism and totalization and in favour of contingency, choice and commitment, temporality, finite perspective. Sartre's thinking took on the look of a strong humanism, based on a view of the subject as an autonomous bestower of meaning on a meaningless world. His focus was on repudiating various forms of determinism (excuse thinking) to the point where his notion of negation (*néant*), constitutive of the subject's autonomy, defined the subject as pure action with no room for receptivity. This is clear in his understanding of the body, and it is here that the differences of these two iterations of the new philosophy crystallize.

In Sartre's ontological discourse there are two incommensurable senses of the body, the body as for-itself (the subjective body) and the body for-others (the objective body). This is evident in his analysis of the body as touching itself, as touching–touched. For him touching and touched are "two essentially different orders of reality . . . different and incommunicable levels of being" (Sartre 1993: 304). A major consequence of this ontological dualism is evident in his phenomenology of tool usage. Tools are extensions of the body's capacities to act. In using a tool, one incorporates the tool into one's capacity, into one's intentionality, to the point where the tool is not noticed. Sartre insists that in thus "interiorizing" the tool, "it loses its character as a technique and is integrated purely and simply in the free surpassing of the given toward ends" (*ibid*.: 523). Merleau-Ponty would respond by pointing out that while the tool in its "character as a technique" may not be noticed in lived experience of its usage, its character does not disappear altogether. If one habitually uses a hammer, one's hand can become calloused; constant labour over a machine can warp one's posture. The body is the point of exchange between subjective and objective, or is rather a "third genus of being" between Sartre's two ontological options. The body, Merleau-Ponty insists, "is both an object for others and a subject for myself" (PP: 167). The touching–touched phenomenon, for Merleau-Ponty, does not involve a "rupture" between two incommunicable modes of reality, but a "fold" where the body experiences itself in two different, but reversible, ways. It is this sort of understanding of the body that he thought necessary for the dialectical exchange between the subject and its world, allowing for the subject to be affected. In remarks he made in *Sense and Non-Sense* about Sartre's view of freedom in *Being and Nothingness*, Merleau-Ponty wrote:

> The question is to know what part freedom plays and whether we can allow it something without giving it everything. We said earlier that *L'Être et le néant* seems to require further development on this point and that one would expect the author to elaborate a theory of passivity. (SNS: 77)

Merleau-Ponty's body-subject was a more modest, ecological subjectivity than Sartre's being-for-itself, with the latter importing into the new philosophy more traditionally modern characteristics. However, as time went on, Sartre's thinking took a dialectical turn, with more of the look of Merleau-Ponty's thinking. But that is another story.

Further reading

Dillon, M. C. 1997. *Merleau-Ponty's Ontology*, 2nd edn. Evanston, IL: Northwestern University Press.
Madison, G. 1981. *The Phenomenology of Merleau-Ponty: A Search for the Limits of Consciousness*. Athens, OH: Ohio University Press.
Schmidt, J. 1985. *Maurice Merleau-Ponty: Between Phenomenology and Structuralism*. London: Macmillan.
Stewart, J. (ed.) 1998. *The Debate Between Sartre and Merleau-Ponty*. Evanston, IL: Northwestern University Press.

FIVE

Between empiricism and intellectualism

Taylor Carman

Merleau-Ponty is best known for his positive account of the bodily nature of perception. Just as crucial to his phenomenology, however, is his negative critique of the ways in which traditional theories tend to misdescribe perception abstractly at the outset, without considering the ways in which it is constituted by the concrete structures and capacities of the body. Specifically, two chief misconceptions loom large, like Scylla and Charybdis, on either side of an adequate account of perceptual experience, threatening to obscure its distinctive character. They are what Merleau-Ponty calls "empiricism" and "intellectualism", and they remain stumbling blocks, perhaps perennial temptations, for theories of perception today.

Empiricism

Empiricism is any view that conceives of perception as based on non-intentional qualitative sensory content – sensations, sense data, so-called "raw feels", *qualia* and so on. Merleau-Ponty's critique of empiricism is twofold. In the first place, he argues, empiricism is descriptively wrong: ordinary perceptual awareness simply is not an awareness of sensations, but of things out in the world – people, situations, events. Second, empiricist theories are incoherent, for the resources they have at their disposal for describing pure sensory content make sense only if we take for granted the full-blown perceptual phenomena they are meant to explain.

The charge of descriptive wrongness is fairly straightforward. As Merleau-Ponty says, the concept of sensation "corresponds to nothing in our experience" (PP: 3). What we see are not mere sense data or *qualia*, but people and things, and often the empty gaps and spaces between them, as well as what the psychologist J. J. Gibson calls "affordances", for example paths, obstacles, barriers, brinks, steps, slopes, shelters and tools (Gibson 1979: 36–41). The "things" we ordinarily see are not abstract, free-floating qualities, but opportunities, threats, dangers – in short, things to do, things to grab, things to avoid. This is in part just to say that perceptual experience is *intentional*, or "of" something. When I have, say, a visual awareness *of* fire, the "of" in that locution is not the same as the "of" in the expression "sensation of pain", where the pain just *is* the sensation. Empiricism goes wrong in collapsing the distinction between the intentional object of my experience, or *what* I perceive, and my experience of it. What I perceive is not (ordinarily) a part or aspect of my perception, but something in the world, distinct from myself.

And yet this theoretical confusion of perceiving and the perceived is not a wholly arbitrary error. Instead, it has its roots in our natural orientation towards the world, whose features we tend to read back into our sensory states when we try to describe those states on reflection. We are normally focused on or "at grips with" (*en prise sur*) our environment, so when we turn our attention to perception itself, we project on to it the qualities of the things we perceive: "We commit what psychologists call the 'experience error', which means that what we know to be in things themselves we immediately take to be in our consciousness of them. We make perception out of things perceived" (PP: 5).

Merleau-Ponty's argument that empiricism is not just incorrect but incoherent is less straightforward, but deeper and more interesting. For the real philosophical problem with empiricism is not just that it happens to be false, but that it cannot possibly be informative. The reason is that the language of sensation is itself parasitic on the language with which we refer to the genuine objects of perception: "When I say that I have before me a red patch, the meaning of the word 'patch' is provided by previous experiences that have taught me the use of the word" (PP: 14).

The Humean principle of the "association of ideas", for example, takes for granted precisely the kind of perceptual coherence it is meant to explain. The mind combines ideas, Hume says, according to three principles: resemblance, contiguity and causality. But to *which* ideas do we apply these principles, and how do we do so? Hume insists that the regular patterns that emerge in our complex ideas would be unaccountable "without some bond of union among them, some associating quality, by which one idea naturally introduces another" (2000: 1.1.4). But this is ambiguous. Does the mind impose order on our ideas just by combining them in particular ways, or do the ideas themselves first exhibit qualities that bring about or motivate the ways in which we associate them with one another? Apparently the latter, but then we must ask what qualities of our ideas can motivate us to associate them as we do. What kinds of things, after all, do we normally associate and group together? Not mere sensations or atomic qualities like *red* or *hot*, but full-fledged things and their concretely contextualized features: the baseball and the basketball, the sock and the shoe, the fire and the burn. Such things are not mere collections of discrete parts, but coherent wholes or ensembles, and their objective coherence is precisely what allows us to isolate aspects or features that we can then associate with one another abstractly:

> It is not indifferent data that set about combining into a thing because *de facto* contiguities or resemblances cause them to associate; it is, on the contrary, because we perceive a grouping as a thing that the analytical attitude can then discern resemblances or continuities. (PP: 16, trans. altered)

The empiricist principle of association thus reverses the true order of explanation, mistaking a consequence of perceptual significance for its ground. As Merleau-Ponty says, "the unity of the thing in perception is not constructed by association, but is a condition of association" (*ibid.*: 17).

The concept of sensation is incoherent, then, inasmuch as empiricists enlist it for two distinct and incompatible purposes. On the one hand, it is meant to capture the phenomenal content of experience. On the other hand, it is supposed to explain how that experience is brought about by stimulations of our sensory surfaces. The reason it fails to satisfy the former descriptive need is precisely its subservience to the latter explanatory demand, and vice versa. Thus when the concept of sensation describes the phenomena adequately, it explains nothing, and when it is subsequently invoked, along with auxiliary hypotheses concerning association and memory, to explain away the manifest phenomena, it no longer describes them as they are.

Intellectualism

Intellectualism, by contrast, is any view that conceives of perception as consisting essentially in the exercise of thought or judgement, whether such judgements are meant to constitute or merely schematize or organize some other, purely sensory content. Roughly, the former version of the view goes back to Descartes and the early-modern rationalists, while the latter is Kantian. In a Kantian vein, for example, William James defines intellectualism as the view that sensations exist, but "are combined by the activity of the Thinking Principle" (1950: II: 27).

For Descartes and Kant, the very fact that we see *things*, as opposed to mere clusters of qualities, is due to our application of the concept of substance to what is given passively to the senses. What we literally see are the features of things, not the things *having* or possessing those features, that is, not some underlying *je ne sais quoi* in which those features are embedded. And so, Descartes writes, "something which I thought I was seeing with my eyes is in fact grasped solely by the faculty of judgement which is in my mind" (1985: AT VII 32). Similarly, Kant argues that the concepts or "categories" of the understanding render the stuff of sensation into an experience of objects: "all synthesis, through which even perception itself becomes possible, stands under the categories, and since experience is cognition through connected perceptions, the categories are conditions of the possibility of experience" (1998: B161).

Merleau-Ponty argues that intellectualism is as misguided and unstable as empiricism, and indeed that the two otherwise seemingly opposed doctrines rest on many of the same bad assumptions concerning the phenomenal character and the bodily basis of perception. But whereas empiricism in effect renders inexplicable the transition from pure sensory quality to the intentionality of attitudes such as belief and judgement, intellectualism simply takes the connection between experience and thought for granted by building judgement into the very definition of perceptual objectivity: "Empiricism cannot see that we need to know what we are looking for, otherwise we would not be looking for it, and intellectualism fails to see that we need to be ignorant of what we are looking for, or equally again we should not be searching" (PP: 28). Intellectualism, that is, fails to acknowledge that there is a problem about how thought can be connected to the world by being grounded in perceptual experiences that are not themselves already forms of thinking. "What intellectualism lacks", Merleau-Ponty observes, "is contingency in the occasions of thought" (*ibid.*).

More recent cognitivist theories of perception have tried to dispense with this problem about the relation between experience and judgement by dispensing with the very idea that anything is really *given* in experience at all, prior to or independent of our judgement about it. Daniel Dennett, for example, insists that there can in principle be no difference between the way things *seem* to us and the way we *think* they seem. For him, quite literally, seeing is believing: to lack a belief about a perceptual experience is simply to lack the experience. Dennett (1991: 132) calls this view "first-person operationalism".

There are, of course, borderline cases between perception and judgement. It is not always easy, or even possible, to say whether an experience is one or the other. We see faces as the faces of either men or women, as either happy or sad. Do we literally *see* their masculinity and femininity or their affective tone, or do we infer gender and mood from something else? You hate anchovies, but is it the actual taste or just the idea of them that gives you the creeps? Intellectualism often thrives on ambiguous cases like these, which tempt us to construe all kinds of intentionality as either explicitly or implicitly judgemental.

But do such borderline cases threaten the very distinction between experience and judgement? To say that there is only a gradual difference between the two, rather than a sharp boundary, is in no way to deny that there are unambiguous instances of each. I perceive the clouds in the sky without any deliberation or commitment of judgement at all, just as I judge that $2 + 2 = 4$ without the faintest glimmer of qualitative feeling. As Merleau-Ponty says,

> Ordinary experience draws a very clear distinction between sensing (*le sentir*) and judgment. For it, judgment is the taking (*prise*) of a position, it aims at knowing something valid for me at every moment of my life, and for other minds, actual or possible; sensing, by contrast, is giving oneself over to appearance without trying to possess it and know its truth. This distinction disappears in intellectualism, because judgment is everywhere pure sensation is not, which is to say everywhere. The testimony of phenomena will therefore everywhere be impugned.
>
> (PP: 34)

Indeed, one ironic consequence of intellectualism is the reaffirmation of one of the most dubious prejudices of the Cartesian conception of the mind, to which materialists such as Dennett are otherwise so hostile, namely the idea that we are incorrigible about our own mental states. For if my consciousness and my beliefs about my consciousness are indistinguishable, it will be impossible for my beliefs to be wrong *about* my experience:

> if we see what we judge, how can we distinguish between true and false perception? How will we then be able to say that the halluciné or the madman "think they see what they do not see"? What will be the difference between "seeing" and "thinking one sees"? (*Ibid*.: 34–5)

There is a difference between seeing and merely thinking one sees, that is, not just because "see" is a success verb, but because things do not always *actually* appear to me the way I *think* they appear, and intellectualism can make no sense of that distinction.

Intellectualism thus begs the questions: at *what* are the operations of the intellect themselves directed?; and how do minds *orient* themselves at the outset *vis-à-vis* their objects? More precisely, what intellectualist theories of perception fail to acknowledge, according to Merleau-Ponty, is the embodiment and situatedness of experience, for they reduce perceptual content to the free-floating cognition of a disembodied subject:

> Perception is thus thought about perceiving. Its incarnation furnishes no positive characteristic that has to be accounted for, and its hæcceity is simply its own ignorance of itself. Reflective analysis becomes a purely regressive doctrine, according to which every perception is just confused intellection, every determination a negation. It thus does away with all problems except one: that of its own beginning. The finitude of a perception, which gives me, as Spinoza put it, "conclusions without premises," the inherence of consciousness in a point of view, all this reduces to my ignorance of myself, to my negative power of not reflecting. But that ignorance, how is it itself possible? (*Ibid*.: 38, trans. altered)

Intellectualism is not just phenomenologically wrong, then, but incoherent, for it pretends to explain appearances whose very existence it cannot consistently acknowledge. And yet descriptions of supposedly constitutive perceptual judgements always turn out to be disguised descriptions of perceptual receptivity. For intellectualism, that is, "Perception is a judgment, but one that is unaware of its own foundations, which amounts to saying that the perceived object is given as a totality and a unity before we have apprehended the intelligible law governing it" (*ibid.*: 42). Here, Merleau-Ponty quotes Descartes: "These and other judgments that I made concerning sensory objects, I was apparently taught to make by nature; for I had already made up my mind that this was how things were, before working out any arguments to prove it" (1985: AT VII 76). What Descartes describes as an innate inclination of the mind, and what Malebranche calls "natural judgment", is just perception itself in its receptive aspect, in contrast to the spontaneity of the intellect (1997: Book One, ch. 7, §IV: 34). "The result", Merleau-Ponty concludes, "is that the intellectualist analysis ends by rendering incomprehensible the perceptual phenomena it is supposed to explain" (PP: 34).

The perceptual ground of all judgement becomes clearer when we consider aspects or Gestalts that shift even while the discrete parts of objects remain constant. As Merleau-Ponty says, "perception is not an act of understanding. I have only to look at a landscape upside down to recognize nothing in it" (PP: 46). Faces and handwriting undergo similar jarring transformations of character when viewed upside down or backwards, yet their objective structures remain the same from a purely intellectual point of view. The sensory stimuli are in a certain sense objectively the same forwards as backwards, right side up as upside down, so the intellectualist supposes the qualitative difference in perceptual aspect must be an artefact of a change of intellectual attitude. You cannot see what is not there, after all, so when a perceptual effect fails to correspond to the supplied stimulus, you must not be literally *seeing* what you seem to see, but merely *thinking* you see it.

But why assume that we can only literally see what directly impinges on our senses? Why not suppose instead that we see things by, say, having them in our peripheral vision, especially in cases where we are sensitized to notice just those salient features that make them relevant to what we are looking at, or looking for? By arbitrarily applying a single preconceived criterion of perceptual success across the board – namely, accurate registration of discrete stimuli – intellectualism systematically ignores the qualitative differences that distinguish our diverse sensory capacities and so underestimates the complexity and sophistication of the perceptual mechanisms involved in bringing the world before our eyes.

For Merleau-Ponty, then, although perception is not grounded in sensations, there is a form of givenness in perception that is irreducible to cognition: "there is a significance of the percept that has no equivalent in the universe of the understanding, a perceptual milieu that is not yet the objective world, a perceptual being that is not yet determinate being" (PP: 46–7). Intellectualism ignores the conceptual indeterminacy of perception and helps itself uncritically to a view of the world as described by the physical sciences: "the real flaw of intellectualism lies precisely in its taking as given the determinate universe of science" (*ibid.*: 47). Only by bracketing that fully objective description of the world, the description that aspires to a view from nowhere, as it were, and stepping back from the theoretical achievements of the sciences to our ordinary situated perspective on our familiar environment can we recover the peculiar naiveté that characterizes the actual quality of our concrete perceptual experience.

The phenomenal field

If perception is neither sensation nor judgement, why have philosophers and psychologists so regularly and so persistently misunderstood it by pressing it into such evidently inadequate conceptual categories? Merleau-Ponty does not rest content with merely criticizing the errors that have plagued traditional theories of perception; he tries also to diagnose those errors by describing the tendencies inherent in ordinary perceptual life that motivate and sustain them. He then offers what he thinks is a more faithful description of the things themselves prior to their distortion in theoretical (and pretheoretical) reflection.

Although the concepts of sensation and judgement are useless as fundamental explanatory notions, perception itself nevertheless clearly has two broadly discernible aspects, which Merleau-Ponty calls, respectively, "sensing" (*sentir*) or "sensoriality" (*sensorialité*) and "knowing" (either *connaître* or *savoir*). These are not the abstract notions of pure impression and pure concept, as one finds in Hume and Kant, but are at home in common-sense, ordinary language and culture. Romantic discourse in literature and the arts, for example, relies heavily on a robust notion of sense and sensibility, just as vague but indispensable notions of judgement are vital to legal and scientific practice.

Thus, when we "sense" something in the familiar and legitimate sense of the word, we *grasp* it: an unburdened wheel *looks* different from a wheel bearing a heavy load; a flame *looks* different to a child – namely hot, dangerous, threatening – after a burn. "Vision", Merleau-Ponty says, playing on the multiple senses of the word *sens*, "is already inhabited by a meaning (*sens*)" (PP: 52). To sense something in this sense is not merely to register or feel it, but to comprehend it, to make sense *of* it. And yet, what the ordinary notion has in common with its bastardized theoretical counterpart, indeed what breathes any life at all into that concept construed merely abstractly, is the suggestion of passivity, receptivity, being given over to the world as it is given to us. This phenomenon is precisely what intellectualism forgets, or suppresses: "A critical philosophy, in the last analysis, accords no importance to the resistance of passivity . . . It thus tacitly assumes that the philosopher's thinking is not subject to any situation" (*ibid.*: 61). What makes sense-experience a kind of experience, rather than an unconstrained form of awareness, Merleau-Ponty maintains, is its subjection to the world. Experience, in this sense, is "the communication of a finite subject with an opaque being from which it emerges, but to which it remains bound (*engagé*)" (*ibid.*: 219).

What, then, in our ordinary experience gave rise to the abstract notion of sensation as pure quality? A very familiar, hence inconspicuous, experience, namely looking intently at an object and momentarily ignoring the background context that presented it to us as something to look at more closely in the first place. The perceptual world could be conceived as consisting of nothing but such qualities only if perception itself were nothing but the relentless, focused inspection of discrete features: "The pure *quale* would be given to us only if the world were a spectacle and one's own body a mechanism that some impartial mind acquainted itself with" (PP: 52).

When I stare directly at a white piece of paper, for example, trying to determine the exact apparent shade of the part of it falling in shadow, Merleau-Ponty says, "I have made the quality appear by fixing my eyes on one portion of the visual field: then and only then have I found myself in the presence of a certain *quale* that absorbs my gaze". Pure sensible qualities are not original ingredients of perception, but artefacts of concentrated attention and reflection:

> The sensible quality, far from being coextensive with perception, is the peculiar product of an attitude of curiosity or observation. It appears when, instead of abandoning my entire gaze to the world, I turn toward the gaze itself, and when I ask myself *exactly what it is I see.* (PP: 226)

Something similar is true of judgement. Explicitly articulated judgements with propositional contents are not conditions of perception, but conditioned achievements built on a more fundamental form of active bodily intelligence that guides our behaviour, including even our most basic ways of perceiving things. Judgement, that is, presupposes a more basic kind of sensory understanding, one that does not involve the application of concepts. Consequently, "Understanding also needs to be redefined, since the general connective function ultimately attributed to it by Kantianism is now spread over the whole of intentional life and no longer suffices to distinguish it" (PP: 53). In the acquisition of a motor skill, for example, "it is the body" – *not the mind* – "that 'understands'" (*ibid.*: 144).

Merleau-Ponty thus wants to draw our attention back to the sensory background underlying our perception of isolated qualities and our formulation of explicit judgements. He calls this background the "phenomenal field", which suggests that it is neither an object *in* our experience nor merely a subjective effect cut off from the world: "This phenomenal field is not an 'inner world', the 'phenomenon' is not a 'state of consciousness' or a 'psychic fact'" (PP: 57). It is, as it were, that aspect of the world always already carved out and made available and familiar to us by our involuntary bodily perceptual capacities and unthinking behaviours. The phenomenal field presents things to us as "infused (*imprégné*) with an immanent meaning (*signification*)" (*ibid.*: 58). How? By having an *intentional* structure, that is, a directional orientation in an environment in a materially inhabited space. So, for example, others are immediately present to us; we see them *as* others, not as objects, certainly not as mere sensory data. What notion of immediacy is this? For Merleau-Ponty, "the immediate is no longer the impression, the object that is one with the subject, but the sense (*sens*), the structure, the spontaneous arrangement of parts" (*ibid.*). Again, what makes this kind of sense *sensible* rather than intellectual, what makes it receptive, is that it constrains us by giving us over to the world. So, although seeing is a kind of understanding, it is bound by what is given to it: "Vision is *a thought subject to a certain field*, and this is what is called a *sense*" (*ibid.*: 217).

Merleau-Ponty's insistence that sensory experience always has the form of a *field*, rather than a mere sum or accumulation of data, is thus a refinement of the seemingly obvious idea that perception is always essentially *perspectival*. To construe a perspective as a field is to appreciate that it is neither a mere collection of objects, a homogeneous segment of space, nor finally somehow just another bundle of sensations or judgements. A field is instead a kind of space or place (*lieu*): it is *where* objects and their qualities appear to us, relative to us. It therefore cannot be understood as a conditioned product of sensations or judgements. Just as space and time were for Kant, so the phenomenal field is for Merleau-Ponty a *transcendental* condition of the possibility of our being perceptually open to the world at all:

> phenomenology, alone among philosophies, speaks of a tran-scendental *field*. This word indicates that reflection never has the whole world and the plurality of monads arrayed and objectified before its gaze and that its view is never other than partial and of limited power. (PP: 61)

Perceptual perspective is not just a geometrical fact about the object-ive position of my sense organs in relation to objects; it is the imma-nent orientation of my experience towards things as ends available to me in virtue of my bodily attitudes and behaviours. It is what makes the perceived world meaningful to me *as* a world:

> the thinking Ego can never abolish its inherence in an individual subject that knows all things in a particular perspective. Reflec-tion can never bring it about that I cease to perceive the sun as two hundred yards away on a misty day, or see it "rise" and "set," or think with the cultural apparatus provided me by my education, my past efforts, my history. (*Ibid.*)

For Merleau-Ponty, that is, the meaningfulness of sense experience is an effect of its cohering around a concrete perspective naturally oriented outwards, away from itself, towards the world.

It is worth remembering, then, that in criticizing empiricist and intellectualist accounts of perception in terms of "sensation" and "judgement", Merleau-Ponty is not denying that our conscious ex-perience is indeed rich and complex in ways that virtually force us to avail ourselves of words like these in describing it. Merleau-Ponty himself has many positive things to say about the perceptual phenom-ena that motivate ordinary talk of such things as sensation, associa-tion, memory, attention and judgement. For of course experience is rife with feeling, internally interwoven, haunted by the past, focused against a background, and intelligent. What Merleau-Ponty criticizes is not our pre-theoretical understanding of what we ordinarily call "sensation" and "judgement", but the technical redeployment of those terms in abstraction from what they are originally called upon to describe. In dismissing the psychological concepts of sensation and judgement, he is arguing not that there is no difference between sens-ing and thinking, but that perception cannot be understood either as the mere passive registration of sense data or as fully free and spontaneous intellectual activity.

The systematic elusiveness of perception

Merleau-Ponty's critiques of empiricism and intellectualism are two aspects of a single effort to describe and conceive of perception not on the model of already familiar kinds of mental states, for example sensations and judgements, but in terms of our bodily orientation in our material surroundings. This shift of perspective is in part a move away from the mentalism of the Cartesian tradition, but it is not just that, for physicalistic theories of consciousness often fare no better in grasping perception as a form of meaningful bodily comportment in an environment. Instead, Merleau-Ponty's phenomenology must be understood as a rejection of individualism, the assumption that perception is an internal event or state of the organism, whether the mind or the brain, which can be described in isolation from its dynamic interactions with its external setting and conditions.

Why have philosophers conceived of perception as something "inside" us, rather than as our outer relation to the world in which we move and live, and which necessarily transcends us? Ironically, Merleau-Ponty suggests, it is because we have grown accustomed to thinking of everything, including ourselves and our fellow human beings, from a wholly objective, third-person point of view. But that third-person perspective essentially abstracts from the very phenomena that render us intelligible to ourselves as first (and second) persons. Experience itself then strikes us as an anomaly, a mystery, an embarrassment to science, something that somehow does not belong in the visible world at all, but must instead be found hidden away in the private recesses of the mind or brain.

Why has it been so difficult to think about perceptual experience without lapsing into these objectivist and subjectivist fallacies? Part of the reason, Merleau-Ponty suggests, has to do with the natural, perhaps inevitable, effect of an essential tendency at work in perception itself, namely our absorption in the world, our directedness towards objects, hence the systematic deflection of our attention away from our own experience. This is no accident, for "it is the essence of consciousness to forget its own phenomena" (PP: 58); "perception masks itself to itself" (VI: 213). Like a vortex, perception constantly pushes us out towards the world and away from itself, and so, as often happens in philosophy, we forget ourselves.

Small wonder, then, that philosophers and psychologists have found perception so hard to describe, or even think about clearly, for it is part of its very nature to *deflect* thought. The phenomenal field is elusive, that is, precisely because its function is to draw us out into the world. The phenomenal field constantly pushes us away from itself, and this is why "Nothing is more difficult than knowing precisely *what we see*", for "perception hides itself from itself" (PP: 58).

What we find in Merleau-Ponty, then, is not just one more in a series of philosophical theories of perception, but a radically new concept of perception and its relation to the world. He sought to realign our entire understanding of perception with phenomena we are always already familiar with before we fit them into conventional categories, pose strange questions about them, and construct theories around them. We learn anew from Merleau-Ponty something we in one sense already knew, if only tacitly, about ourselves. His work thus performs the recollective function that Plato ascribed to philosophy, namely reminding us in a flash of insight what we feel we must already have understood, but had somehow forgotten owing to our unreflective immersion in the world.

Further reading

Carman, T. 2008. *Merleau-Ponty*. London: Routledge.
Dillon, M. C. 1997. *Merleau-Ponty's Ontology*, 2nd edn. Evanston, IL: Northwestern University Press.
Kelly, S. D. 2005. "Seeing Things in Merleau-Ponty". In *The Cambridge Companion to Merleau-Ponty*, T. Carman & M. Hansen (eds), 74–110. Cambridge: Cambridge University Press.
Taylor, C. 2005. "Merleau-Ponty and the Epistemological Picture". In *The Cambridge Companion to Merleau-Ponty*, T. Carman & M. Hansen (eds), 26–49. Cambridge: Cambridge University Press.

SIX

Psychoanalysis

Beata Stawarska

The reader of Merleau-Ponty can trace a thread running through his writings, from the earliest *The Structure of Behavior* up to the unfinished and posthumously published *The Visible and the Invisible*. This thread weaves together the philosopher's commitment to phenomenology and lived experience, along with psychoanalytic theory and its preoccupations with the regions of human life that transcend rational and deliberate planning and thought. These two strands may at first sight appear to derive from differing if not radically opposing worldviews. Classical phenomenology, founded by Edmund Husserl, is a philosophy of consciousness where the totality of human activity is modelled on intentional acts of the ego as it relates to objects. A paradigmatic example of such a relation is visual perception, where the eye provides the subjective pole from which rays of gaze issue, while the perceived object, such as a cube, provides the terminus of the gaze. Even though it is the object that is the deliberate focus of visual perception, the perceiving subject is necessarily co-present. Acts of consciousness are therefore controlled by a central agency, which attends to its object in view of obtaining clear knowledge.

Psychoanalysis, on the other hand, unveils regions of human life that are not subject to deliberate control, which are not transparently known, and to which it is difficult to ascribe an individual agent acting purposefully to attain a predetermined goal. Dreams, slips of the tongue, neurotic symptoms, belong to the murky domain of the unconscious, and so seem by definition to transcend the narrow confines of phenomenological consciousness. And yet, Merleau-Ponty (PhF) argues, *contra* such a cursory reading, phenomenology and psychoanalysis do not stand at the opposing ends of the spectrum but are inextricably intertwined. On the one hand, psychoanalysis helps to thicken and deepen the meaning of human existence by transcending the classical subject–act–object structure of pure consciousness. On the other hand, phenomenology helps to refine psychoanalytic concepts and free them from a mechanistic causal frame of reference used by Freud to interpret his findings. Phenomenology and psychoanalysis are therefore natural allies standing in a relation of mutual dependence and enlightenment. As Merleau-Ponty's writings show, both disciplines become transformed in relation to the other, and so are internally rather than externally related.

Towards the end of his life, Merleau-Ponty was invited to write a preface to *L'Oeuvre de Freud* by Angelo Louis Hesnard (1886–1969), a senior Freudian psychoanalyst and president of the French Society for Psychoanalysis, who pioneered a renewal of interest in Freud in postwar France. Hesnard wrote in his *L'Oeuvre* that "Freud, by his discoveries, had opened the way for a new philosophy and . . . his doctrine and method are neighbors of a concrete philosophy whose relatively recent success is considerable: phenomenology" (PhF: 12). It is therefore unsurprising that Hesnard found it fit to request that Merleau-Ponty, whose philosophical appropriations as well as critical misgivings about Freud's project Hesnard greatly valued, preface the treatise devoted to Freudian psychoanalysis. Merleau-Ponty opens the preface noting the significant lines of convergence between phenomenology and psychoanalysis, but cautioning – in agreement with Hesnard – that psychoanalysis needs to be separated "from a scientistic or objectivist ideology" (*ibid.*: 67). This separation, Merleau-Ponty adds, was present in his own philosophical work from the beginning. Let me elaborate on this point in reference to relevant texts.

Merleau-Ponty's earliest manuscript, *The Structure of Behavior* (1942), is devoted to articulating the relations between consciousness and nature, organic as well as psychological and social (SB: 3). Such a project is clearly of an interdisciplinary nature, and Merleau-Ponty engages natural as well as human sciences as he spells out the place of conscious human thought and action in the natural world. Psychoanalysis is one of the schools of thought in psychology the philosopher calls upon (together with Gestalt psychology), but his discussion in this early text is limited to Freud and the tone of his comments tends to be critical. Merleau-Ponty is particularly outspoken regarding Freud's aspirations to model psychoanalysis on physics in order to guarantee its scientific status. Consider in this regard that Freud conceived of psychoanalysis as *metapsychology*, i.e. as a scientific endeavour aimed to rectify the constructions of metaphysics by exposing the deep psychological sources of mythological and religious beliefs in supernatural phenomena – beliefs he likened to paranoiac delusions projected on to the external world. Freud's objective was then to "transform *metaphysics* into *metapsychology*" (Freud 1975: 322). The product of this transformation was a highly theoretical ensemble of conceptual models, including the notion of a psychical apparatus divided into agencies (the unconscious, preconscious and consciousness in his early mapping of the mind, and the id, the ego and the super-ego in the later model), and a theory of instinctual drives caught in inescapable antagonism (the polarity of sexuality and self-preservation in his early theory and of life and death drives in his later work). Importantly, Freud argued that a complete metapsychological interpretation of a psychical process would capture its three interrelated aspects: the dynamic (regarded in terms of the conflict and combination of instinctual forces), the topographical (regarded in terms of its figurative location within the psychical apparatus – the unconscious, preconscious and conscious, or the id, ego and super-ego), and last, and most pertinently to Merleau-Ponty's criticism, the economic. The economic perspective stipulates that psychical processes consist in the circulation and distribution of given quotas of instinctual energy, typically libido, and that these quantities are subject to fluctuations and can in principle be measured. Even though Freud conceded that the exact nature of this energy was an unknown, he contended also that the science of the mind will be incomplete without a detailed economic perspective in place. He devoted the bulk of his early work to cashing out mental process in terms of quantities of excitation circulating along neuronal pathways. It is primarily to this economic perspective on human life adopted by Freud that Merleau-Ponty vehemently objects.

Consider Freud's theory of dream interpretation in this regard. On the one hand, Freud needs to be praised for departing from a physiological theory that views dreams as meaningless psychic expressions of somatic processes occurring during sleep. Freud revolutionized our understanding of the mind by expanding the conception of meaning beyond logical and rational thought. Dreams are meaningful thought processes, according to Freud, but they are in need of interpretation. Their manifest content reported by the dreamer in the first recital of the dream is in need of analysis so as to expose the layers of latent thoughts that contributed in diverse ways to make the final product. The dreamer is typically asked to freely associate on the basis of the recollected dream material so as to fill in the blanks in the dream narrative that would otherwise appear incoherent. Now, Merleau-Ponty comments:

> It has been clearly shown how, faced with the contrast between the subject's first recital of the dream and the second recital which analysis reveals, Freud believed it necessary to actualize the latter in the form of latent content within an ensemble of *unconscious forces* and mental entities which enter into conflict with the *counter-forces* of the censor; the manifest content of the dream would result from this sort of *energic action*.
>
> (SB: 177, emphasis added)

It is to these metaphors of forces that the philosopher objects. By representing the life of the mind in terms of an interplay of instinctual tendencies entering into a nexus of causal interactions Freud resorts to "explanations in the third person" (*ibid.*: 178), i.e. he shifts focus from the experience of the dreamer who recollects and interprets a personal event in the psychoanalytic session to the aforementioned "scientistic or objectivist ideology" of a dispassionate non-participant observer who merely records the interplays of energetic fluctuations and could in principle measure the quotas of energy involved. This perspective of materialistic realism, which makes Freud view human conduct on a par with physical processes studied in natural science, leads him to impose a mechanistic causal interpretation on to pathological and non-pathological behaviour alike. A neurotic complex is viewed as a symptom causally produced by a traumatic experience; a dream is viewed as an event caused by a childhood memory (*ibid.*). Now it is difficult to understand how causal determinants that may be unknown to the experiencing subject (because they are repressed or forgotten) could enter the life of consciousness and organize the patterns of meaning in human conduct from within. Furthermore, a neurotic complex or a dream is, on Freud's own admission, not only a product of material from the past but also "conditioned by the whole attitude of the consciousness which avoids thinking about it in order not to have to integrate and be responsible for it" (*ibid.*). Rather than posit unidirectional causal vectors directed from past to present as well as external soma to psyche relations to explain human conduct, it is therefore more fitting to speak of "degrees of integration" of human conduct, where pathology testifies to a higher degree of fragmentation and to the presence of rigid semi-independent attitudes (complexes, neurotic symptoms) that resist entering into the larger synthesis of the person's behavioural repertoire and are not subject to the passage of time but appear locked in a repetitive cycle. To use the term from Merleau-Ponty's contemporary, Sartre, we need an "existential psychoanalysis" to recast Freud's powerful insights in terms of personal existence rather than impersonal mechanics.

Merleau-Ponty's suspicion in regard to Freud's physicalistic account of human conduct survives in his later work. For example, his lecture on the "Child's Relations with Others" (PrP), which Merleau-Ponty delivered as Chair of Child Psychology at the Sorbonne, testifies to the ambiguity in Freud's usage of libido as a physiological process (especially in the "Three Essays on the Theory of Sexuality") and points to a more refined and philosophically useful conception of sexuality worked out by Freud in his later works (*Beyond the Pleasure Principle, The Ego and the Id*). This latter conception informs Merleau-Ponty's own discussion of sexuality (discussed below). In "Child's Relations with Others", Merleau-Ponty also engages the French psychoanalyst Jacques Lacan's theory of the so-called mirror stage. According to Lacan, between the ages of six to eighteen months, the child identifies with the image of its bodily Gestalt, typically when observing its own reflection in the mirror. This visual identification lays the foundation of what is to become the child's ego, and provides a sense of bodily unity and mastery, contrasted with the child's initial state of powerlessness and motor incoordination. Even though Lacan's account reiterates some of the discussion about the acquisition of the visual image of the body by Wallon, Merleau-Ponty emphasizes that Lacan's psychoanalytic analysis is unique and preferable because "it emphasizes the affective significance of the phenomenon" (PrP: 137). In Lacan's account, it is less the case of the child having to understand that her body image is reflected in the mirror while her felt body is found in its proper location; it is rather the case of the child being fascinated and captivated by her reflection. The body image, like any visual image, extends a promise of domination and control, which exerts the fascinating effect on the child that a purely cognitive account cannot capture. Furthermore, if the mirror phase involved only the understanding that the virtual reflection in the mirror indicates the real body proper, it should be sapped of any special significance and we would therefore be hard pressed to explain why this reflection may continue to have the fascinating quality of a double of oneself even for an adult, and why the experience of a double may play out in one's interpersonal life (*ibid.*: 138–9). Lacan's psychoanalytic account, which highlights the affectively charged and inherently ambiguous status of the mirror image for both the child and the adult, provides therefore a more accurate reading of human identity than a purely cognitive one.

Turning now to Merleau-Ponty's monumental treatise, *Phenomenology of Perception*, it is fair to say that his discussion of sexuality in this monograph is the most outspoken expression of his profound indebtedness to psychoanalysis. The reader of *Phenomenology* may at first be hard pressed to identify specific references to psychoanalysis in this treatise. For example, the unconscious is only occasionally evoked, and the determining influence appears to be Husserl's phenomenology as a science of consciousness. Husserl's phenomenological framework appears to guarantee uninhibited insight into the life of consciousness in its multitude of intentional relations to objectivities, and to univocally privilege self-awareness, transparency and activity. Needless to say, by adopting a determined focus on perception, Merleau-Ponty challenges this established framework. By positing the primacy of perception over and against intellectual thought, he introduces an element of passivity, receptivity and ineradicable dependence on embodied structures of sensibility that are not the results of an individual decision but belong rather to our facticity shared with other embodied perceivers and to our rootedness in this world. Merleau-Ponty's take on consciousness is therefore far removed from the received Cartesian conception and compatible in fact with the Freudian notion of the unconscious. Indeed, if the unconscious is rarely mentioned by name in *Phenomenology*, it is because it serves to describe the very perceptual consciousness in its ambiguity, opacity, multiplicity of meanings, and unending quest for interpretation. Merleau-Ponty's thesis of the primacy of perception overlaps with Freud's thesis of the primacy of unconscious processes and motivations in human conduct. It is crucial in this regard not to misunderstand Freud's conception of the unconscious as a carbon copy of traditional consciousness, sharing the latter's *modus operandi* but devoid of awareness. In his attempts to justify the notion of the unconscious, Freud clearly stated that he did not intend to postulate a second unconscious consciousness; what typifies the latent mental processes uncovered by psychoanalysis are their "characteristics and peculiarities which seem alien to us, or even incredible, and which run directly counter to the attributes of consciousness with which we are familiar" (Freud 1984: 172). The unconscious notably rejects the logical principle of contradiction and ignores chronological ordering of events in time. Ultimately, then, it is the non-rational *modus operandi* that captures the specificity of the unconscious, rather than lack of conscious awareness. Dreams, neurotic symptoms, slips of the tongue, etc., are after all manifest – even though obscurely and in need of interpretation – to consciousness. That is why Freud eventually abandoned the conscious/unconscious distinction as the basis for charting out separate regions of the mind and adopted a new id–ego–super-ego topology. The unconscious is viewed increasingly less as a secret treasure casket hidden in the inner recesses of the mind (neatly demarcated from waking thought and action) and more as a pervasive element seeping into all areas of human existence. The very distinctions between rational and non-rational activity, sanity and madness, perception and fantasy, get blurred in the process.

This latter conception of the unconscious as pervasive element of consciousness itself significantly informed Merleau-Ponty's own thinking about the nature of perception in particular and human existence in general. To be sure, the very notion of the unconscious gets redefined in the process, especially by being anchored in the sensible and desiring body of the perceiver. Whereas the reader of Freud's highly theoretical and speculative writings may be left with the impression that unconscious processes apply primarily to the energetic transactions conducted within the machinery of the mind, in Merleau-Ponty's writings the embodied and embedded nature of the unconscious is unmistakably clear. It is especially well articulated in his discussion of sexuality (PP: ch. 5) and Freud's direct influence on Merleau-Ponty is best documented there.

In this chapter, Merleau-Ponty cautions against understanding sexuality as a bundle of psychological and physiological facts, third-person processes occurring in the mind and the body. Sexuality has to do with consciousness and it is an expression of our freedom (PP: 167). However, it is a peculiar type of consciousness, which is not rational, or fully cognizant of its own intentions. Sexuality should not be understood as a *cogitatio* aiming at a *cogitatum* (*ibid.*: 157) – but rather as a body-to-body relation embedded in the world. Like perception and motility, sexuality should be understood as an original intentionality of consciousness (*ibid.*); it is a source of vitality and fruitfulness in our experience.

Sexuality is therefore not a separate category; not a "peripheral involuntary action" nor an "autonomous cycle" (*ibid.*), but rather co-extensive with existence as such. It forms the "current of existence" at work in perception, which firmly anchors the libidinal body in the world shared with other embodied and desiring perceivers. It explains why perception may carry an erotic charge and provide a source of sensuous pleasure without necessarily culminating in a sexual act in a narrow sense. To be sure, if sexuality is so pervasive and expansive on Merleau-Ponty's reading, there is a danger of the loss of meaning. If all existence is sexual, then stating this fact becomes a tautology (*ibid.*: 158). Sexuality must have a specific meaning that is not interchangeable with existence – but neither is it separate from it. In Merleau-Ponty's words, "if words are to have any meaning, the sexual life is a sector of our life bearing a special relation to the existence of sex" (*ibid.*: 159). Some practices are unambiguously sexual and there are clear areas of concentration of sexuality. Yet sexuality is also an ambiguous atmosphere (*ibid.*: 169) – diffuse like an odour or sound (*ibid.*: 168), without a punctual location. The difference between sex and sexuality, a particular body and general existence, is therefore in intensity or degree, but not in kind. We never leap out of sexuality, just as we do not leap out of existence. Even celibacy counts as an expression of sexuality – sexuality is still a sexual orientation, "an attitude of escapism and solitude" that still takes up and makes explicit a sexual situation (*ibid.*: 169).

Merleau-Ponty openly credits psychoanalysis with this expansive conception of sexual existence:

> Here we concur with the most lasting discoveries of psychoanalysis. Whatever the theoretical declarations of Freud may have been, psychoanalytic research is in fact led to an explanation of man, not in terms of his sexual substructure, but to a discovery in sexuality of relations and attitudes which had previously been held to reside *in consciousness*. Thus the significance of psychoanalysis is less to make psychology biological than to discover a dialectical process in functions thought of as "purely bodily", and to reintegrate sexuality into the human being. (*Ibid.*: 157–8)

Having dispelled the biological conception, psychoanalysis can regard sexuality as a site of meaning, even though the meaning is intrinsically in need of interpretation. Hence a neurotic symptom such as sexual "frigidity" should be understood in existential and not only anatomical terms (*ibid.*: 158). The refusal to engage in sexual intercourse on the woman's part, as well as sexual impotence in a man, need to be thematized as an existential stance, infused with meaning and related to personal history and projects for the future, even though these relations may be unclear to the person her/himself. Merleau-Ponty agrees with psychoanalysis that even seemingly unintentional acts, such as forgetting where the present from one's spouse is, display (however obscure) meaning and intentionality (*ibid.*: 162). Forgetfulness consists in a strategy of avoidance. When reconciled with the spouse, the person finds the book (*ibid.*). The incident of forgetting is an act of consciousness, but the latter is expanded beyond Descartes's conception of clear and distinct knowledge.

In his endorsement of Freud's conception of sexuality, Merleau-Ponty stresses that the sexual is not the genital and that the libido is not an instinct (PP: 158). Both statements should enable Freud and Merleau-Ponty to extend the meaning of sexuality beyond the dominant conception as heterosexual desire culminating in intercourse and the production of offspring. Some feminist philosophers have questioned the ability of the psychoanalytic/existential conception to accomplish this professed objective. To explain why, consider the libido–instinct distinction first. Freud famously stated that libido is a drive (*Trieb*, from *treiben* – to push), and not an instinct (*Instinkt*). Instinct is a hereditary behaviour pattern peculiar to animal species, varying little between individuals, and unfolding according to a temporal scheme. For example, animal sexuality follows predetermined mating seasons, is marked by species-specific courtship rituals, and there are specific parenting duties assigned to the members of either sex. On the other hand, Freud argued that human sexuality does not exhibit such fixed patterns. As a persistent trait of human existence, sexuality exhibits variations based on familial individual and cultural differences in sexual practice and object-choice. In psychoanalysis, the sexual drive is therefore a constant but relatively malleable force, uniquely shaped by the twists and turns of personal biography, in contradistinction to the predetermined animal instinct.

Consider now the remaining disjunction between the sexual and the genital. According to Freud's classic statement, sexuality exists originally in a polymorphous state, with sexual energy inhabiting diverse disconnected erogenous zones. These zones become erogenous through stimulation: for example, the oral zone is predisposed as a site of sexual pleasure through breast-feeding; the phallus and the clitoris are zones of pleasurable sensations, even in infancy. This polymorphous diversity becomes typically subject to genital synthesis during puberty, where the heterogeneous sites of pleasure become subsumed under the unitary goal of heterosexual intercourse and re-production. Even though Freud stated that humans are born bisexual, he offered a teleological and prescriptive narrative of sexual development arguing that a normally developing human being acquires a preference for the opposite sex. Hence, while in redressing the disjunctions between animal instinct/human drive and the genital/the sexual Freud (and Merleau-Ponty, given his endorsement) could have fully challenged received notions of "normal" and "natural" sexuality, they ultimately failed to achieve this end. As feminist writers have since argued, the understanding of heterosexuality as normal construes pervasive, socially sanctioned and historically sedimented cultural practices and institutions as inescapable natural/biological phenomena pre-existing culture and history. To the extent that this tradition continues to have a hold on Freud's and Merleau-Ponty's theories of sexuality, their openness and expansiveness remain proportionately limited.

Even though Merleau-Ponty, like Freud, assumes the naturalness of heterosexuality, his philosophical account of sexuality differs from that of Freud in significant respects. Merleau-Ponty's philosophy is not reliant on the notion of the unconscious as a site of drives determining conscious conduct from the outside, but rather extends the range of consciousness to cover conduct whose motivations and meaning may be obscure, even to oneself, and in need of interpretation. He expands the range of the erotic beyond the mapping of the erogenous zones on the body proper to the erotic perception that pervades the relation between the body and the world. Merleau-Ponty's theory therefore both reappropriates and transcends Freud's theory, in line with the phenomenological commitment to embodied consciousness, inescapably embedded in the world.

Merleau-Ponty's insights from psychoanalysis included in his Sorbonne lecture ("Child's Relations with Others") and the sexuality chapter from *Perception* are taken up as well as significantly revised in his lectures at the Collège de France and in his final unfinished manuscript, *The Visible and the Invisible*. Tracing these developments and revisions regarding psychoanalysis throws light on the larger philosophical turn in Merleau-Ponty's thinking from the anthropocentric perspective of the individual human body adopted in his analyses of perceptual consciousness to the ontology of the flesh developed in the later work. The course notes from Merleau-Ponty's 1954–55 Collège de France lectures on "The Problem of Passivity: Sleep, the Unconscious, Memory" as well as "Nature and Logos: The Human Body" are an obvious choice for a discussion of the psychoanalytic influence on Merleau-Ponty's evolving thought, but more widely available are the lecture notes published in *Themes from the Lectures at the Collège de France* (TL).

In these lectures, Merleau-Ponty moves away from his earlier interpretation of the unconscious in terms of broadly construed incarnated consciousness to that of carnality, of which one's body proper is an instance but not a privileged point of departure. To be sure, the terminology used in the "Passivity" chapter is reminiscent of discussions from *Phenomenology*. In his analysis of sleep and dreams, Merleau-Ponty insists that these phenomena should be interpreted as modalities of perceptual activity laden with traces of the past – rather than, as Sartre would have it, pure nothingness and mental void suspended from the environing world. Sleeping consciousness is "cluttered with the debris of past and present" (TL: 48), and the weight of our dreams testifies to the relation the oneiric consciousness holds to the personal past and to the complex ways in which it is woven into the person's present life. The distinction between dreaming and wakeful consciousness should not therefore be cast in terms of absence and presence of reality, and the unconscious should be regarded as a type of perceiving consciousness (*ibid.*: 50).

In the concluding chapter on "The Human Body", however, Merleau-Ponty cautions that "we must think of the human body (and not consciousness) as that which perceives nature which it also inhabits" (*ibid.*: 128). This objective requires an "esthesiology", i.e. a study of the body of the perceiving animal situated in an environment and inextricably interrelated with the bodies of others. To maintain the point of view of consciousness, even if redefined in terms of perception, motility and sexuality, still runs the risk of conceiving the body and nature as objects surveyed by a subject. To avoid this danger, Merleau-Ponty increasingly preferred to adopt the ontological viewpoint of corporeality and the flesh of which the body proper is one among multiple instantiations. Corporeality turns out to be an entity with two faces or "sides". Thus the body proper is a sensible and it is the "sensing"; it can be seen and it can see itself; it can be touched and it can touch itself, and, in this latter respect, it comprises an aspect inaccessible to others, open in principle only to itself. The body proper embraces a philosophy of the flesh as the visibility of the invisible (*ibid.*: 129).

Continuous with the flesh, the body proper communicates with the world at large and is no longer rigidly circumscribed by the contours of the bodily form. Merleau-Ponty invokes "a logic of implication and promiscuity" (*ibid.*: 50) to capture this one-in-another (*Ineinander*) of carnality and the undividedness between the inside and the outside, which testifies to the permissive nature of being we are immersed in prior to adopting the reflective stance of an observer. Importantly, the unconscious gets redefined in the process as an ontological category reflective of the ongoing transactions and mutual encroachments between the self and the (natural as well as social) world. Merleau-Ponty found the work of Melanie Klein to be more helpful than Freud's for capturing this broader ontological ramifications of our mundane existence. He explains:

> The theoretical concepts of Freudianism are corrected and affirmed once they are understood, as suggested in the work of Melanie Klein, in terms of corporeality taken as itself the search of the external in the internal and of the internal in the external, that is, as a global and universal power of incorporation.
>
> (TL: 129–30)

This ontologically construed conception of the unconscious can only be accomplished within the perspective of a philosophy of the flesh as the basic element and starting point of enquiry. Merleau-Ponty's final unfinished work on the philosophy of the flesh from *The Visible and the Invisible* is therefore at least in part a creative response to the limitations of the Freudian notion of the unconscious and a constructive attempt to provide the foundations of an ontological psychology that casts Freud's innovative insights in a more philosophically appropriate lexicon. Merleau-Ponty stresses that "the philosophy of Freud is not a philosophy of the body, but of the flesh – The Id, the unconscious – and the Ego (correlative) to be understood on the basis of flesh" (VI: 270). "A philosophy of the flesh is the condition without which psychoanalysis remains anthropology" (*ibid.*: 267). That means that the unconscious must not be thematized in terms of individual mental processes in the head, not as the body proper and its conscious subjectivity opposed to objects, but rather a more basic category of being as carnality. Within this larger ontological framework, one's own body is inextricably connected to other bodies, just as the body of the child is connected via the umbilical cord to the body of the mother. Hence the imperative: "Do a psychoanalysis of Nature: it is the flesh, the mother" (*ibid.*) so as to recover this non-subjective notion of embodiment as intercorporeality.

Crucially, and in the guise of a conclusion to this chapter, it is the psychoanalytic conception of the unconscious that provides the theoretical resources with which philosophy can move beyond the subject-centred perspective of classical phenomenology to which Merleau-Ponty continued to adhere in his early work, notably *Phenomenology of Perception*. The unconscious discloses an impersonal sub-rational spontaneity at the heart of our lives that refuses to be captured by the "I think", and so it decentralizes the conscious epistemic subject of classical phenomenology. At the same time, it is the philosophical conception of the flesh rather than Freud's notion of the mental apparatus that provides "certain means of expression that [psychoanalysis] needs to be completely itself" (PP: 58). As announced in the opening paragraph, Merleau-Ponty's project therefore engages philosophical reflection and psychoanalytic theory in a critical as well as illuminating reciprocal relation, which transforms both traditions of enquiry from within by helping to refine and revise their basic concepts, and to cast their insights and discoveries in the most appropriate terms. Psychoanalysis may need phenomenology to fully realize its own potential, but the reverse turns out to be true as well.

Further reading

Butler, J. 1989. "Sexual Ideology and Phenomenological Description". In *The Thinking Muse: Feminism and Modern French Philosophy*, J. Allen & I. M. Young (eds), 85–100. Bloomington, IN: Indiana University Press.

Hoeller, K. (ed.) 1993. *Merleau-Ponty and Psychology*. Atlantic Highlands, NJ: Humanities Press.

Olkowski, D. & J. Morley (eds) 1999. *Merleau-Ponty, Interiority and Exteriority, Psychic Life, and the World*. Albany, NY: State University of New York Press.

SEVEN

Philosophy of history

Sonia Kruks

How are we to make sense of history? This is a pivotal question for Merleau-Ponty, and one that he poses at several different, though interwoven, levels. These levels include our personal and our intersubjective lives and the more general level of what he calls "public history" (TL: 39–45). At the former levels he raises questions concerning how individually situated and intersubjective selves are instantiated, shaped, and shape themselves in time. At the latter level, that of "public history", he asks how we are to make sense of large-scale historical processes – the temporal transformations of societies and states, the transitions between large-scale epochs, and whether or not we may discern a clear directionality, or even progress, in human societies. Although these levels are, for Merleau-Ponty, interconnected, it is his exploration of history at the large-scale "public" level that is the primary topic of this chapter.

Our common-sense views of history of this "public", or general, kind are most often subtended by one of two kinds of assumption. We often conceive history as having a cumulative, or pre-given, trajectory that unfolds over time – as the necessary "progress" of freedom, or reason, or human well-being, for example. Or else we see it as essentially random and unpredictable, as the outcome of diverse actions, contingent events and conjunctures, as exemplified in the claim that the assassination of Archduke Ferdinand "caused" the First World War. Both of these common-sense views of history also inform positions within the philosophy of history, with Hegel (1770–1831) arguably formulating the classic argument for the former conception and Nietzsche (1844–1900) for the latter. Reformulations of the

Hegelian conception of history have, since the mid-nineteenth century, informed much Marxist theory (and practice), while more recent poststructuralist accounts of the ruptured and discontinuous nature of history (notably Foucault's) extend from the Nietzschean conception.

Merleau-Ponty argues that neither conception is adequate and that each, in a different way, fails to grasp the complexity and ambiguity of history. Against what we may call the Nietzschean view (although Merleau-Ponty himself does not often explicitly refer to Nietzsche), he insists that "[t]here is no history where the course of events is a series of episodes without unity". Yet, against the Hegelian notion of history as the logical unfolding over time of the Idea (*Geist*, also translated as Mind), he also asserts that there is no history where history is deemed to be "a struggle already decided in the heaven of ideas" (TL: 29). History is neither random nor predetermined, Merleau-Ponty insists; rather, it is "where there is a logic *within* contingence, a reason *within* unreason" (*ibid.*: 29–30). Today, although many liberal notions of history as a progress towards greater freedom or justice persist, with the decline of Marxism and the ascendancy of poststructuralist theory arguments for the discontinuous and contingent nature of history have become more pervasive. However, when Merleau-Ponty was writing, in the 1940s and 1950s, his concern as he developed his own account of history was less to rebut Nietzschean than Hegelian- and Marxist-inspired views.

Merleau-Ponty's concerns were both philosophically and politically driven. Philosophically, there was a dramatic growth of interest in Hegel in France in the 1930s, when Merleau-Ponty was a student. In particular, the seminars of the Russian émigré scholar, Alexandre Kojève, some of which Merleau-Ponty attended, made Hegel a pivotal figure for Merleau-Ponty's generation of thinkers. As Merleau-Ponty puts it: "interpreting Hegel means taking a stand on all the great philosophical, political, and religious problems of our century" (SNS: 64). Reading Hegel raised above all the question of the relationship between ideas and history, and so of the status of philosophy itself. Politically, Merleau-Ponty was a committed socialist in the 1940s and, in *Humanism and Terror* (1947), he offered what he called "critical support" to the French Communist Party and its pro-Soviet policies. Thus the history of the Russian Revolution and its slide into Stalinist terror also drove his concern with history, and figured centrally in his critique of philosophical claims that we may be assured of the forward march of history.

In developing his own account of history, Merleau-Ponty begins from Hegel. But his readings of Hegel are deliberately equivocal. On the one hand, Hegel, or at least "the textbook Hegel", is an idealist thinker who subordinates the living flux of history to a pre-ordained system or Idea, who "reduced history to the history of the spirit" and "found the final synthesis heralded and guaranteed in his own consciousness . . . and in the very realization of his philosophy" (SNS: 81). On the other hand, one may still retrieve from Hegel – and especially from the early Hegel – a more "existential" account of historical dialectic as lived and ambiguous, an account that profoundly informs Merleau-Ponty's own account of human existence and history. Marx, he argues, is similarly equivocal. There is a Marx (and Marxism) that has strong affinities with the textbook Hegel (inspiring later Soviet Marxism); and there is another Marx whose insights inform Merleau-Ponty's own "existential" conception of history.

The idealist Hegel

Merleau-Ponty gives us a good general portrait of the "textbook", idealist, Hegel in his inaugural address at the Collège de France (1952). The Hegel in this account fails to realize the limits of philosophy. He does not recognize the fact that philosophy and history are both forms of human practice and that the philosopher is situated *in* history and thus cannot claim to view it objectively. Thus, this Hegel ends by giving philosophy priority over history – and consequently over human existence: "For Hegel philosophy is absolute knowledge, system, totality, the history of which the philosopher speaks is not really history, that is to say, something which one does. It is rather universal history, fully comprehended, finished, dead" (EP: 48). Hegel sometimes regards the philosopher as the man who simply reads history, since "the real is rational"; at other times he makes the philosopher the subject of history. But either way, "since history has been staged by him, he finds in it only the sense that he has already placed there" (*ibid.*: 49–50). In subordinating history to the Universal, to the "Idea", Hegel creates a "dream" of history and there is no place in that dream for human beings as individual freedoms, as contingent existences. No longer is Hegel's philosophy the description of human existence in its concrete singularities and multiple and ambiguous meanings. It refuses recognition to such existence in the name of its own dream-world intellectual system.

72

For Merleau-Ponty, what constitutes human existence and distinguishes human beings from other species is their capacity for transcendence, for negation. We continually "project" ourselves into the future and, acting in relation to both the natural and the social world, we create meanings only to continually pass beyond them. Flux, creation, a dialectic with the world in which both freedom and constraint give meanings to actions, are what make us human. Although this conception clearly owes much to Hegel, the textbook Hegel ends by destroying it, for in subordinating existence to the final synthesis, he ultimately denies man his negativity and thus his capacity for freedom and transcendence. Man becomes instead an object, a victim of the "cunning of reason", especially in Hegel's later works. Historical epochs cease to be considered intrinsically significant as manifestations of human existence, but are treated only as stages in the development of the "Idea", stages in which the men of the time are the helpless victims (hence objects) of historical necessity. Thus, Merleau-Ponty notes, for example, that in the *History of Philosophy* Hegel considers Oriental thought only as a "moment" within the development of the "Idea". Because the "Idea" is said to find its final realization in Western philosophy, there exists in this work an assertion as to the absolute superiority of Western thought, and a dubious failure to consider the intrinsic significance of Oriental thought (S: 137).

Merleau-Ponty insists that, in privileging philosophy as the driving force of history, Hegel also ends by destroying the proper function of philosophy itself. That is, he "embalms" philosophy and cuts it off from its roots in lived experience. "Hegel", he writes, "is the museum. He is, if you wish, all philosophies, but deprived of their finiteness and power of impact, embalmed, transformed, he believes, into themselves, but really transformed into Hegel" (S: 82). To be human, Merleau-Ponty argues, is to be "a place of unrest" (SNS: 66), a continual and contingent movement of free transcendence, and philosophy must both reflect on and partake of this movement. Should it deny the contingency of human existence in the name of the Idea, philosophy becomes non-philosophical. Thus Merleau-Ponty's wise philosopher "does not place his hope in any destiny, even a favorable one, but in something belonging to us which is not destiny – in the contingency of our history. The denial of this is a fixed (non-philosophical) position" (EP: 44).

Merleau-Ponty's critique of the idealist Hegel is not only of philosophical but also of profound political import. Hegel's final synthesis not only asserts the superiority of Western philosophy, but also of Western political institutions. It is in the modern Western state, as described in *The Philosophy of Right*, that Hegel sees the concrete expression of the "Idea". Moreover, as the final synthesis and end of history, the Hegelian state is bound to be oppressive towards its own members. Because it is the Idea made manifest, it – and *de facto* its officials, the "universal class" – can brook no dissent. "The later Hegel", Merleau-Ponty writes in *Humanism and Terror*, "kept this designation [the "universal class"] for the officials of the authoritarian state who survey history's meaning for everyone else and create humanity through force and war. In a word, Hegel institutionalizes Terror . . . [S]ince Reason, after all, once in power, becomes violence, [he] puts his trust in violence alone to unite men" (HT: 150).

Hegel's argument for the necessary progress of history towards its final pre-given end later reappears in history in other guises. It appears in a "materialist" form in the proclaimed self-certainties of "orthodox" Communist Party Marxism, both during and after the Russian Revolution. Merleau-Ponty argues that Marx, like Hegel, is an equivocal thinker. An "existential" account of history may be drawn from him his work but, true to its Hegelian origins, it also invites a reading of the inevitable, pre-given unfolding of history in which individual agency and contingency have no place. Thus, since 1917, in the name of communism as the final end of history, the authoritarian and terroristic tendencies incipient in Hegelian philosophy have become historically manifest as the justification of revolutionary violence. "Cunning, deception, bloodshed, and dictatorship are justified if they bring the proletariat into power and to that extent alone", Merleau-Ponty writes (HT: xix) – but the problem is that (*contra* the self-proclaimed certainties of this Hegelianized version of the Marxian dialectic of history) we can never be sure that they will do so. Likewise, Merleau-Ponty challenges Western "liberal humanist" conceptions of history that view it as the progress of freedom, for, in self-righteously defending its principles, liberalism has also become a dangerous idealism. By ignoring, in the name of abstract principles, the concrete realties and the ambiguities of specific situations, liberalism has become "an ideology of war" (*ibid.*: xxiv). It serves as a dangerous justification for colonial and anti-communist violence.

The existential Hegel

But if Hegel stands as both root and paradigm for dangerous visions of history as the necessary march of progress towards an ideal, he is also the source for a very different vision of history: Merleau-Ponty's own. In a lecture of 1947, published as "Hegel's Existentialism" (SNS: 63–70), Merleau-Ponty develops a reading of Hegel's *Phenomenology of Mind* that locates it as the point of origin for his own (and other) existential phenomenology. This is a Hegel who is attentive to the concrete, one who does not subordinate existence to the Idea. He "does not propose to connect concepts but to reveal the immanent logic of human experience in all its sectors" (*ibid*.: 65). Although he may ultimately have been concerned with developing a total philosophical system, this Hegel is equally interested in describing each step in the unfolding of human existence for its own *intrinsic* significance. As Merleau-Ponty put it, Hegel's *Phenomenology* "does not try to fit all history into a framework of pre-established logic but attempts to bring each doctrine and each era back to life and to let itself be guided by their internal logic with such impartiality that all concern with system seems forgotten" (*ibid*.).

On Merleau-Ponty's reading, the Hegelian description of the history of the emergence of human self-consciousness also originates the existential notions of "responsibility" and the "project": Hegel's thought is "existential" because it views a human life as "a life which is its own responsibility and which tries to understand itself". As an individual "project", he shows, a life is created in a dialectic between subjective "self-certainty" and objective truth, as we continually test our subjective intentions against the world and modify them. Such a dialectic must be open, indefinite: if ever "subjective certainty finally equals objective truth", and if ever the "final stage" of history is actually attained, then "man, deprived of movement, would be like an animal – man, as opposed to the pebble which is what it is, is defined as a place of unrest (*Unruhe*), a constant effort to get back to himself and consequently by his refusal to limit himself to one or another of his determinations" (SNS: 66).

Thus, Merleau-Ponty argues, when this existential Hegel speaks of absolute knowledge he does not conceive of it as the "final stage" or as the "end" of human development, nor as the completion of the dialectic, or the end of history. Rather, "absolute knowledge" is a "way of life", in which consciousness "at last becomes equal to its spontaneous life and regains its self possession" (SNS: 64). This is also to say that it invokes a reason that acknowledges the irrational in human life. For such a knowledge, history is not the triumphant march of reason but rather a complex dialectic of "*sens et non-sens*" (sense and non-sense), that is of meaning and non-meaning, of direction and lack of direction. History will be marked by indeterminacies, by random events and chance conjunctures.

But if this is so, then are we not in the presence of the second of the "common-sense" views of history mentioned at the beginning of this chapter: that history is so essentially unpredictable that no logic, no direction, or progress – no *sens* – is discernible within it? Or, in its post-Nietzschean and more recent poststructuralist formulations, is not history discontinuous, episodic, ruptured, an assemblage of random events and conjunctures? Merleau-Ponty rejects such views, for what he sets out to develop is an account of history that may give their due both to its *sen* and its *non-sens*. Again, it is to the "existential" Hegel that Merleau-Ponty refers us for a first formulation of such a project, for this Hegel is

> the inventor of that Reason broader than the understanding, which can respect the variety and singularity of individual consciousnesses, civilizations, ways of thinking, and historical contingency, but which nevertheless does not give up the attempt to master them in order to guide them to their own truth.
>
> (SNS: 63)

But the idealist Hegel later came to privilege the Idea, and in its name to suppress the particularities of concrete human existence. Thus, it is by turning to the "young" Marx – the proponent of a conception of human existence that better grasps how embodiment and our relations with nature are integral to consciousness and to human relations – that Merleau-Ponty develops his own initial account of history. Later, in the 1950s, it is with regard to "orthodox" Marxism in action that he becomes increasingly pessimistic about the possibility of determining the *sens* of history – though he never gives up on it entirely.

Marx, Marxism and history

Following the "young" Marx (the author, in the 1840s, of the "Economic and Philosophical Manuscripts", the "Theses on Feuerbach" and other key texts of a "humanistic" Marxism), Merleau-Ponty calls the human activity through which meanings emerge in history "praxis". Praxis is an active and engaged form of reason, unlike conventional philosophy. It emerges as we produce the world around us, and it is always in contact with the world and other people. In contrast to the detached, "contemplative" reason of philosophy, the Marxian notion of praxis describes human beings as the makers of their own world, and it thus affirms individuals (and not some version of the Idea) to be the source of reason and truth. Thus consciousness here is not an attribute of a "subject" that stands "outside" and "objectively" observes the material and social world; rather it is always itself materially and socially suffused. Because consciousness is in the world, it is always particular. Consequently, this Marxism, says Merleau-Ponty, makes individuals "the subject of history" (SNS: 80). If history is made by individuals and if its possibilities are open, then individuals are responsible agents and they must decide what to do. Hence, as soon as questions must be posed about the direction of history, "one invites the individual to understand and decide; in the last analysis one puts him back in control of his life and agrees that the meaning history will have for him depends on the meaning he sees in it" (*ibid.*: 79).

But if history has many diverse meanings seen by many different individuals, does not a problematic descent into subjectivism and relativism follow? If multiple, individual perspectives may each equally claim to be correct, then must we not conclude, after all, that history has no coherent direction at all, that it is *non-sens*? While insisting on the significance of individual thought and action in making history, Merleau-Ponty endeavours to steer a course between such relativism at one extreme and, at the other, the claims (be they "textbook" Hegelian, "orthodox" Marxist or "abstract" liberal) that the *sens* of history is indubitably assured. Thus in saying that history is open and subject to multiple interpretations, and in saying that its course is never predetermined, Merleau-Ponty is not thereby saying that we may navigate it however we may happen to choose, or that the course of history is wholly unknowable or contingent. To understand Merleau-Ponty's own views of the historical dialectic as one of *sens* and *non-sens*, it will be helpful briefly to refer to some of his ideas on "personal" history, on how individual lives are at once free and constrained. To do this I turn briefly to Merleau-Ponty's discussion of freedom in *Phenomenology of Perception*.

In *Phenomenology of Perception* Merleau-Ponty portrays human existence as always embodied as well as conscious. We are each a "body-subject" rooted in the natural and social world and, consequently, neither consciousness nor freedom may fully transcend the "givens" of the world. It follows that a subjective wish, when it cannot open into the intended action (or "praxis") in the world, is not to be confused with freedom. Thus, for example, "the cripple" who wishes to rescue a drowning person but cannot and "the strong swimmer" who actually does so "do not have the same experience of autonomy" (PP: 436). Thus "the very notion of freedom demands that our decision should plunge into the future, that something should be *done* by it, that the subsequent instant should benefit from its predecessor and though not necessitated, should at least be sought out by it" (*ibid.*: 437, trans. altered). To wish, or to desire, but without the possibility of effectively engaging in action in the world is not freedom; it is rather to dream. Similarly, mere wishes about how "public" history should develop and realistic judgements as to its actual possibilities must not be confused. Not all the meanings that individuals may attribute to history will enable them to "plunge into the future", or to engage in the world. Thus there *are* grounds – not absolutely certain ones, but still reasonable ones – from which we may evaluate the different meanings different individuals attribute to particular historical situations. Even though our judgements may turn out to be mistaken, and history may prove us wrong, still there are more or less justifiable choices to be made in any situation. Thus Merleau-Ponty rejects the radical relativism that says all evaluations and choices are of equal worth.

In order to make the more justifiable choices we need to attend to the weight of the past as it inheres in the present. For the past indicates probable – though never inevitable – outlines of a future. This is so both at the levels of "personal" and of "public" history. Thus in *Phenomenology of Perception*, with regard to personal history, Merleau-Ponty rejects Sartre's claim that I am free at any moment to change how to act. For Sartre, either I must be wholly free to change my behaviour, or else I am determined, an "object". But Merleau-Ponty rejects such stark alternatives: they represent an untenable dualism that is put into question by our status as embodied subjects. Against Sartre's claim that I am "free" to abandon the inferiority complex that I have had for twenty years, Merleau-Ponty retorts that this is not "probable". On the contrary, "generality and probability are real phenomena", he insists (PP: 442). Once we recognize that our existence is situated, that it is inseparable from our body, our surroundings, our past, and so forth, then we do not have to accept Sartre's "either/or", his claim that we are either free or determined. That is, probability exists as the weight, or "sedimentation" of the past, of what Merleau-Ponty calls "institution", upon us. By "institution" Merleau-Ponty refers to

> those events in experience which endow it with durable dimensions, in relation to which a whole series of other experiences will acquire meaning, will form an intelligible series or a history

– or again those events which sediment in me a meaning, not just as survivals or residues but as the invitation to a sequel, the demand for a future. (TL: 40–41, trans. altered)

Institution describes the ways we carry our past (for example, an inferiority complex) so as to invite, but not to determine, a particular kind of future.

Likewise, when we come to consider public history, Merleau-Ponty suggests that, without being able to make the assured predictions of the textbook Hegel or orthodox Marxism, we can plausibly anticipate certain directions to the future. This is because, here too, "institutions", meaningful stabilities, and so certain trajectories, emerge from the past and indicate a likely future. Thus Marx, in Merleau-Ponty's view, correctly suggests that economic phenomena, although not causal, or determinative of history, do offer a "historical anchorage" to other phenomena, for, in his reading of Marx,

economic life is not a separate order to which the other orders may be reduced: it is Marxism's way of representing the *inertia* of human life; it is here that conceptions are registered and achieve *stability* . . . economic life is at the same time the historical carrier of mental structures, just as our body maintains the basic features of our behavior beneath our varying moods.

(SNS: 108, emphasis added)

Marx avoids a reductive determinism, yet nevertheless offers a plausible sketch for the future: he offers a reading of history that provides tools to navigate towards a more human future, to navigate between necessitarian doctrines and theories of history as wholly contingent. Marxism, Merleau-Ponty insisted in 1947, "is not a philosophy of history; it is *the* philosophy of history and to renounce it is to dig the grave of reason in history. After that there remain only dreams or adventures" (HT: 153).

History after Marxism

But plausibility and probability admit of degree, and so our evaluations of events and processes, and also of philosophies, may reasonably alter. Over time, and especially with regard to his claim that Marxism is *the* philosophy of history and his hypothesis that, for all its flaws, Soviet-style communism still bore an emancipatory potential, Merleau-Ponty came to re-evaluate his judgements. In 1947, in *Humanism and Terror*, although deeply troubled by the already-visible violence of the Soviet regime, he still considered this regime a more likely bearer of a future of human freedom than Western capitalism. "There are *perspectives*," he wrote,

> but as the word implies, this involves only a horizon of probabilities, comparable to our perceptual horizon which can, as we approach it and it becomes presents to us, reveal in itself to be quite different from what we were expecting. Only the major features are certain, or, more exactly, certain possibilities are excluded: for example, a definite stabilization of capitalism is excluded. But how and by what paths socialism will become a reality is left to a conjecture of events. (HT: 55)

However, by 1955, in *Adventures of the Dialectic*, Merleau-Ponty concluded that the many "detours" of socialism had now permanently deflected it from its potential ends. Moreover, he was no longer convinced that the stabilization of capitalism would not be a "major feature" of the future. Thus Merleau-Ponty came to change his evaluation of the humanistic potential of Marxism and to end his critical support for the Soviet Union.

These shifts in his political evaluations not only altered Merleau-Ponty's assessment of Marxism but also of the relationship between philosophy and history. In the Preface to *Signs* (1960), one of the last essays he completed before his death in 1961, Merleau-Ponty argued that there was a greater complexity to the relationship between philosophy and history than his previous appropriation of Marx's notion of praxis had implied. Given that Marxism can no longer claim to provide a privileged reading of history, he writes that "the relationship between philosophy and history is less simple than was believed. It is in a strict sense an action at a distance, each from the depths of its difference requiring intermingling and promiscuity", adding "we have not yet learned the proper uses of this encroachment" (S: 13). Merleau-Ponty is far more pessimistic about the world he finds around him in 1960 than he was in the late 1940s. However, he still refuses to abandon the claim that there is *sens* as well as *nonsens* in this world. Rather, he notes that his very pessimism may be explained (though not explained away) historically. "Everything we believed to be thought through, and thought through correctly . . . has all fallen into ruin", he writes gloomily of his generation of leftist intellectuals. "But", he adds immediately, "we should be careful. What we call disorder and ruin, others who are younger live as the natural order of things; and perhaps with ingenuity they are going to master it precisely because they no longer seek their bearings where we took ours" (ibid.: 23). History has moved on, and although the sedimented meanings of a previous era may still weigh counterproductively on those who lived through it, now other new meanings are emerging. Again invoking the need to navigate between both subjectivism and an account of history as objective necessity, Merleau-Ponty remarks towards the end of the essay that "there is equal weakness in blaming ourselves alone and believing only in external causes" (ibid.: 35). It is equally misguided either to blame solely oneself for one's errors (for that would be to attribute them purely to one's own consciousness) or to blame them on external necessity (which would be once again to deny the place of concrete individuals in making history).

By 1960 Merleau-Ponty regarded the works of both Hegel and Marx as "classics". Classics are works of which one can no longer say that they are "true" or "false"; rather they are works which one must address "as obligatory steps for those who want to go further". One does not take classics literally, "and yet new facts are never absolutely outside their province but call forth new echoes from them and reveal new lustres in them" (S: 11). For us, today, perhaps Merleau-Ponty has also become a classic: his work is now a key site for considering history as neither the necessary unfolding of a pre-given logic, nor the random clash of subjective meanings, contingent actions and events. If we want to think about the ambiguities of history as at once *sens* and *non-sens*, to consider history as shaped at once by reason and by chance, then Merleau-Ponty must still remain our starting point.

Further reading

Key works by Merleau-Ponty on history: AD, EP (section V), HT, S (Preface), SNS ("Hegel's Existentialism", "Concerning Marxism", "Marxism and Philosophy"), TL (chs 4 and 5).
Kruks, S. 1981. *The Political Philosophy of Merleau-Ponty*. Brighton: Harvester.
Miller, J. 1979. *History and Human Existence: From Marx to Merleau-Ponty*. Berkeley, CA: University of California Press.
O'Neill, J. 1970. *Perception, Expression and History: The Social Phenomenology of Human History*. Berkeley, CA: University of California Press.
Whiteside, K. 1988. *Merleau-Ponty and the Foundation of an Existentialist Politics*. Princeton, NJ: Princeton University Press.

EIGHT

Politics and the political

Diana Coole

Merleau-Ponty was an intensely political thinker, who took seriously his role as a public intellectual and wrote as a man of the Left. He published many books and articles on politics, including astute analyses of current events as well as more general reflections on the direction of collective life in the mid-twentieth century. While he was not a political theorist in any conventional sense, he believed that philosophers have a civic responsibility to engage with contemporary issues, providing the critical distance and interrogative zeal that journalists, activists or the public typically lack. They have a duty "to demand enlightenment" and "to explain the manoeuvres, to dissipate the myths" that constitute everyday political life, while also aiming "to inspire a politics" by experimenting with new concepts and forms of coexistence (EP: 63; HT: xxix; TD: 12).

Paradoxically, it is the very concreteness his existentialist commitments required that helps explain the relative neglect of Merleau-Ponty's political studies today, despite renewed interest in other aspects of his philosophy. His concerns are no longer our own. Yet I would argue that just as one cannot grasp the full import of his interventions without understanding something of the philosophy that orients them, nor is it possible to appreciate his philosophy without recognizing the political concerns that motivated it. Associating the modern lifeworld with a rationalist mode of being-in-the-world, he condemned its ethos of subjective mastery, its tendency to reification and closure, and its proclivity for nihilism. But he found one of its most tragic manifestations in the excessive violence that modern political regimes practise in their pursuit of humanism. Underlying these regimes' shortcomings, Merleau-Ponty concluded, is a failure to understand the nature of the political or to recognize the particular virtuosity that is the vocation of the political actor.

Merleau-Ponty's work is thus political in the widest sense of pursuing a transformation of modern experience. But it is also political in a narrower sense of trying to show those who do engage with this risky political realm how they might negotiate its ambiguities and sheer complexity in a more reasonable way. Crucial to both levels, he maintained, is recognition of irreducible contingency. He struggled throughout his career to sketch the ontology of this contingent interworld where violence and communication, power and reason, entwine and proliferate across collective life. This understanding of the political and of the kind of political engagement it summons is an enduring aspect of his political thinking and one of the reasons for returning to his political philosophy today.

Merleau-Ponty's political experience

The events Merleau-Ponty commented on were mainly those of postwar Europe during the 1940s and 1950s. Experiences of the Nazi Occupation remained painfully vivid memories in France (Merleau-Ponty had himself participated in the Resistance), illustrating the tragic personal choices individuals are sometimes called upon to make in politics and posing the question of why the liberal French state had proven so impotent in the face of fascist aggression. Now the cold war was being fought out in an increasingly Manichean way, with the space for nuances and ambiguities being closed down by ideological foes demanding that France take sides. Merleau-Ponty urged caution while criticizing both protagonists, revealing their hypocrisy while describing the lived experiences their values actually supported. Meanwhile, he observed France's fraught journey towards modernization. Economic development was reproducing class injustice and changing conditions were revealing the anachronism of the French political elite, as well as the moribund nature of the Republic's political system and of its attitude towards others. The war in Algeria and the violent process of decolonization in North Africa, which occupied Merleau-Ponty's thoughts as the 1950s wore on, only reinforced his sense that French politics was adrift and that signs of progressive forces were at least well hidden.

This period of French history is brought to life by the third volume of Simone de Beauvoir's autobiography, *Force of Circumstance*

(1963). In it we witness her friend Maurice Merleau-Ponty playing his role in a narrative of commitment, disappointment and quarrels among erstwhile comrades. Although he never joined the Communist Party, Merleau-Ponty was part of that generation of French intellectuals – among them Sartre and de Beauvoir – who were trying to revitalize Marxism by practising a critical, humanist version that was indebted to Hegel and to the recent publication of Marx's youthful writings, but also to the phenomenology of Husserl and Heidegger. Merleau-Ponty would identify dialectics and existentialism as the two essential philosophical themes of the twentieth century (S: 155). Although he developed these in a distinctive phenomenological way, he would remain faithful to them throughout his career, despite the later influence of structuralism on his work. In particular, they inspired his commitment to investigating and criticizing lived experience from a position that was self-consciously and thus reflexively situated within it. He would eventually call this approach "hyperdialectics" (VI: 89–95).

Anti-humanists would soon dismiss these dialectical, phenomenological and existentialist approaches as dependent on a philosophy of the subject. Yet Merleau-Ponty's version already anticipated many of his critics' arguments, rendering his own writings considerably less vulnerable to their criticisms than were those of Marx, Husserl or Sartre; in some respects he might even be designated a poststructuralist *avant la lettre* (Busch & Gallagher 1992: xii; Hass & Olkowski 2000: 13). Yet it was the capacity of the former approaches to facilitate critical engagement in politics as it unfolds within everyday experiences that helped Merleau-Ponty recognize that the difficulties he discerned in French politics were symptomatic of a broader problematic in modernity. As the world-historical aspirations of Marxist revolutionary politics faltered, so Europe as a whole seemed to be suffering a crisis of identity and a loss of meaning. Here Merleau-Ponty seems to have been influenced – as were his contemporaries Adorno and Horkheimer and other early members of the Frankfurt School – by a particular combination of Nietzschean, Husserlian and Weberian pessimism, as well as by the Left's disillusionment with Marxism. If he still shared Marx's materialist antipathy towards liberal capitalism, he also recognized a cultural and political malaise he associated with the disappearance of a viable alternative and with the loss of criteria or capacities for practising a progressive politics.

While he did not succumb entirely to the political gloom that would render the critical theorists' critiques so total as to be politically paralysing, Merleau-Ponty did retreat somewhat from political engagement after the Korean War, which he blamed on Soviet aggression. This was the occasion for his quarrel with Sartre (whose support for the Communists during the war relied on a dangerous idealist fantasy, in Merleau-Ponty's opinion); his provisional shift to supporting the parliamentary, non-communist Left (and a "new" or "Weberian" liberalism) and his resignation from the editorial committee of *Les Temps modernes*, which had been the main instrument for his public voice since 1945. While he would continue to intervene in political debates, those concerning North Africa in particular, Merleau-Ponty suggested that silence was sometimes a more appropriate response when discussion had become especially closed and events were particularly nonsensical (Goehr 2005; Stewart 1998).

Yet his analyses of mid-twentieth-century modernity were not entirely devoid of hope, and this seems to be attributable to Merleau-Ponty's sense that appreciation of contingency was growing, thanks to the success of existentialism and phenomenology in combating rationalist certainties. His analyses of modern political regimes suggested that their limitations could be traced to the rationalist presuppositions that underpin their projects and undermine their understanding of the nature of politics. He therefore concluded that appreciating the role of contingency in collective life was the route to overcoming some fundamental prejudices and their violent effects, where more narrowly political changes would only repeat past failings. Modernity's very foundations must be reconfigured, and this would require nothing less than a return to ontology (VI: 165) in order to describe how existence emerges and coexistence is engendered in (or as) a hazardous, contingent interworld.

The main "prejudice" to be challenged here was Cartesian (and Kantian) rationalism, with its ontological presuppositions concerning mind–body dualism and the subject–object opposition that is its epistemological corollary. It is his rejection of the realist (empiricist) and idealist (intellectualist) approaches that are the legacy of such assumptions that structures all Merleau-Ponty's critical interventions. This is equally – indeed especially – true of his political critiques, where he observed the way these dualisms and the orientations associated with them translate into irrational and violent political strategies, as well as an instrumental and dehumanizing treatment of nature and of others.

The political critiques

In addition to various articles that are now published mainly in *Sense and Non-Sense* (1948) and *Signs* (1960), Merleau-Ponty wrote two books specifically about politics: *Humanism and Terror* (1947) and *Adventures of the Dialectic* (1955). Both volumes are composed of a series of linked essays that tackle issues connected with cold war politics and modern regimes, but which also examine the political philosophies that support them. The political and theoretical criticisms are inseparable here, and this inseparability is indeed indicative of Merleau-Ponty's belief that practices and ideas are dialectically interwoven.

While the earlier book is more obviously inspired by Marx's critique of bourgeois society and is unequivocal in its condemnation of liberal capitalism, the later one is more circumspect in its judgements of liberal democracy but less equivocal in its treatment of Marxist politics. This shift in his political support has encouraged some commentators to present Merleau-Ponty as a thinker who became more conservative over time (e.g. Madison 1988: 72; Cooper 1979). But my own view is that his basic commitments remained consistent here. His abiding aim was to judge political regimes existentially, that is, according to the kind of lived relationships – the "human bond" or existential signature – they actually support rather than according to their self-professed values. Only then, he believed, could they be compared and evaluated according to a common criterion. A "truer" way of coexisting would be one that encourages the enrichment of relationships through communication, differentiation and complexity, as well as the questioning and experimenting that are valued once the provisional, contingent and limited nature of all relative solutions to coexistence is appreciated. The material conditions of existence are a crucial element in any such solution. This partly explains his fascination with the Soviet Union, whose sociological and political forms were still taking shape. What changed during the early 1950s was a clearer sense of what communist regimes actually meant for everyday life and the geopolitical circumstances in which Merleau-Ponty's own analyses were interpreted (Coole 2003).

Yet it is nonetheless true that these developments did prompt Merleau-Ponty to realize that he had not always remained faithful to the phenomenological imperative of interrogating every presupposition. In particular, he had taken certain aspects of Marxism for granted (as Marx had himself retained unquestioned naturalist presuppositions regarding human essence and its *telos*) that must now be subjected to deeper scrutiny. Most of *Adventures of the Dialectic* is accordingly devoted to an analysis of fundamental errors among dialectical misadventurers from Marx, via Lukács (who sometimes also serves as a proxy for the younger Merleau-Ponty), Lenin and Trotsky, to Sartre. It shows how they oscillated between realist and idealist assumptions that are anathema to dialectics and manifest themselves disastrously in political practice.

It was the effects of these kinds of dualist thinking that had already structured *Humanism and Terror*. Here Merleau-Ponty had focused on the dangers of enacting a politics that presumes an opposition between means and ends, or between intentions and consequences. While he generally saw liberal regimes as more idealist in focusing on universal human values, and their communist counterparts as more positivist in their emphasis on constructing the material conditions needed for an egalitarian society, his main concern was that neither recognized how, in politics, principles and outcomes are inseparable. Despite their apparent differences, these regimes both practised a politics of the subject.

Kantian-inspired liberalism (exemplified by the pre-war French state) too readily assumes men of good will who are amenable to consensus and whose values can simply be imposed on collective life (SNS: 32). Unfortunately, "violence will not be expelled by locking ourselves within the judicial dream of liberalism" (HT: 34), for this normativity militates against the necessity of dirtying one's hands and thus leaves unjust socio-economic structures unchallenged (S: 217). It fails to recognize that embodied actors inhabit an intersubjective domain where reason and violence, freedom and power, conscience and events are inseparable, and politics is a risky undertaking that has to be made under conditions of adversity. Failing to appreciate the contingency of the political and thus the interpretive skill, compromises and strategic flexibility it requires, this sort of liberalism can readily switch from quietism to a dangerous moralism, whose attempt at imposing its values on recalcitrant events often leads to excessive violence (HT: 119, 149). This is why "Machiavelli is worth more than Kant" (*ibid.*: 104).

In the case of the liberal state, there is also a failure to recognize its provisionality and limitations. "Its nature is violent, nor does it hesitate to impose itself through violence in accordance with the old theory of the secular arm" (*ibid.*: xxiv). Racism, exploitation and colonial violence are all endemic in liberal-democratic systems, Merleau-Ponty observes. Its humanist values serve as an alibi for unemployment and war; they do not "filter down to the common man" (*ibid.*: 175). From the perspective of existentialist analysis, these regimes therefore fail to live up to their own ideals. Even when he lost hope that communism might yet reform itself, he still insisted that "the disgraces of both systems are entered on a complex and 'probabilistic' balance sheet, and a critique of one of the systems cannot by itself ground one's choice of the other" (AD: 181).

Yet communist actors fare no better in Merleau-Ponty's analysis, inasmuch as they focus purely on the outcome of acts. If they subscribe to a Marxist philosophy of history that guarantees them success, then their interpretation of history's requirements still demands a subjective reading that is no less rationalist if it imposes a preconceived meaning on events, rather than plunging into the contingencies of an ambiguously emerging present (HT: 93; AD: 71). A broken "dialectic in action responds to adversity either by means of terror exercised in the name of a hidden truth or by opportunism" (*ibid.*: 95). Under Stalin, the dialectic had become merely an ideological point of honour, where political actors no longer acted dialectically by communicating with the masses who make history or by reflecting on the detours and changing significance of their acts. Instead they, too, tried to impose their will on society rather than engaging with the contingencies of intersubjective life. In the process, revolutionary violence had been institutionalized as terror and justified by an appeal to the necessity of objective facts.

Although his critics sometimes presented Merleau-Ponty as a naive apologist for Stalinism, he explains in *Adventures of the Dialectic* that inasmuch as he had advocated a "wait and see" stance in 1947, this was predicated on wondering whether other communist regimes might yet take a different direction – whether "we shall see a new type of society, which has yet to be studied" (HT: 142) – while opportunities for a more democratic style of working-class praxis had still seemed possible in Western Europe during the ferment of the immediate postwar period (*ibid.*: xxiii, 158; AD 228f). But he had already acknowledged in 1947 that despite a paucity of reliable data, it had become possible "to construct a picture of Soviet life which is the opposite of proletarian humanism" (HT: 136). By the time Merleau-Ponty wrote "The U.S.S.R. and the Camps" in 1950 (S), it was clear that their ten million inmates, coupled with evidence of new hierarchies and the kind of bureaucratization against which Weber had warned, undermined any possibility of labelling the Soviet Union socialist (S: 265). The objectivist aspect of Soviet practice was apparent in its way of treating society as a second nature, to be manipulated by "the type of action a technician would make, like that of an engi-

neer who builds a bridge" (AD: 63, 95). Again, this was antithetical
to a dialectical manner of negotiating the political and material force
field.

Despite these criticisms, Merleau-Ponty maintained that the sociology of communist regimes was "entirely left to be done" (ibid.: 224)
and that although Marxism was not true as such, it did remain a useful perspective from which to interpret history (ibid.: 180, 225, 227;
S: 9f, 12). Following Khrushchev's reforms and communism's becoming the choice of some ex-colonial states as a route to modernization, Merleau-Ponty did not anyway consider his judgement or the
system's significance to be a closed issue. One still needed "sharp
eyes" to interpret its direction and its changing contours (AD: 224;
S: 5). The same was true, of course, of liberal capitalism, and he
remained alert to its neo-colonial and ecological costs as economic
modernization gathered pace (S: 4, 12). Interviewed in 1960, he
opined that "everything remains to be done or undone" because
philosophy's traditional approaches are unable to "express what
the world is now living through" (TD: 9f; PP: 241). Revitalizing the
dialectic in light of contingency was central to this task. This would
facilitate an alternative sense of the political and suggest an exemplary way of practising politics.

Political ontology

In order to undertake politics in a reasonable way, Merleau-Ponty
believed that it is first necessary to acknowledge the ineluctable presence of the non-rational. This is not an argument for humanity's
irrationality, but a consequence of accepting the embodied nature
of political actors. It is perception rather than reason that is now
primary, with reason emerging (and remaining) inseparable from
its corporeal, practical provenance. It is in the emergence of perceptual forms, where the phenomenal body interacts with its milieu to
co-compose provisional but meaningful unities, that significance first
appears and (co)existence proliferates. This phenomenological ontology has important implications for Merleau-Ponty's understanding
of politics. It suggests a resolutely non-Cartesian process whereby
meaning and matter are irreducibly entwined. This is why the kind of
dualist presuppositions that underpin rationalist regimes are untenable. The violent and inefficacious politics that relies on subject–
object opposition, and that alternates between idealist and objectivist
approaches to collective life, can now be challenged in the name of the

lifeworld wherein coexistence appears and intersubjectivity is forged. This, for Merleau-Ponty, *is* the domain of the political, and it is a consequence of our being embodied actors within an intercorporeal milieu.

The intentional body that phenomenology describes entails a degree of irremediable and pre-personal opacity, but also a rich texture of intercorporeal relationships and communications that operate on non-cognitive (although not necessarily on pre-cultural) as well as symbolic levels. I have tried elsewhere to pursue the implications of this claim in regard to embodied interlocutors who engage in deliberative practices, since their irreducible corporeality has important implications for the interplay of reason and power in democratic contexts (Coole 2007a). Other thinkers recognize the potential of Merleau-Ponty's work for investigating the phenomenology of race, ethnicity and gender (see Chapter 18). Although he did not write about body politics as such, he alerts us to the political significance of corporeality and to the efficacy yet vulnerability of flesh that is itself a contingent process of becoming. Embodiment situates political actors as beings-in-the-world; they inhabit a pre-personal, intercorporeal realm where encroachment is endemic and perspectives remain partial. It means that their intentions – whether corporeal or reflective – are caught up in an interworld to whose more enduring structures, habits and meanings they contribute and on which they sometimes improvise creatively. Yet this intersubjective milieu always outruns, constrains, forms and excites them in a more or less anonymous way that eludes full understanding or control.

This is why the oppositions that frame the tragedy of the political can never be resolved by separating ideals from facts or intentions from consequences. The challenge of collective action revolves around the ineluctable interplay of personal commitments and their unintended consequences. Social scientists typically tackle this conundrum by distinguishing between agency and structure and then reconstructing their relationship. But Merleau-Ponty seems to have concluded that nothing less than a new ontology of the political would be necessary: one that recognizes an intersubjective, intercorporeal interworld – the "between" – as the realm of coexistence in its own right. The challenge would be to grasp this dense, multi-layered field of relationships or forces – this "flesh of the world" where perspectives blend and reason appears (PP: xix; VI: 84) – and to describe its choreography.

It is possible to elicit a novel sense of agency from this later work, inasmuch as it implies abandoning the ontology of rational individuals that typically underlies accounts of agency in political studies, as well as the teleological presumptions about collective agency that marred Marxism. Instead, the phenomenologist traces the hazardous appearing of agent-oriented capacities – capacities for meaning, reflexivity, expression, improvisation, communication – that emerge contingently within the interworld, where they only sometimes acquire the kind of singularity that brings political efficacy. Such capacities are not properties of an ontological subject, but expressions of immanently generative flesh (Coole 2005; Archer 2000: 127–37). Capacities for political agency emerge within the force field of collective life and the task of the phenomenologist (or political actor) is to seek signs of potentially transgressive or transformative capacities within the ambiguities and complexities of this field. Although Merleau-Ponty did not live to explore the implications of this ontology, it suggests the basis from a radically new understanding of politics and the political.

It is important to keep in mind that flesh remained for Merleau-Ponty a worldly notion: a realm of lived, intercorporeal, intersubjective experience. It is not, he insisted, "pure" Being but "the system of perspectives that open onto it". Being is not laid out before me as a spectator but unfolds "at the intersection of . . . my acts and at the intersection of my acts with those of the others", such that "the sensible world and the historical world" are "always intermundane spaces", a "pell-mell ensemble of bodies and minds, promiscuity of visages, words, actions, with, between them all, that cohesion which cannot be denied them since they are all differences, extreme divergences of one same something" (VI: 84). The thinker who would best appreciate the implications of this description for the political is Foucault, whose account of a volatile field of forces where power and resistance incite one another is in many ways anticipated by Merleau-Ponty's flesh. But it is the latter who seeks guidance for political agency in this dense, reversible field.

The phenomenology of political practice

If it is the philosopher's responsibility to plunge into the labyrinth of coexistence in order to interpret its emergent significance and to track the ambiguous emergence of agentic capacities that might challenge its closures and reifications, then political actors must engage in a rather similar practice. As Merleau-Ponty explains, political commitment of any sort means working with existing forces and understanding, perhaps reorienting, them. It therefore requires not only "our goodwill and our choice but our knowledge, our labor, our criticism, our preference and our complete presence" (AD: 232). Because actors deal more immediately with the contingencies of everyday power relations, their interventions carry greater risks and require more audacity.

The thinkers with whom Merleau-Ponty found most affinity here were Machiavelli, Marx and Weber. What they shared, at least in their more phenomenological moments, was precisely their appreciation that politics is a realm of contingency and adversity, where reason has to be engendered and is never guaranteed. They recognized, too, that the political is a distinctive domain of collective life that requires its own kind of virtuosity or vocation, where violence cannot be eliminated by fiat. It is Machiavelli, Merleau-Ponty claims in his "Note on Machiavelli", who "introduces us to the milieu proper to politics and allows us to estimate the task we are faced with if we want to bring some truth to it" (S: 214). This Machiavelli recognized that power "is not naked force, but neither is it the honest delegation of individual wills" (*ibid*.: 212f). He saw how political life unfolds in a symbolic realm of appearances and dissimulations, where power seduces and communicates as well as constrains through naked force, and he described "that knot of collective life in which pure morality can be cruel and pure politics requires something like a morality" (*ibid*.: 211). It is in light of this understanding, predicated on the view that "history is a struggle and politics a relationship to men rather than principles", that Merleau-Ponty defines *virtù* as "a means of living with others" (*ibid*.: 214, 219).

This ability is in part hermeneutical: the astute actor does not try to impose her will on events; rather, because she lives her times acutely she is able to perceive the "significance and pattern within a given situation" (HT: 63). She recognizes that this *sens* (meaning and direction) is no cunning of reason to be deciphered, yet history is not meaningless either. The desires and anxieties of myriad actors are meshed in their everyday interactions, where they weave a web in which vectors and constellations can be discerned. Although success is never guaranteed, action is not therefore bereft of signs and clues to guide it. History teaches us "errors to avoid" and actors must continuously reflect upon the unpredictable effects of their acts. Those who communicate with others and live their times well can increase their chances of acting efficaciously and humanely.

It is this sense of politics that Merleau-Ponty also discerns in Marxism at its best. This Marxism is not a grand narrative but a "reading of ongoing history" that orients itself around existing forces, where values and facts unfold within a "network of events". This non-teleological Marxism rests "on the profound idea that human perspectives, however relative, are absolute because there is nothing else and no destiny". It underpinned the art of "the great Marxists of 1917" who "deciphered history while it was taking place and projected its trends through decisions that avoided equally any subjective folly or *amor fati*" (HT: 18, 53, 58). In short, this "rigorous and consistent Marxism" recognized the density of human relations. It practised a "theory of historical comprehension . . . and of creative choice"; it questioned history regarding its emergent *sens* (AD: 29). Merleau-Ponty spoke in this context of a "Weberian Marxism" to denote those revolutionaries who "lived their time" with insight and passion (*ibid.*: 5). Like the intentional body that interacts with the visible world or Weber in his creative intuition of ideal types, the capacities of such agents resemble those of the pianist who "deciphers an unknown piece of music" by gaining a feeling for its internal logic and patterns (SNS: 93). This allows them to improvise without acting gratuitously. If Weber shares something with Machiavelli here, it is his recognition that collective life is a realm of violence without guarantees. One who has a vocation for politics must be willing to compromise, but without losing sight of the principles for which action is undertaken. This last caveat is crucial and it is in this context that Merleau-Ponty praises a dialectical, "Marxist Machiavellianism" (HT: 120; S: 221; EP: 59). It is good ends (a regime where coexistence can flourish) that distinguish mere opportunism or "vulgar relativism" from an exemplary political flexibility, yet the latter cannot flourish once it gets trapped in a means–ends dichotomy. Instead it is necessary to recognize politics as an ongoing process that folds back on itself critically, reflexively.

If Machiavelli's *Fortuna* is closer to Merleau-Ponty's sense of contingency than it is to fate, it is because chance "takes shape only when we give up understanding and willing" (S: 218). On Merleau-Ponty's account, the political virtuosity described by the Italian humanist resembles the phenomenological or dialectical art that he commends as an effective way of navigating the reversals and uncertainties of the political interworld. This was, after all, the treacherous field of forces he had found himself negotiating when he intervened in cold-war politics. He had tried to exemplify the lessons he wanted to teach us about engaging with politics in a contingent world, through the subtleties of his own intervention.

Further reading

Coole, D. 2007. *Merleau-Ponty and Modern Politics after Anti-Humanism*. Lanham, MD: Rowman & Littlefield.

Crossley, N. 1994. *The Politics of Subjectivity: Between Foucault and Merleau-Ponty*. Aldershot: Ashgate.

Kruks, S. 1981. *The Political Philosophy of Merleau-Ponty*. Brighton: Harvester.

Lefort, C. 2005. "Thinking Politics". In *The Cambridge Companion to Merleau-Ponty*, T. Carman & M. Hansen (eds), 352–79. Cambridge: Cambridge University Press.

Whiteside, K. 1988. *Merleau-Ponty and the Foundation of an Existential Politics*. Princeton, NJ: Princeton University Press.

NINE

Art and aesthetics
Hugh J. Silverman

Unlike his erstwhile friend Jean-Paul Sartre, Merleau-Ponty was neither a playwright nor a novelist. However, as a philosopher of perception, he would often comment on the various arts, especially poetry, painting, music and film, the artists who created them, and the experience of understanding them. Sartre had already written about the imagination as distinct from perception and expression in *Imagination* (1936) and *The Psychology of Imagination* (1940), but also in *Being and Nothingness* (1943). Sartre had already published his first novel *Nausea* (1938) and, during the war, several plays: *No Exit, The Flies, Dirty Hands*. Meanwhile in 1939, Merleau-Ponty completed *The Structure of Behavior* (1942), in which there is hardly a mention of aesthetic matters. By contrast, his *Phenomenology of Perception* (1945) is interfused with passing references to Cézanne and Van Gogh, to Proust, Balzac, Valéry and Stendhal, and to Beethoven's Ninth Symphony and its musical performance.

In *Phenomenology of Perception*, appeals to painters, novelists, musical performances are all in aid of explaining how phenomenological experience – of the body, of language, of time, of vision – articulates embodied being-in-the-world. In the important Preface he remarks:

> If phenomenology was a movement before becoming a doctrine or a philosophical system, this was attributable neither to accident, nor to fraudulent intent. It is as painstaking as the works of Balzac, Proust, Valéry, or Cézanne – by reason of the same kind of attentiveness and wonder, the same demand for awareness,

the same will to seize the meaning of the world or of history as
that meaning comes into being. In this way it merges into the
general effort of modern thought.   (PP: xxi)

The sense(s) of expressing the world

Merleau-Ponty's first serious forays into aesthetic experience came
in the years following the conclusion of the war when he taught at
the University of Lyon (1945–48). Examples from aesthetics and the
psychology of communication occupied about one-third of his course
programme. In the second year, he offered a course on "Aesthetics
and Modern Painting". As I note in the Translator's Preface to *Consciousness and the Acquisition of Language*, "the course on aesthetics
ranges from a consideration of contemporary aesthetics and a discussion of Cézanne, cinema, cubism, Malraux to the significance of
the psychology of art" (CAL: xxxiii–xl). In 1947–48, Merleau-Ponty
again taught a course on "Aesthetics", focusing on modern poetry
and in particular on the French Symbolists (Baudelaire, Rimbaud,
Mallarmé). He "tried to articulate the essence of poetry, with emphasis on Sartre's interpretation of Baudelaire and Valéry's study of
Mallarmé" (*ibid*.: xxxviii). Both Sartre's *Baudelaire* and his *What Is
Literature?* appeared in 1947.

   In these three years before his 1948 appointment as Professor
of Child Psychology and Pedagogy at the Sorbonne, Merleau-Ponty
explored how the experience of the artist or writer could be understood phenomenologically. Detailed studies of Cézanne's painting,
Sartre's and Simone de Beauvoir's novels, and the New Cinema – pol-
ished and published in *Sense and Non-Sense* (1948) – stand in sharp
contrast to his fleeting comments on aesthetic matters throughout
Phenomenology of Perception.

   In "Cézanne's Doubt", Merleau-Ponty takes special care to develop the phenomenological–psychological experience of the artist
when confronting the immediate task of his artistic practice. He
begins his study of Cézanne with a quote from a letter Cézanne had
written in 1906 (at the age of 67, one month before his death):

   I was in such a state of mental agitation, in such great confusion
   that for a time I feared my weak reason would not survive . . .
   Now it seems I am better and that I see more clearly the direction my studies are taking. Will I ever arrive at the goal, so

intensely sought and so long pursued? I am still learning from
nature, and it seems to me I am making slow progress.

(SNS: 9)

Cézanne, Merleau-Ponty writes, worked feverishly – "alone, without
students, without admiration from his family, without encourage-
ment from his critics" (*ibid.*). Furthermore: "his extremely close
attention to nature and to color, the inhuman character of his paintings (he said that a face should be painted as an object), his devotion
to the visible world; all of these would then only represent a flight
from the human world, the alienation of his humanity" (*ibid.*: 10).
Yet, "the meaning of his work cannot be determined from his life"
(*ibid.*). Merleau-Ponty elaborated in detail the number of colours he
used on his palette, his use of colour over outline, and the technique
of making light emanate from objects. He "abandoned himself to the
chaos of sensations" (*ibid.*: 13). Cézanne, Merleau-Ponty writes, "did
not think he had to choose between feeling and thought, between
order and chaos". He "makes a basic distinction not between 'the
senses' and 'the understanding' but rather between the spontaneous
organization of the things we perceive and the human organization
of ideas and sciences" (*ibid.*). This distinction between the natural or
even vital order and the human order had already been the focus of
the penultimate chapter of *The Structure of Behavior* (1942).

Cézanne's experience exemplified Merleau-Ponty's own account
of synaesthetic perception – the crossing over of the various senses –
which he elaborates at length in *Phenomenology of Perception* (PP:
228–9). He writes:

Cézanne does not try to use colour to *suggest* the tactile sensations which would give shape and depth. These distinctions
between touch and sight are unknown in primordial perception.
It is only as a result of a science of the human body that we
finally learn to distinguish between our senses.   (SNS: 15)

This native synaesthesia in Cézanne's artistic practice – phenomenologically described and experienced – is inaccessible to psycho-
physiological distinctions.

The lived object is not rediscovered or constructed on the basis
of the contributions of the senses; rather, it presents itself to
us from the start as the center from which these contributions
radiate. We *see* the depth, the smoothness, the softness, the

hardness of objects; Cézanne even claimed that we see their odor.   (*Ibid.*)

Merleau-Ponty delights in showing that the artist can present this lived embodied phenomenal field through painting:

> If the painter is to express the world, the arrangement of his colours must carry with it an indivisible whole, or else his picture will only hint at things and will not give them in the imperious unity, the presence, the insurpassable plenitude which is for us the definition of the real. That is why each brush-stroke must satisfy an infinite number of conditions . . . expressing what *exists* [as] an endless task.   (*Ibid.*)

Merleau-Ponty sees phenomenology as coinciding with Cézanne's "process of expressing" as a painter.

Similarly, Merleau-Ponty turns to Leonardo da Vinci as understood by the poet–essayist Paul Valéry and by his contemporary Sigmund Freud. Da Vinci's obsessions and his inability to finish his painting projects were reflections of his father abandoning him. But Merleau-Ponty shows that the psychoanalyst's "hermeneutic musings" (accounts of da Vinci's fantasies of his mother's breast depicted as a vulture in his painting *The Virgin and Child with St Anne*) do not take away from one's "freedom". Rather, psychoanalysis, he says, "teaches us to think of this freedom concretely, as a creative repetition of ourselves, always, in retrospect, faithful to ourselves" (SNS: 25). Linking da Vinci's expressions of freedom to Cézanne's life project: "it was in the world that he had to realize his freedom, with colors upon a canvas" (*ibid.*). "Freedom" was, of course, a persistent theme for both Merleau-Ponty and Sartre (and many others) as the oppressive occupation of Paris reached its conclusion in 1945. Sartre's 1947 account of the "free writer" enacting the "freedom of the reader" through the depiction of freedom in the literary work (*What Is Literature?*) is matched by Merleau-Ponty's conviction that the artist – Cézanne as well as da Vinci – expresses freedom through the sensuous materialities of colours on a canvas.

Besides "Cézanne's Doubt", *Sense and Non-Sense* contains three other essays in aesthetics. "Metaphysics and the Novel" concerns Simone de Beauvoir's novel *L'Invitée* (1943) – a thinly disguised fictionalized account of Sartre's affair with the young Olga Kosakievicz that challenged her own relationship with Sartre. Merleau-Ponty reads through the intrigue of the triadic relationship and the manner in which the relationship between Pierre and Françoise was threatened by Pierre's relationship with the younger 20-year-old Xavière. Françoise and Pierre "have established such sincerity between them, have constructed such a machine of language, that they are together even when living apart from each other and can remain free in their union" (SNS: 31). "Man is metaphysical in his very being", writes Merleau-Ponty, "in his loves, in his hates, in his individual and collective history" (*ibid.*: 28).

From now on, Merleau-Ponty boldly affirms, "the tasks of literature and philosophy can no longer be separated" (*ibid.*). Merleau-Ponty and his friends were convinced that de Beauvoir's and Sartre's novels were so philosophically charged that one could read them in tandem with their philosophies and even develop philosophies out of them. "When one is concerned with giving voice to the experience of the world and showing how consciousness escapes into the world, one can no longer credit oneself with attaining a perfect transparence of expression" (*ibid.*). Here the philosophical gives way to the literary:

> Philosophical expression assumes the same ambiguities as literary expression, if the world is such that it cannot be expressed except in "stories" and, as it were, pointed at. One will not only witness the appearance of hybrid modes of expression but the novel and the theater will become thoroughly metaphysical, even if not a single word is used from the vocabulary of philosophy. (*Ibid.*)

Unlike Sartre and de Beauvoir, Merleau-Ponty did not write novels or plays. He was the quintessential philosopher, and yet he recognized the importance of the literary becoming philosophical and the philosophical becoming literary. His ongoing aesthetic themes of expression and freedom could now be enacted in a comprehensive way through literary philosophizing.

"A Scandalous Author" explores how Sartre's literary art can develop a whole moral and social theory. *No Exit*, the *Roads to Freedom* novels, and even the earlier 1938 *Nausea* demonstrate how theories of expression and freedom can be formulated in aesthetic terms. Sartre's plays and novels could be described as the very enactment of Merleau-Ponty's notions of expression and freedom. He cites Sartre as saying "When people speak to me about freedom, it is as if they were speaking about myself," which Merleau-Ponty interprets as Sartre identifying "himself with that transparency or that agility

which is not of the world and which . . . makes freedom 'mortal'"
(SNS: 47).

Despite this strong commitment to painting and literature as expressing human freedom, he also includes (in *Sense and Non-Sense*)
an essay entitled "The Film and the New Psychology". A movie, he
claims, is not thought, but rather perceived. The "new psychology"
is officially the Gestalt psychology of Köhler, Koffka, Gelb and
Goldstein that had fascinated Merleau-Ponty for over a decade.
Gestalt psychology teaches that what we see is never reducible to
the perception of isolated elements. *Aesthesis*, sense-experience,
embodied perception spontaneously grasps wholes despite the presentation of discrete imaged filmic elements. We don't distinguish
between signs and their significance, Merleau-Ponty claims, since the
world presents itself as always already organized into signifying
wholes. The film is "not a sum total of images but a temporal *Gestalt*"
(SNS: 54). In cinema, perception is temporal and not just visual.
Phenomenology of Perception had already demonstrated that temporality is prospection in retrospection and retrospection in prospection (PP: 414). The experience of related frames in a film links
the past moments to those of the future and vice versa. Sitting in the
movie house experiencing a film – with the coexistence of others in
the theatre – a lived perceptual network takes place. Both the philosopher and the movie-maker belong to a common generation,
indicating that both thought and the technical cinematic effort are
heading in the same direction (SNS: 59).

Indirect language, style and the speaking subject

The second significant phase in Merleau-Ponty's aesthetic theory
comes as he completes his four-year stint as Professor of Child
Psychology and Pedagogy. During those years, he had focused on
the child's language acquisition, the child's relations with others, the
child's experience of others, the psycho-sociology of the child, and the
role of phenomenology in the constitution of the human sciences. But
in 1951–52, as Merleau-Ponty was elected to the Chair of Philosophy
at the Collège de France, he sought to elaborate a radically new
way of thinking about language and aesthetic experience. He distinguished between "indirect language" (non-direct, non-formulaic,
non-argumentative, non-thetic speech) and "the algorithm" (the
scientific, reductive, quantitative ways of thinking about language
and expression). Building on "The Body as Expression, and Speech"

chapter in *Phenomenology of Perception*, Merleau-Ponty's *The Prose of the World* shows that indirect language is expressive and that embodied expression includes gesture and painting as well as verbal communication. The "speaking subject" (*le sujet parlant*) does not express thought. Speaking speech (*la parole*) is the speaker's expressive thought (PP: 180). The speaking subject communicates not by "representation" or "thought" but "with a certain style of being and with the 'world' at which he directs his aim" (*ibid.*: 183).

In *The Prose of the World*, Merleau-Ponty is worried about those who argue for a "pure language" – a linguistic idealism in which all the elements are formed as conventional signs. Language would include only "ready-made phrases". But language is constantly faced with the prospect of expressing what has never yet been seen, new definitions, new symbols. The ideal of a self-contained language would exclude anything that is not fully explicit. One "never means to say more than one does say and no more is said than one means" (PW: 5). Ultimately, the algorithm is a "revolt against language in its existing state and a refusal to depend upon the confusions of everyday language" (*ibid.*). This myth of a universal language (the algorithm) will have to contain within it everything that it will have to express. This claim to self-sufficiency, univocity and universality of language on the part of the algorithm overlooks how language is experienced, lived, expressed. "One of the effects of language", Merleau-Ponty notes, "is to efface itself to the extent that its expression comes across" (*ibid.*: 9).

Meaning (or sense) is not the simple linguistic signification that is lexically given. Meaning (as *sens*) is not observable, consumable, all-encompassing. *Sens* cannot be reduced to an univocal meaning. "When someone – an author or a friend – succeeds in expressing himself, the signs are immediately forgotten; all that remains is the meaning. The perfection of language lies in its capacity to pass unnoticed" (PW: 10). Merleau-Ponty claims that there are two languages: (1) "language after the fact, or language as an institution, which effaces itself in order to yield the meaning . . . it conveys"; and (2) "the language which creates itself in its expressive acts, which sweeps me on from the signs toward meaning – sedimented [or spoken] language (*le langage parlé*) and [speaking] speech (*le langage parlant*)" (*ibid.*). Merleau-Ponty here is distinguishing between the active speaking of a language and the given, sedimented, conventional language or speech that we use in order to understand one another directly. When reading Stendhal, he says that the reader is brought within the imaginary self even to the extent that the reader would be able to say: "I am

Stendhal". The book takes possession of the reader. The reader brings a sedimented, spoken language (*un langage parlé*) with him or her as accepted relations between signs and familiar significations come into play. Another language, namely speaking speech (*le langage parlant*) is the living, active "call to the unprejudiced reader" (*ibid.*: 13). "Once I have acquired this language (spoken language), I can easily delude myself into believing that I could have understood it by myself, because it has transformed me and made me capable of understanding it" (*ibid.*).

In literary experience, expression belongs to both spoken language and speaking language. But pure, spoken, conventional language is not one thing and the living, speaking, literary language something else. They are both aspects of expression. Aesthetic experience can never be uniquely one or the other but is always infused with both. The meaning produced by literary uses of speech can also be found in everyday language. Both involve the production and expression of sense, namely, the embodied enactment of language. Literary language drives speaking subjects to express themselves in new ways, and yet there is an ambiguity to their expressivity. He even says that expressing oneself is paradoxical since it grows from already established and thoroughly evident expressions. However, we detach ourselves from these conventional expressions so that they can be new enough to arouse attention. This novel manner of expression arising from a uniqueness of speaking is what Merleau-Ponty calls "style".

"Style" – invoked in *Sense and Non-Sense* – is now a key concept in his aesthetic theory. And indirect language is embedded in this notion of style. Truly expressive language cannot choose only one sign for an already defined signification. Speech and expression that "tends toward" is crucial to Merleau-Ponty's notion of creative communication, including that of the literary artist, the painter or the musician. Just as the child "tended toward" its first words out of babble, the writer "tends toward" expression often without providing a reductive univocal singular meaning. While Merleau-Ponty resists treating painting as a language, he claims that "the writer's task is to choose, assemble, wield, and torment the intruments [of phrasing, syntax, literary genres, modes of narrative] in such a way that they induce the same sentiment of life that dwells in the writer at every moment, deployed henceforth in an imaginary world and in the transparent body of language" (PW: 48). Similarly, classical painting presupposes a relationship between the painter and the viewer of the paintings. But in modern painting, as André Malraux claims, painting as a "creative" expression was quite new. And Merleau-Ponty agrees that there is "only one subject in painting, namely, the painter himself" (*ibid*.: 5) – a key theme that returns in Merleau-Ponty's last published essay "Eye and Mind" (PrP: 159). However, Merleau-Ponty qualifies this claim by stating that the subject of the paintings is not just the painter himself, but rather his "original relation to the world", namely, his "style" (PW: 56). Merleau-Ponty writes elegantly:

> Style is what makes all signification possible. Before signs or emblems become for everyone, even the artist, the simple index of already given significations, there must be that fruitful moment when signs have given form to experience or when an operant and latent meaning finds the emblems which should liberate it, making it manageable for the artist and accessible to others. (*Ibid*.: 58)

Style, for Merleau-Ponty, is the expression of indirect language. Artistic expression cannot be reformulated in conventional (direct) language, for "expression always goes beyond what it transforms by bringing it into a composition which changes its meaning" (*ibid*.: 69).

The arts transform a culture's relation to its past. This novelty of expression makes a tacit culture go beyond its limits. Unlike the writer who is obliged to use an established language, the painter is engaged in radically refashioning language. Painting is unable to speak; in this sense, it remains indirect. Horace in his *Ars Poetica* offered the simile "*ut pictura poesis*" (a poem is like a painting). Lessing's *Laocoön* shows that a poem is more effective than the fixed, static, plastic arts. Merleau-Ponty distinguishes the writer's language from the language of painting. The spirit of painting is a "spirit extended to itself" (PW: 101). The writer's language is called upon to "pursue self-possession, to master through criticism the secret of its own inventions of style, to talk about speech instead of only using it" (*ibid*.). Painting, however, has a temporality such that a painting can be experienced centuries later without having been initiated into the originating civilization. Writing, by contrast, "begins to communicate its most lasting sense to us only after it has introduced us to circumstances and arguments long since past" (*ibid*.: 102). In short, Merleau-Ponty revises Lessing's claim about time – appealing to a different sense of temporality. Lessing privileges literary art because it can describe an event over time while sculpture or painting can capture only a key moment in the event. Merleau-Ponty sees painting as situated in a historical moment (and yet transcending that moment) while literary art requires that it articulate its temporal–historical place in time.

Literary language and speaking speech

Two essays that were collected together in *Signs* (1960) – "Indirect Language and the Voices of Silence" and "On the Phenomenology of Language" – were actually written at the same time as *The Prose of the World* in 1951–52. "Indirect Language and the Voices of Silence" begins with the statement: "we have learned from Saussure . . . that, taken singly, signs do not signify anything, and that each one of them does not so much express a meaning as mark a divergence of meaning between itself and other signs" (S: 39). Here Merleau-Ponty expresses his definitive debt to the semiological thinker who helped him rebalance his phenomenological perspectives (Silverman 1997). Ultimately, without the contribution of Saussurean semiology, he doubtless could not have developed his theory of expression as a signifying activity, and hence his aesthetic theory would have most probably taken a different direction. In "Indirect Language and the Voices of Silence", he claims:

> A language sometimes remains a long time [emergent] with transformations which are to come; and the enumeration of the means of expression in a language does not have any meaning, since those which fall into disuse continue to lead a diminished life in the language and since the place of those which are to replace them is sometimes already marked out – even if only in the form of a gap, a need, or a tendency. (S: 41)

Meanings often do not have a strict space of their own. They are often located in the interstices and hence rife with a certain transformative power. Meanings arise "at the edge of signs" (*ibid.*). In this respect, Merleau-Ponty often cited Brunelleschi, architect of the Florentine cathedral (*duomo*) cupola. Does Brunelleschi belong to the medieval world of closed spaces or did he discover the "universal space" of the Renaissance? The language of Brunelleschi's architecture is transformed over time. The meaning of his architectural space appears at the intersection of, and in the intervals between, architectural identities, between signifiers, between determinate sign structures. Architectural meanings are like linguistic meanings – they arise only in that any one sign is profiled against other signs. There is no place in this circulation of meaning for a pure meaning. Similarly, the writer has no text to which he can compare his writing, no language prior to language (*ibid.*: 43). Hence Merleau-Ponty asserts that all language is indirect or allusive. No meaning can prevail over the others, no expression can consume the others, no sign can stand outside all signs as the determinate, guiding, univocal sign for all others. Resonating with Heidegger's (1976) famous "*die Sprache spricht*" (language speaks), Merleau-Ponty writes: "language speaks peremptorily when it gives up trying to express the thing itself" (S: 44). And later: "language speaks, and the voices of painting are the voices of silence" (*ibid.*: 81). The painter reaches across the silent world of lines and colours, and offers an unformulated power of deciphering only after we have enjoyed the work (*ibid.*: 45). The painter speaks through a tacit language as expressive speech. This tacit language is the painter's style. Citing Renoir's *The Bathers*, Merleau-Ponty notes that the painter "questioned the visible and made something visible", namely, the world and the blue water of the Mediterranean sea. Through our incarnate, bodily gesture towards the world an order of relations appears that is unknown to pure physiology and biology. Similarly, the writer dwells in an already speaking world of elaborated signs. Expression is given life in an already speaking world.

Summaries of Merleau-Ponty's courses at the Collège de France for the 1952–60 period were officially deposited at the Collège as a review of his work each year, later published as *Themes from the Lectures* (TL). His first courses clearly carried on the aesthetic theory that was taking shape in *The Prose of the World*. In "The Literary Use of Language" (1953), Merleau-Ponty offers – as he did implicitly in *The Prose of the World* – a response to Sartre's 1947 *What Is Literature?* He does so by appeal to Valéry and Stendhal. By contrast to Sartre, who thought poetry was nothing other than the presentation of objects in the world – exemplars of the in-itself – and unable to appeal to the free reader, Merleau-Ponty offers an affirmative account of poetry. He claims that poetry cannot be rejected simply because it does not pretend to say something (TL: 15). Poetry does not convey signification by effacing itself – not because it has no signification or meaning, but because it has more than one signification. This multiplicity of meaning accounts for its richness and vitality.

In his 1954 course "The Problem of Speech", carrying on this theme with respect to the writer, and in particular Proust, he points out that "the writer takes everyday language and makes it deliver the prelogical participation of landscapes, localities, and gestures, of men among themselves and with us" (TL: 25). Hence the writer's work is one of language rather than "thought".

His task is to produce a system of signs whose internal articulation reproduces the contours of experience . . . Literary speech
expresses the world in so far as it has been given to someone to
live it and at the same time it absorbs the world and poses itself
as its proper goal.   (*Ibid.*)

From the titles of the 1955–56 courses – "Institution in Personal
and Public History" and "The Problem of Passivity" (TL) – one might
think that he had left aesthetic theory behind. But this is far from the
case. The former course focuses on the dialectic between the institut-
ing subject and the instituted subject, namely the institution. And here
he draws his examples from Proust and Kafka. Both of these writers
were confronted with either a search (as in Kafka) or a indefinite
elaboration (as in Proust). Proust in particular offers a *via negativa*
of love that takes place in the context of sadness – even if based in
separation and jealousy. "The Problem of Passivity" elaborates
varieties of passivity – dream, memory, sleeping, the unconscious – as
articulated in Freud with his "layers of signification", and in Proust
with his memorial consciousness of past events and experiences,
such as Marcel's memories of those bodily sensations of pleasure
watching Albertine asleep on the couch before him.

Proust recurs throughout Merleau-Ponty's writings from *Phenomenology of Perception* to his 1958–59 course on "Philosophy
Today". Proust's novels are an illustration of how non-philosophy
– indirect language – is the articulation of the very possibility of
philosophy. Hence Merleau-Ponty often appeals to Rimbaud and
Mallarmé (the poets who interrupt the parallelism between signifier
and signified), to Proust, Joyce, Hemingway and Faulkner (who offer
an indirect signification), and to Cézanne (who offers a perceived,
amorphous world which survives not by default but by excess) and
Klee (whose abstraction is the terrifying world of the concrete in
memory, of the search for transcendence). In each of these cases,
the arts demonstrate that philosophy is nascent and emergent as non-
philosophy. Aesthetic experience, like the experience of history, is
non-philosophy as it opens up a space for philosophy.

Aesthetic visibility as non-philosophy

In the final phase of Merleau-Ponty's aesthetic theory, the celebrated
"Eye and Mind" (PrP) demonstrates another way of describing the
expression of the artist as non-philosophy. In this wonderful essay,

Merleau-Ponty sets the stage for the work that did not see the light of day during his lifetime – *The Visible and the Invisible* – but that would have shown his shift from the phenomenological account of perception to the ontological appeal to interrogation of the visible world. The painter, and Cézanne, in particular, returns not as the doubting artist unsure of his abilities, perceptions and practice, but as the one who, in the words of Valéry, "brings his body" to what he is about to paint. He places himself before the scene – often the Mont St Victoire in Aix-en-Provence – where he attempts to make visible what he sees, to confront the scene of vision with his seeing, which remains invisible to him. As hard as he may try, he cannot see his own seeing. The visible mountain off in the distance, however, begins to take shape on his canvas. The visibility that marks the relation between his invisible seeing and the visible scene as he looks at the mountain becomes a new visibility as he watches the mountain appear on his canvas. This new visibility matches the prior visibility of the visible mountain off in the distance but with a style that pertains to Cézanne the artist. His style is his expressivity, and his expressivity is his seeing the world in terms of this new visibility.

Cézanne painted more than sixty self-portraits during his long life as a painter. Merleau-Ponty suggests that he was attempting, in effect, to capture his own seeing, his own invisible vision, as he looks into the mirror that he places before him so that he can produce a self-portrait. The eyes are always looking forwards, looking at the viewer of the painting, just as Cézanne looked into the mirror and saw the eyes looking that he so desperately wanted to capture in the moment of seeing. Whether he could capture his own seeing, his own invisible in relation to the visible, his very visibility, he nevertheless took this infinite task as one that should be the fulfilment of his whole life project.

The essay is entitled "Eye and Mind" because the "eye" of the painter, the one who sees and who seeks to make his relationship to what he sees a new visibility that arises as a visible on the canvas, is the enactment of aesthetic expression, of an unachievable self-identity, of autobiographical textuality (Silverman 1994: Ch. 15). The "mind" (*esprit*) of the scientist will have to take a step backwards so as to not get wrapped up in a personal relationship with the things that are to be studied. The scientist's enterprise would be undermined were he or she to be engaged too closely with the materials at hand. The painter by contrast paints by getting his or her hands dirty – full of paints and other materials – so that he or she is able to fulfil the task at hand.

Embodied but now thought of in terms of "brute" or "raw" being, visibility has replaced the earlier phenomenological formulations. Visibility, and the interrogation of visibility in the writings of the philosopher, will be the frame of the painterly scene – opening up a space in which the experience of the visible can take place. Visibility – or tangibility, if one follows the readings of this text by Irigaray and Derrida – will be the event of non-philosophy as it presents itself for interrogation, for the placing between the visible and the invisible in order to make room for visibility, for philosophizing. This transformed ontological aesthetic promises to become the future of aesthetic theory for years to come.

Further reading

Dillon, M. (ed.) 1997. *Ecart & Différance: Merleau-Ponty and Derrida on Seeing and Writing*. Amherst, NY: Prometheus.

Fóti, V. (ed.) 1996. *Merleau-Ponty: Difference, Materiality, Painting*. Atlantic Highlands, NJ: Humanities Press.

Lawlor, L. 2006. "Un écart infime (Part II): Merleau-Ponty's 'Mixturism'". In *The Implications of Immanence: Toward a New Concept of Life*, 70–86. New York: Fordham University Press.

Silverman, H. J. 1994. *Textualities: Between Hermeneutics and Deconstruction*. London: Routledge.

Silverman, H. J. 1997. *Inscriptions: After Phenomenology and Structuralism*. Evanston, IL: Northwestern University Press.

PART III

Inventions

TEN

Body
David Morris

The body is at the heart of Merleau-Ponty's philosophy. The theme is anticipated by the study of animal and human behaviour in *The Structure of Behavior* (1942) and is central to *Phenomenology of Perception* (1945), which is our focus. Against Descartes and the usual contemporary view of the body as a biomedical object or as a vehicle of consciousness, the *Phenomenology* demonstrates that one *is* one's body. There is no ontological separation between the experiencing "I" and the body as one lives it. Indeed, the lived body is one's intentional opening to the world, through which alone one experiences meaningful things in the first place.

Merleau-Ponty's philosophy of the body is therefore no mere study of a neutral object, but an investigation of one's existence as a philosopher. So the body is a key methodological term, equal in significance to Descartes's *cogito*. But the *cogito* would close philosophical problems by having the philosophizing "I" certify itself from within. In contrast, Merleau-Ponty poses philosophy's initial question – "Who am I?" – within a body open to the world. This inherently exposes philosophy to living, perceptual, emotional, sexual and expressive drives, to other people, to lived space and time – it uncovers philosophy's permanent openness to what Merleau-Ponty later calls the pre-philosophical or pre-theoretical (cf. N: 72; S: 164–5; PrP: 3–6). Merleau-Ponty thus radicalizes philosophical method, since his philosophy begins by installing itself in and being responsible to a pre-philosophical setting that exceeds it.

While Merleau-Ponty's later writings no longer focus on the body as such, they do not abandon the themes of openness and radical

111

method. Rather, they trace these to levels deeper than the body, for example to nature or flesh. We could say that Merleau-Ponty's philosophy forever plays in "the key of body", a key resonant with pre-philosophical being. This chapter reveals the body as a key concept by showing how the body and Merleau-Ponty's radical method overlap across his philosophy.

This overlap is foreshadowed in *The Structure of Behavior*'s study of the relation between consciousness and nature. Merleau-Ponty urges that neither classical rationalism nor empiricism can grant full integrity to both consciousness and nature in the same moment, so neither can give a robust account of how the two are related. He therefore turns to the phenomenon of structure, to the meaningful organization that arises within the responsive behaviours of physical systems, animals and human beings. By exposing a meaning within the movements of nature, the discovery of structure reverses the Cartesian, empiricist and reductionist eradication of Aristotle's intelligible forms. This reversal anticipates what the *Phenomenology* discovers in perception and the lived body: being already has meaning prior to philosophical reflection. And Merleau-Ponty's strategy in *The Structure of Behavior* anticipates his signature method: solving problems by opening philosophy to already meaningful phenomena that push philosophy beyond classical conceptual alternatives and badly formulated questions.

Given this strategy, Merleau-Ponty's philosophy is ripe for phenomenology, which aims to dismantle philosophical prejudices by attending to the testimony of the things themselves. But he radicalizes phenomenology by showing how the testimony of things emerges on a perceptual, bodily level prior to reflection. Phenomenology cannot just reflect on the phenomena as given: it must go further back, through what Merleau-Ponty calls radical reflection. Radical reflection involves us in "a creative operation which itself participates in the facticity of that [unreflective] experience" from which philosophy begins (PP: 61). That is, radical reflection anchors itself in the unreflective by showing how it is engendered in a creative operation that at once gives birth to meaningful things and to our conceptual reflections upon them. We must, then, first of all study the creative operation that enables philosophical reflection and the meaningful field of phenomena in which it takes place.

For Merleau-Ponty, this radical methodological project inherently overlaps with a philosophy of the body. This is because the body reveals itself as our very way of being in the phenomenal field. Further, bodily phenomena especially challenge traditional conceptual divisions, opening us to an articulation of being older than philosophical thinking. That is, the body invites the radicalization of our concepts by way of being the root (*radix*, in the Latin) of the creative operation that opens the phenomenal field.

To grasp these points, we need to reconstruct some of Merleau-Ponty's central observations about the body. His first claim (PP: Pt 1, chs 1–2) is that the body escapes traditional conceptual divisions between subject and object, and between first-person and third-person perspectives, a claim he then develops by drawing on experimental data and description of disrupted bodily experience, for example the experience of phantom limbs by amputees. In the usual run of experience some of us, especially the "philosophers", might think it plausible to conceive our bodies as mere objects or as accoutrements of subjectivity. But in experiments, illness and disruptions, something pre-philosophical can intrude and testify against this subject–object distinction. Specifically, illness reveals itself not simply as an absence of the proper function of an objective body or its parts, but as a vividly experienced change in one's access to the world. This is especially the case in drastic or chronic illness. Such an illness changes what one can hope for, project and do in one's world, and correlatively changes the sense of oneself, even one's consciousness. But this change is irreducible to objective modifications of the biological body, for these are mediated by attitudes to the world and ourselves, by habits and projects. For example, someone who experiences a bodily modification, even a drastic one, as simply giving a new "normal" will have a different outlook from someone experiencing it as wholly hobbling past habits, projects and norms. Conversely, someone whose meaningful habits, existential projects and hopes are undermined by family may experience this as a felt bodily inability to eat or move in meaningful ways. One's bodily experience and one's meaningful existential projects change in entwining ways. And one's existential projects are not pure projections of subjectivity, for they can be modulated by changes rising from the organic level (e.g. by a prosthesis that gives a new way of moving).

The body exceeds ontological categories of subjectivity versus objectivity, presence versus absence and so on; it appears neither as a biological object nor as a mere vehicle of subjectivity. "I *am* my body" (PP: 150), and my body is not an objective body but a lived body (*corps vécu*), irreducibly saturated with and supportive of my lived attitudes to the world, a body with a "momentum of existence" (habitual projections of meaning) that exceeds any biomedically objectified "body at this moment" (cf. *ibid*.: 82). The lived body –

which is what we will henceforth mean by "body" – is thus what Merleau-Ponty calls an "inborn complex". This "complex" has the sort of meaning at the crux of a Freudian complex. But in the body as inborn complex, meaning does not arise at a psychological level; it is born at an organic level that is pre-personal, which is thence modulated through one's bodily engagement with the intersubjective world, engendering a complex personal relation to the world (cf. PP: 82–5).

Altogether the body as inborn complex is to be understood as the locus of our "being in the world" (*être au monde*) (*ibid.*: 78–81). Merleau-Ponty adapts this term from Heidegger's conception of "being-in-the-world" (*in-der-Welt-sein*). Heidegger's term names an ontological structure fundamental to beings such as ourselves; its hyphenated construction flags the indissoluble reciprocity of our being, the world and the relation of being-in. For Heidegger, this ontological structure is irreducibly meaningful, and irreducible to traditional subject–object dualisms. Merleau-Ponty's claim that the body is the locus of being in the world is highly significant, for on the one hand it says that the body itself protests against traditional conceptual divisions and demands a new ontology. On the other hand, it says that being in the world can be grasped through the lived body. As Merleau-Ponty puts it, "the ambiguity of being in the world is translated by that of the body, and this is understood through [the ambiguity] of time" (PP: 85). Merleau-Ponty radicalizes philosophy by finding pre-philosophical being and the ontological at issue within the body itself.

So far we have seen that the body mediates meaning, is mediated by meaning, and is thus our opening to meaningful being. But how is this so? How is the body the root, the *radix*, of meaningful being? Merleau-Ponty's claim that the ambiguity of meaningful being is "to be understood through [the ambiguity] of time" gives us a clue, when put together with his study of "The Spatiality of One's Own Body and Motility". There he shows that the body is not merely "*in* space, or *in* time", but "*inhabits* [*habite*] space and time" (PP: 139, emphasis in original). A New Yorker does not merely occupy coordinates (8th and 93rd, say) in a neutral container, but lives in New York, maps it out and learns routes through it in relation to her projects, thereby engendering the New York she inhabits. So too the body is not merely in space, but inhabits space by moving through it. The body's inhabitation of space is thus a matter of time and movement. Indeed, as we shall see, for Merleau-Ponty perceptual meaning is importantly rooted in bodily movement. So "the ambiguity of being in the world is translated by that of the body, and this is understood through that of time" because the meaning of being is in part engendered in a moving body.

Here we approach a central discovery of the *Phenomenology*, namely *motor intentionality*. Husserl's phenomenology famously showed that all consciousness is consciousness *of* something. Consciousness is not a purely interior event entirely present to itself in a given moment; rather each act of consciousness has its meaning through an internal, open relation to a meant object. To perceive or imagine a die, for example, is not to have entirely present in oneself a representation of a die in its totality; it is to perceive or imagine one cluster of die-faces as characteristically leading to other die-face clusters, in interaction with one's perceiving or imagining activity. The very meaning of die thus inherently refers to a complex of die-face interactions having their locus in a die-object. The meaning is about and springs from the die as meant object. This "aboutness" of meaning is what Husserl calls "intentionality". While Merleau-Ponty endorses intentionality as a crucial Husserlian discovery, he writes that "[i]n our opinion Husserl's originality lies beyond the notion of intentionality; it is to be found in the elaboration of this notion and in the discovery, beneath the intentionality of representation, of a deeper intentionality which others have called existence" (PP: 121 n. 5). What Merleau-Ponty effectively does is show how intentionality as existence is bodily, by revealing it as motor (moving) intentionality (*intentionnalité motrice*, cf. *ibid.*: 110). This is to say (1) that bodily movement is itself laden with meaning and intentionality, and (2) that intentionality and meaning lie in movement. Let us take up these points in order.

On the one hand, studies of movement pathologies show that in certain cases someone can execute a meaningful action such as grasping a tool to use it, but cannot point to something in the same location if they have no use for it. For Merleau-Ponty, phenomena of this sort evince a distinction between two sorts of space, which we might call practical space and geometrical space. That someone can operate in practical space, can relate to things and sites as topics of meaningful deeds, yet cannot relate to things as located in an abstract geometrical space suggests that our practical, moving relation to things has an autonomy irreducible to vectors of movement in geometrical space. For example, the seasoned driver's hand relates to the car's turn signal not as so many inches from the steering wheel, but as to be moved in the practice of making a turn. The turn signal is part of a practical space lived by the driver, as a particular Central

Park path is part of a New Yorker's lived route to work. Neither needs to nor typically does relate to these as things objectively located in geometrical space; rather they inhabit a practical space correlative to their living movements. This is why Merleau-Ponty says that the body is not neutrally *in* space but *inhabits* or *enlivens* (*habite*) space. Bodily movement shows that it is itself invested with a meaning bearing upon things: bodily movement is not the translation of an object in a Cartesian coordinate system, but the carrying out of meaningful projects that cut across meaning-laden things and places. So we can understand "motility as basic intentionality. Consciousness is in the first place not a matter of 'I think that' but of 'I can'" (PP: 137). Bodily movement itself is meaningfully "about" things, is intentional.

On the other hand, in being about things, bodily intentionality is what vests them with meaning: perceptual synthesis is not purely cognitive; it is a moving activity. Merleau-Ponty develops this point through study of what he calls the "body schema" (the centrality of the body schema is obscured in the English by Smith's inattention to Merleau-Ponty's careful distinction between body image and body schema). When reaching for something, our limbs do not move in a disordered way; nor do we first make rough shoulder and forearm movements that bring the hand near things and only then make finer wrist, palm and finger movements. In reaching for a bath sponge, from the start the fingers prepare to lightly squash it, while in reaching for the tap the fingers prepare to grasp and turn it. The person lifting a box that looks heavy but is in fact light may clumsily jerk it from the floor because their movement is geared to it as heavy.

Roughly, the body schema is that in virtue of which a bodily movement is a finely coordinated ensemble of motions intentionally organized in advance towards targets that are to be meaningfully moved. This schema is crucial to our sense of the perceptual identity and unity of things. When rolling a marble between your thumb and index finger, you perceive a single, spherical thing. This is quite remarkable, for your digits touch separate surfaces that in purely sensory terms have nothing to do with one another. Just as we might ask why two eyes looking at things from separate angles give one vision of one world, we might ask why you feel one marble rather than two separate things. The rationalist or empiricist would suggest that you pull off this trick by synthesizing sensory inputs, such that the experienced marble is a result of a cognitive synthesis. Merleau-Ponty, however, emphasizes that this synthesis is rooted in bodily movement itself. In Husserl's analysis, the die's identity is given in the way one cluster of die-faces leads to another, with reference to the die as intentional object. Here this analysis is translated into bodily movement: it is the way one index-finger-feel characteristically leads to another, in counterpart to thumb-feels, the way the marble continually offers itself to rolling between digits, that gives a sense of the marble's unity; and all of this is with reference to the marble itself as interactive with schematized bodily movement. The marble's perceived, meaningful identity is achieved in a synthesis inseparable from the moving body and things. Note that such a "synthesis in the flesh" does not just give us a sense of things but of our body: to feel one marble is to correlatively feel one's hand as having a moving unity; illusions that make one see or feel a fragmented or doubled world (as when handling a marble with crossed fingers, in which case one often feels a doubled marble) may also distort one's experience of one's body. As Merleau-Ponty puts it: "The synthesis of the object is here effected, then, through the synthesis of one's own body, it is the reply or correlative to it, and it is literally the same thing to perceive one single marble and to use two fingers as one single organ." The theory of the body schema is, then, "implicitly, a theory of perception", for the body schema is what enables "syntheses in the flesh" (PP: 205–6). These syntheses are not confined to the tactile realm. For Merleau-Ponty, binocular fusion and even the perception of colour and lighting levels involve moving and scanning relations to things. As he puts it, one must look in order to see (*ibid.*: 232, cf. Kelly 2005). More, the sorts of meanings engendered within bodily movement are not restricted to perception. The chapter on "Space" suggests that dream meanings are invested with a similarly bodily intentionality, and his account of bodily expression and the "tacit *cogito*" suggest that bodily movement is ultimately behind *all* meaning.

How could bodily movement possibly harbour and engender meaning? Within the *Phenomenology* a clue to this problem is found in the study of habit, especially in the final pages of "The Spatiality of the Body", where Merleau-Ponty writes that "habit expresses our power of dilating our being in the world, or changing our existence by appropriating fresh instruments" (PP: 143). This tells us two things. First, a change in habit, in our patterns of movement, is a change to *our way of being in the world* – a claim that would be utterly extraordinary if we were not already pursuing the problem of how meaning is engendered within bodily movement. Second, working in the other direction, movement engenders meaning because it is *not* reducible to changes in the body as a mere biomechanical thing wholly present to itself (in the "body at this moment") because it is the movement of a body inherently shot through with habits. In virtue of my habits, I do not live and move in relation to things as grasped by objective science within geometrical space; I live and move in a space of practical things correlative to my anticipations (e.g. the turn signal). Things are thus reflective of my habits and projects, of the ways that I work and rework my movements toward an anticipated world, in ways that transcend mere biology, via the temporality of the body. These ways of moving, captured in habits, are what give my body its schema. Movement is vested with meaning because it stems from a kind of transcending in the flesh, because the body is, ontologically, a locus of self-transcending. This self-transcending is realized in domains of habit acquisition, expression and intersubjectivity that open and invest our bodies with something more than is what is given in mere biomechanical determinations (cf. Russon 2003).

In short, Merleau-Ponty, in both *The Structure of Behavior* and *Phenomenology of Perception*, insists that being has a meaning. The *Phenomenology* shows that being has a meaning in virtue of an intentionality in movement underwritten by a body schema. But the body schema engenders meaning in virtue of being ontologically open to a temporality of the body (in habit and perceptual learning), to space (in movement), to language (in expression) and to others (in intersubjectivity).

Let us now step back and connect our results with the larger philosophical issues with which we began. In the *Critique of Pure Reason* Kant answers the question of how we experience being as meaningful by showing how reason subsumes intuitions (roughly, sense data) under concepts, via schemata (roughly, recipes for fitting intuitions to concepts). But Kant argues that the operation of schemata ultimately requires something creatively added by the imagination. Both Deleuze and Heidegger lament that Kant confined this creative operation to the subject, rather than finding it in *being*. For Heidegger, the creative operation of the imagination in Kant would open reason to the sort of temporality of being central to Heidegger's ontology (1997: 10). The above suggests that in Merleau-Ponty the imagination is placed in the ontological openness of the body as being in the world. The creative operation that yields schema and gives being meaning is an operation of the body in its temporal, spatial, habitual, expressive and intersubjective openness to its world. This is why we can say that the body is the site of the "creative operation which itself participates in the facticity of . . . [unreflective] experience" (PP: 61), a creative operation that turns unreflective experience into a meaningful phenomenal field. The body is a sort of hollow or fold (cf. *ibid*.: 215; SB: 161–2; N: 210, 218), a place within being that opens being, from within, to meaning, or rather, that appropriates an older meaning already limned in this opening.

What is innovative in Merleau-Ponty's *Phenomenology* is the way that the root or *radix* of this opening is the moving body. This leads to the method of radical reflection mentioned at the outset. If the meaning of being is engendered within the open being of the body, then philosophy cannot pretend to begin from a *cogito* closed on to itself. Philosophy must begin in a radical responsibility to an openness that perpetually exceeds it. The chapter on "Sense Experience" (which in some ways reworks, in terms of a philosophy of the body, the connection that Kant forged between the meaning of being and transcendental reflection) ends by making this methodological point. In an extraordinary sentence Merleau-Ponty writes: "Hence reflection does not itself grasp its full meaning unless it refers to the unreflective fund of experience which it presupposes, upon which it draws, and which constitutes for it a kind of original past, a past which has never been present" (PP: 242). Reflection draws on an original past which has never been present, which Merleau-Ponty first finds marked in our bodily being. This means that philosophy and being could never have been closed, that both are constitutively open and self-transcending.

It remains to be asked how the body and being have this sort of openness. In the *Phenomenology* this openness remains an existential fact uncovered through a phenomenology of subjective experience. But from the above perspective, his later philosophical investigations of nature, flesh, expression, institution and so on precisely look like new versions of the question about the openness of being that he first poses in terms of the body. Merleau-Ponty's distinctive philosophical gesture is his effort to locate the openness and source of being's meaning in something precedent to and exceeding the philosopher, in the body, nature, flesh – something not simply within our consciousness – and to do so via a radical reflection that begins within this openness (in *The Visible and the Invisible*'s terms, via an interrogation from within chiasmatic being). This is why we can say that the body is forever at the heart of Merleau-Ponty's philosophy, that his philosophy is truly a philosophy *of* the body, a philosophy that is not only about the body, but that springs from the body as emblem of an opening that exceeds us.

Further reading

Casey, E. S. 1984. "Habitual Body and Memory in Merleau-Ponty", *Man and World* **17**, 279–97.

Gallagher, S. 1986. "Lived Body and Environment", *Research in Phenomenology* **16**, 139–70.

Gallagher, S. 1995. "Body Schema and Intentionality". In *The Body and the Self*, J. L. Bermúdez, A. Marcel & N. Eilan (eds), 225–44. Cambridge, MA: MIT Press.

Kelly, S. D. 2005. "Seeing Things in Merleau-Ponty". In *The Cambridge Companion to Merleau-Ponty*, T. Carman & M. Hansen (eds), 74–110. Cambridge: Cambridge University Press.

ELEVEN

Perception

David R. Cerbone

As the title to his central work – *Phenomenology of Perception* – indicates, perceptual experience is a, if not the, central topic of Merleau-Ponty's philosophy. The title indicates additionally that his approach to that topic is phenomenological. Merleau-Ponty insists that a phenomenology of perception is absolutely vital for arriving at an understanding of perception's place in our overarching conception of ourselves and the world around us. Too often, he thinks, perceptual experience has been overlooked or mischaracterized so that its founding role has not been fully appreciated; too often, philosophers and scientists have tried to characterize perception in terms that are both descriptively inadequate and explanatorily inert. Such descriptions of experience tend to introduce notions – sensations, stimuli, judgements – that are not really present in our perceptual experience, and such explanations tend to appeal to processes that owe their sense to the prior workings of perception. Too often, in other words, the philosopher or the scientist describes perceptual experience "as one might describe the fauna of a distant land – without being aware that he himself perceives, that he is the perceiving subject and that perception as he lives it belies everything that he says of perception in general" (PP: 207). As a result, researchers do not fully appreciate that "all knowledge takes its place within the horizons opened up by perception", and so that "there can be no question of describing perception itself as one of the facts thrown up in the world, since we can never fill up, in the picture of the world, that gap which we ourselves are, and by which it comes into existence for someone, since perception is the 'flaw' in this 'great diamond'" (*ibid.*).

We can see in these remarks an insistence on both the *autonomy* and *authority* of perceptual experience. These twin notions in turn suggest that a wholly different approach to perception is needed. Merleau-Ponty's "return to phenomena" is his attempt to bring perceptual experience more clearly into view. Phenomenology "must begin by reawakening the basic experience of the world" (PP: viii) so as "to return to that world which precedes knowledge" (*ibid.*: ix). That Merleau-Ponty characterizes the return to phenomena as a return to the *world* indicates that he does not share Husserl's conception of phenomenology: Merleau-Ponty's return is not Husserl's reduction. Indeed, Merleau-Ponty contends that "the most important lesson which the reduction teaches us is the impossibility of a complete reduction" (*ibid.*: xiv). The return to phenomena, to perceptual experience as it is lived through, is not a retreat to the standpoint of "pure consciousness", an "inner sphere" that can be isolated from the goings-on in the world.

Empiricism, intellectualism and the integrity of perception

According to Merleau-Ponty, philosophers and scientists have largely failed in their attempts to describe and explain perception. These failures are in large part informed by a pair of "traditional prejudices", which he refers to under the headings of "empiricism" and "intellectualism". Part of the task of making a "return to phenomena" is overcoming these twin prejudices, thereby removing the distortions and outright falsifications that prevent our getting clear about perception. The first prejudice, empiricism, may be understood as involving four main ideas:

1. Perception involves the receipt or recording of some kind of simple sensory *units* or *atoms*, e.g. ideas of light and colour, simple sensations, retinal stimuli, that are in some way *less* than the things we typically say we see, e.g. apples, tables, chairs. These simple sensory units are both qualitatively and quantitatively independent of one another.

2. Each sensory faculty or modality serves as an independent "channel" of such sensory units – the faculty of sight records ideas of light and colour, the faculty of touch ideas of hardness and resistance, and so on – such that what I see is not literally the same thing that I touch.

3. The perception of the things we typically say we see, hear, smell, touch and taste, e.g. apples, tables, chairs, is as an outcome, product or result of the reception and combining of the more basic units of experience. Our perception of ordinary things is a matter of our having "observed" that these sensory units "go together" or "accompany" one another, and so we "account them one distinct thing," such as *an* apple, *a* table and so on.

4. Affective, emotional qualities are further additions to, or continuations of, perceptual experience proper that are "excited by" perceptual experience but not a part of it.

The following passage, from a central text in the classical empiricist tradition, Berkeley's *A Treatise Concerning the Principles of Human Knowledge*, nicely summarizes these four ideas:

> By sight I have the ideas of light and colors, with their several degrees and variations. By touch I perceive, for example, hard and soft, heat and cold, motion and resistance, and all these more or less either as to quantity or degree. Smelling furnishes me with odors, the palate with tastes, and hearing conveys sounds to the mind in all their variety of tone and composition. And as several of these are observed to accompany each other, they come to be marked by one name, and so to be reputed as one thing. Thus, for example, a certain color, taste, smell, figure, and consistence having been observed to go together, are accounted one distinct thing signified by the name "*apple*"; other collections of ideas constitute a stone, a tree, a book, and the like sensible things – which as they are pleasing or disagreeable excite the passions of love, hatred, joy, grief, and so forth.
>
> (1950: §1)

It should be noted that Berkeley's theory of perception can very easily be "physicalized", which involves replacing his now-antiquated talk of various kinds of "ideas" with a variety of physical stimuli.

Merleau-Ponty's first point against this empiricist picture of perception is that our immediate experience does not involve an awareness of any such individual sensory units. Consider visual experience: here, we do not have, in the first instance, pure sensations of light and colour, but instead we see, and say we see, things, and we do not even see things in isolation, but instead see them within a scene and so against a background. I see, for example, my red-and-white coffee cup, not sensations of red and white, and I see the cup *on* my desk, so that the surface of the desk and various other things on the desk serve as the backdrop. Merleau-Ponty contends that "the perceptual 'something' is always in the middle of something else, it always forms part of a 'field'" (PP: 4). The most basic description of the most basic perceptual experience involves the ideas of both figure and ground.

This first point is not anything like a knock-down objection to empiricism, since empiricism claims to be offering an explanatory theory of perception, which gives the building blocks of perceptual experience. Of course, when we perceive, these building blocks are already, as it were, built up into something more complex; nonetheless, empiricism claims that careful analysis will show that there are these building blocks, indeed there must be given the separation among the various sensory "inputs". Although this move deflects the initial objection, Merleau-Ponty's principal claim is that empiricism is not merely descriptively inadequate, but, more strongly, that its descriptive inadequacies make it theoretically unsalvageable. That is, his claim is that if one were to start with such atomistic building blocks, such simple sensations, ideas or stimuli, then one could never recover ordinary experience, since the latter contains features that are not reducible to empiricism's sensory building blocks and whatever relations are possible among them. In other words, if empiricism were correct about the basic building blocks of perceptual experience, then the kind of perceptual experience we do in fact enjoy would be impossible.

Consider again Merleau-Ponty's contention that even the most simple form of visual experience involves the notions of figure and ground: even seeing a simple shape or a bare patch of colour involves seeing it against a background from which it is separated. We do not first experience a number (how many?) of independent sensations that then get grouped together. Not only do we not experience the shape-and-background in this way; we *could* not, since we would then be unable to account for how the sensations combine to make up what we see. To see this, consider how the various features of the shape-and-background scene are related to one another: the shape stands out from the background; the shape has edges that clearly delineate it and separate it from what surrounds it; the edges *belong* to the shape, not to the background, as does all of the area the edges enclose. Perceiving the shape-and-background involves seeing the shape as *on* the background, so that the background is seen as running underneath the shape, much as I see the surface of my desk spreading under the coffee cup resting on it.

The problem for the empiricist is one of accounting for these features of the experience, of explaining how all the independent sensory atoms are grouped together in just this way. How, for example, does the empiricist account for the idea of all the area making up the shape belonging together? Why are the edges of the figure not seen as belonging to the surrounding background, rather than to the area within? Clearly the edges *are* seen as so belonging, but what is mysterious on the empiricist account is how this comes about. The notion of the non-shape sensory elements forming a background is even more mysterious, since the sense of the background as continuing *behind* the figure is one for which, necessarily, no sensory atoms can be adduced: such atoms, as lying behind the figure, would be unsensed and so could not play a role in the construction of the perceptual experience. Of course, the empiricist may appeal to a mechanism such as association to account for how sensations get grouped together. Over time, sensations are observed to go together (roundness with red, for example, which become associated as one apple), and so what I see now is more or less automatically grouped in accordance with past associations (having had lots of sensations of red accompanied by sensations of round, I now seem to see the one apple directly or immediately). On one reading, this appeal to association is circular, since it helps itself to the notion of qualities being observed to go together, and the empiricist owes us an account of *how* these observations come about (and, especially, in the particular way that they do). Equally circular are any appeals by the empiricist to memory in accounting for the grouping of sensations in a particular way: to say, with respect to a particular experience, that the arrangement is due to the memory of things having been experienced in accord with that arrangement only pushes further back the problem of explaining the basic idea of experiencing sensations in an arrangement. Merleau-Ponty says at one point that "an impression can never by itself be associated with another impression" (PP: 17), which means that no associative mechanism the empiricist might propose will appear as anything more than arbitrary, or, to the extent that it does, the account will lapse into circularity.

For Merleau-Ponty, the underlying problem with the project of trying to reconstruct perceptual experience using the materials available on the empiricist account is that the various features of the picture are internally related to one another, whereas sensations or sensory atoms, given their independence, can only be externally related to one another. Merleau-Ponty's contention is that one can never recreate or account for internal relations on the basis of external relations. Consider one of Merleau-Ponty's own examples: seeing a patch of woolly red carpet. Such an experience cannot be construed as the combination of the sensation of red plus the sensation of woolliness, because the red one perceives would not be *this* red were it not also woolly (and likewise for the woolliness). The features of the perception infuse and inform one another, and so cannot be treated as autonomous elements, standing only in external relations to one another. As Merleau-Ponty says:

> Synaesthetic perception is the rule, and we are unaware of it only because scientific knowledge shifts the centre of gravity of experience, so that we have unlearned how to see, hear, and generally speaking, feel, in order to deduce, from our bodily organization and the world as the physicist conceives it, what we are to see, hear and feel. (PP: 229)

Succinctly put, the empiricist ignores what we might call the "integrity of perception", which stresses the priority of the whole over the parts, such that the parts are not independent, antecedently given elements, but are internally connected to each other and to the whole that comprises them: "When we come back to phenomena we find, as a basic layer of experience, a whole already pregnant with an irreducible meaning, not sensations with gaps between them" (*ibid.*: 21–2).

The empiricist account of perception as a matter of receiving stimuli and possessing sensations renders experience as something altogether passive and inert, a series of events that arise in a causal, quasi-mechanical fashion. Small wonder, then, that what it countenances as the components of perceptual experience is insufficient to capture perception as it is lived. Indeed, empiricism seems to overlook entirely the fact that perceptual experience is lived by someone who perceives. Perceptual experience is not merely the passive recording of stimuli, a faithful reproduction of the surrounding environment, but an activity, as is signalled, for example, by the many active terms we use in connection with perception. Even if we restrict our attention to visual experience, we find, for example, such active notions as looking, watching, scanning, searching, noticing, finding, attending, investigating, focusing, glancing, peeking, gazing and peering. The second of the twin "traditional prejudices", which Merleau-Ponty dubs "intellectualism", has the virtue of emphasizing the role of the subject who perceives in the act of perception, and its conception of perception as the achievement of an active subject is one to which

Merleau-Ponty is not entirely unsympathetic. At the same time, as his labelling of intellectualism as a "prejudice" indicates, its account of perception remains problematic.

Intellectualism's central claim is that all perceptual experience involves judgement, and so to perceive anything at all consists of the making of a judgement with respect to that thing. Perceptual experience, as centrally involving judgement, thus centrally involves the subject who does the judging, thereby making perceptual experience active through and through. Merleau-Ponty holds that judgement is secondary with respect to perceptual experience, and so argues that it falsifies the character of perceptual experience to see judgement as an ever-present feature. Consider the case of the Müller-Lyer illusion. Even once we have determined that the lines enclosed by the arrows are indeed equal, and so upon seeing them, judge that they are equal, it still remains the case that we *see* the lines as not being equal (nor, again, exactly unequal either). As our gaze takes in the lines and the arrows, we almost seem to see the lines change their length (even though we *know* that nothing like this is happening). If perception and judgement were equivalent, then the lines should appear equal once we have been informed of the illusion. That they do not, but instead present themselves with a kind of indeterminacy, held in tension between being equal and unequal, undermines the contention that perception is pervaded by judgement. By insisting on the primacy of judgement, the intellectualist effaces these kinds of tensions and indeterminacies in the act of perception, thereby rendering perceptual experience as more frozen and static than it really is and must be. Intellectualism is thus an overreaction to the lifeless, mechanical model offered by the empiricist.

Although intellectualism presents itself as, and is in some respects, an antidote to empiricism, correcting the errors and distortions present in the empiricist's conception of perception, part of the problem with the intellectualist position is that it shares too much with the empiricist view it claims to reject. As Merleau-Ponty notes, "Judgment is often introduced as *what sensation lacks* to make perception possible" (PP: 32). The problem here is that the introduction of judgement, as making up for what sensation lacks, still shows a commitment to sensations as an ingredient or component of perceptual experience: "Perception becomes an 'interpretation' of the signs that our senses provide in accordance with the bodily *stimuli*, a 'hypothesis' that the mind evolves to 'explain its impressions to itself'" (*ibid.*: 33). By only adding on to the empiricist conception of perception, rather than abandoning it altogether, intellectualism thus inherits the same problems and liabilities inherent in the view it seeks to displace.

Merleau-Ponty's critique of the "traditional prejudices" informing many prevalent (then and now) conceptions of perception in both philosophy and psychology, as well as his insistence on what I've been calling the integrity of perception, opens on to a wider array of phenomena to be described. In particular, what both of the traditional prejudices obscure from view is a proper appreciation of the *embodied* character of perceptual experience: the integrity of perception is informed by, and founded on, the integrity of bodily self-experience, which neither empiricism nor intellectualism recognizes. We have seen that the empiricist's account of perception treats perception as the endpoint of a causal, mechanical process (the receipt of stimuli, the presence of sensations before the mind), whereas the intellectualist treats perception as a species of judgement. In the case of the empiricist, the body is itself treated as a mechanism, or perhaps an assemblage of mechanisms, causally connected with the surrounding world via the "bombardment" of light rays and molecules, a conduit of sensations; the intellectualist account of perception, bound up as it is with the mental act of judgement, treats the perceiving subject as only accidentally or contingently embodied, with all the organizing and schematizing work of perceptual experience taking place within the confines of consciousness. Just as the twin prejudices can be shown ultimately to share a picture of perception as involving stimuli or sensations as a key ingredient, so too the two share a conception of the body as merely one material entity among others, playing only a causal role in the production of perceptual experience. Where they differ is on whether anything more is needed than the workings of such causal mechanisms for there to be perceptual experience. To counteract this mechanical, wholly causal conception of the body, Merleau-Ponty's "return to phenomena", which begins with a description of the integrity of perception, quickly develops in *Phenomenology of Perception* into a phenomenology of the body and bodily self-experience.

Merleau-Ponty claims, provocatively, that "consciousness is in the first place not a matter of 'I think that' but of 'I can'" (PP: 137), and this claim is central to his account of perceptual experience. According to Merleau-Ponty, the world is manifest in experience in accordance with our bodily structure and skills: things are manifest as near or far, here or there, in reach or out of reach, above or below, available or unavailable, usable or unusable, inviting or repulsive, and so on in relation to our ways of inhabiting the world, and such inhabitation is always bodily in nature. Things are not encountered primarily in terms of a detached gaze, as though our main relation to the world were one of staring; on the contrary, things are manifest, arrayed before and around us, in relation to our bodily abilities, our many ways of getting a *grip* on the things we encounter. I use the word "grip" here both literally and figuratively, as when I grip the pen, coffee cup, hammer, steering wheel, etc., in my hands (literal) and when I "get a grip" on things and situations, putting things in order, getting things under control, and optimizing my perceptual access (figurative). The latter, more figurative, kind of grip involves myriad bodily skills. When looking at things, we variously bring them or ourselves closer or otherwise increase our distance, depending on the thing (compare looking at a coin versus looking at the façade of a building) in order to get the best view:

> If I draw the object closer to me or turn it round in my fingers in order "to see it better", this is because each attitude of my body is for me, immediately, the power of achieving a certain spectacle, and because each spectacle is what it is for me in a certain kinaesthetic situation. In other words, because my body is permanently stationed before things in order to perceive them and, conversely, appearances are always enveloped for me in a certain bodily attitude. In so far, therefore, as I know the relation of appearances to the kinaesthetic situation, this is not in virtue of any law or in terms of any formula, but to the extent that I have a body, and that through that body I am at grips with the world. (PP: 303)

To perceive, to be embodied, to be "at grips with the world", are not three separate or separable notions for Merleau-Ponty, but are three overlapping, interconnected, internally related aspects of our existence. The "return to phenomena" reveals this overlapping and interconnected unity of consciousness, embodiment and the world made manifest through our embodied experience. Merleau-Ponty calls this unity the "intentional arc", which informs every aspect of our experience:

> Let us therefore say . . . that the life of consciousness – cognitive life, the life of desire or perceptual life – is subtended by an "intentional arc" which projects round about us our past, our future, our human setting, our physical, ideological and moral situation, or rather results in our being situated in all these

respects. It is this intentional arc which brings about the unity of the senses, of intelligence, of sensibility and motility.

(PP: 136)

Perceptual faith

Already in *Phenomenology of Perception*, Merleau-Ponty sees perceptual experience as resistant to analysis: the "primary layer of sense experience which is discovered only provided that we really coincide with the act of perception and break with the critical attitude" cannot be conceived "after the fashion of analytical reflection" (PP: 238–9). A paradox thus lies at the heart of his phenomenological project, as Merleau-Ponty himself acknowledges: "The task of radical reflection, the kind that aims at self-comprehension, consists, paradoxically enough, in recovering the unreflective experience of the world . . . and displaying reflection as one possibility of my being" (*ibid.*: 241). In his unfinished *The Visible and the Invisible*, this "paradox" is further explored and developed in his extended ruminations on *perceptual faith* and the "difficulties and contradictions" that arise when one tries to grasp it explicitly:

> We see the things themselves, the world is what we see: formulae of this kind express a faith common to the natural man and the philosopher – the moment he opens his eyes; they refer to a deep-seated set of mute "opinions" implicated in our lives. But what is strange about this faith is that if we seek to articulate it into theses or statements, if we ask ourselves what is this *we*, what *seeing* is, and what *thing* or *world* is, we enter into a labyrinth of difficulties and contradictions. (VI: 3)

The faith that permeates perceptual experience evanesces upon analysis, which yields up images that populate the interiority of our mental lives and objects that stand apart, confined to an exterior realm beyond the reach of any such images. From the standpoint of reflection, perceptual faith looks not only ungrounded, but unintelligible, since it is unclear how the proximity of mind and world it assures can even be conceived: although perception and world coexist "without difficulty in the exercise of life, once reduced to theses and to propositions they destroy one another and leave us in confusion" (VI: 8).

The task of a philosophy of perception, if it is not to be a mere "philosophy of thought" that forecloses any "openness upon being" (*ibid.*: 89), is to bring into view "the mute experience from which we draw what we say" (*ibid.*: 88). The philosophy of perception must, in other words, put into words what is essentially wordless, without thereby distorting or falsifying. Reflection must recover the non- or pre-reflective, without imposing or incorporating what belongs only to reflection:

> If therefore reflection is not to presume upon what it finds and condemn itself to putting into the things what it will then pretend to find in them, it must suspend the faith in the world only so as to *see it*, only so as to read in it the route it has followed in becoming a world for us; it must seek in the world itself the secret of our perceptual bond with it. It must use words not according to their pre-established signification, but *in order to state* this prelogical bond. (*Ibid.*: 38)

Just as Merleau-Ponty, in *Phenomenology of Perception*, avoids the falsifying dichotomies of subjective and objective, sensation and judgement, *The Visible and the Invisible* likewise refuses dichotomous thinking (for-itself and in-itself, being and nothingness, experience and object). Even "perception" turns out to be one of the "notions" an exploration of perceptual faith must avoid, along with "acts of consciousness", "states of consciousness", "matter" and "form", as all of these invite, without yet stating, the kinds of dichotomies and divisions that make perceptual experience unthinkable. Instead, "like the natural man, we situate ourselves in ourselves *and* in the things, in ourselves *and* in the other, at the point where, by a sort of *chiasm*, we become the others and we become world" (VI: 160).

Further reading

Carman, T. & M. Hansen (eds) 2005. *The Cambridge Companion to Merleau-Ponty*. Cambridge: Cambridge University Press.

Cerbone, D. R. 2006. *Understanding Phenomenology*. Chesham: Acumen.

Dillon, M. C. 1997. *Merleau-Ponty's Ontology*, 2nd edn. Evanston, IL: Northwestern Univesity Press.

TWELVE

Ambiguity

Gail Weiss

Merleau-Ponty's references to "ambiguity" appear throughout his works, most frequently in *Phenomenology* of *Perception*, and so it is not surprising that the concept of ambiguity is often understood to be central not only to his earlier but also to his later philosophy. In what follows, I shall first offer an analysis of specific passages from *Phenomenology* of *Perception* where Merleau-Ponty invokes the ambiguity of human experience to illustrate what his noted commentator, Alphonse de Waelhens, calls his "philosophy of the ambiguous" in the second French edition of *The Structure of Behavior*. I shall then show how Merleau-Ponty's descriptions of ambiguity directly influence Simone de Beauvoir's understanding of the ambiguity of human existence as the ground for existentialist ethics. Finally, I shall suggest that the notion of ambiguity, as he develops it throughout his *oeuvre*, provides a crucial link among other key concepts he introduces including anonymity, reversibility and the flesh.

Merleau-Ponty's conceptions of ambiguity

One of the most famous passages in which Merleau-Ponty appeals to the ambiguity of human existence appears in the middle of *Phenomenology of Perception* in the chapter entitled "The Body as Expression, and Speech" when he addresses the age-old question regarding whether it is nature or culture that has the primary influence on human conduct:

Everything is both manufactured and natural in man, as it were, in the sense that there is not a word, not a form of behavior which does not owe something to purely biological being – and which at the same time does not elude the simplicity of animal life, and cause forms of vital behavior to deviate from their pre-ordained direction, through a sort of *leakage* and through a *genius for ambiguity* which might serve to define man.

(PP: 189, emphasis added)

Here Merleau-Ponty identifies ambiguity with the irreducibility of human behaviour to nature on the one hand or to culture on the other. Human behaviour, he suggests, is both natural and cultural simultaneously and, for this reason, presents itself as ambiguous. In his words: "It is no more natural, and no less conventional, to shout in anger or to kiss in love than to call a table a table" (*ibid.*). The ambiguity he is describing is also evidenced through this absence of a hard-and-fast distinction between linguistic and non-linguistic gestures. Both types of gestures are embodied responses to the world of our concern, which call forth the responses of others, an additional source of ambiguity that I shall address shortly.

Moreover, for Merleau-Ponty, "the experience of our own body . . . reveals to us an ambiguous mode of existing" (PP: 198). This is because I live my body in the first person, that is, subjectively, yet at the same time my bodily experience outruns my subjective awareness. Thus I inhabit an impersonal generality that links me to other bodies that function similarly to my own. As he states:

Whether it is a question of another's body or my own, I have no means of knowing the human body other than that of living it, which means taking up on my own account the drama which is being played out in it, and losing myself in it. I am my body, at least wholly to the extent that I possess experience, and yet at the same time my body is as it were a "natural" subject, a provisional sketch of my total being. (*Ibid.*)

Merleau-Ponty explicates the impersonal dimensions of embodied experience further in a subsequent discussion of how our bodily intentionality extends beyond any act of consciousness:

In so far as I have hands, feet, a body, I sustain around me intentions which are not dependent upon my decisions and which affect my surroundings in a way which I do not choose. These intentions are general in a double sense: firstly in the sense that they constitute a system in which all possible objects are simultaneously included; if the mountain appears high and upright, the tree appears small and sloping; and furthermore in the sense that they are not simply mine, they originate from other than myself, and I am not surprised to find them in all psychophysical subjects organized as I am.　　　　　　　(*Ibid.*: 440)

Taken together, these passages introduce several aspects of the ambiguity of human experience that function simultaneously but are not reducible to one another. First, there is the ambiguity initially discussed that derives from the always intertwined contributions of both nature and culture to human behaviour. Second, there is the ambiguity of bodily experience in so far as it is both subjective and, at the same time, is pervaded by what Merleau-Ponty calls an "atmosphere of generality" that connects one to all other bodies, human and non-human, that are co-present with one in the world. From this latter perspective, my body appears as a natural object just like other natural objects, but, of course, it is never merely a natural object but always the subject of my perceptions, the centre of my conscious (as well as pre-reflective) experience. This leads us to a third way in which bodily experience is ambiguous, namely, through the *cooperation* of both conscious intentions and pre-reflective bodily intentions that together orient one towards the world of one's concern.

There are at least two interrelated sources of bodily intentionality that Merleau-Ponty is identifying in the above passages that also contribute to the ambiguity of our experience: the first stems from the natural expressivity of my body, its ongoing capacity to respond to the world towards which it is perpetually directed in a manner that outstrips my conscious awareness and specific motor projects. The second reflects the fact that my bodily intentions are not unique to my body alone, but arise as a result of the particular *type* of body I have and thus are shared by other human bodies that also display a vertical posture, five sensory modalities, and specific gestural capacities (both linguistic and non-linguistic). Recognizing the continual interplay that takes place between my own gestures and the gestures of others, starting with infants' early responsivity to, and imitations of, their caretakers' gestures, brings us to a related source of ambiguity that lurks "between the lines" in these passages, namely, the interrelationship between the subjective and intersubjective dimensions of human experience. Merleau-Ponty provides an extended discussion of the development in early childhood of this imitative interplay of gestures, and the attendant "confusion" of self and other in "The Child's Relations with Others" (PrP: 141–51).

Some of the most moving descriptions of the indissoluble, ambiguous connection between my subjective experience and my relationships with others appear in the final chapter of *Phenomenology of Perception* on "Freedom". Invoking (and then deconstructing) Sartre's crucial distinction between being-for-itself and being-for-others, Merleau-Ponty argues:

> I must apprehend myself from the onset as centred in a way outside myself, and my individual existence must diffuse round itself, so to speak, an existence in quality. The For-Themselves – me for myself and the other for himself – must stand out against a background of For Others – I for the other and the other for me. My life must have a significance which I do not constitute; there must strictly speaking be an intersubjectivity; each one of us must be both anonymous in the sense of absolutely individual, and anonymous in the sense of absolutely general. Our being in the world, is the concrete bearer of this double anonymity. (PP: 448)

Not only does being-for-itself always emerge against a background of being-for-others but Merleau-Ponty's understanding of being-for-others emphasizes a reciprocity that is missing from Sartre's account. While Sartre's descriptions in *Being and Nothingness* imply that the self oscillates between being-for-itself and being-for-others as if these were separate experiences, Merleau-Ponty insists that I exist for the other and the other also exists for me concurrently without either experience being privileged. He develops this point further in the following famous passage from the concluding pages of *Phenomenology of Perception*:

> For what is given, is not one fragment of time followed by another, one individual flux, then another; it is the taking up of each subjectivity by itself, and of subjectivities by each other in the generality of a single nature, the cohesion of an intersubjective life and a world. The present mediates between the For Oneself and the For Others, between individuality and generality. True reflection presents me to myself not as idle and inaccessible subjectivity, but as identical with my presence in the world and to others, as I am now realizing it: I am all that I see, I am an intersubjective field, not despite my body and

historical situation, but, on the contrary, by being this body and this situation, and through them, all the rest.   (PP: 452)

Here, the ambiguities of human experience are interconnected and multiplied, extending from the complex interrelationships between subjectivity and intersubjectivity, individuality and generality, to the dynamic interplay between my body and my historical situation, our intersubjective life and the world. Implied in these aspects of ambiguity and apparent in the quotation above is a temporal ambiguity where, for Merleau-Ponty, I am not contained in the "now" of the present; rather, "my living present opens upon a past which nevertheless I am no longer living through, and a future which I do not yet live" (*ibid.*: 433). As the interweaving of all three temporal modalities, the living present exhibits a dynamic, synthetic unity that preserves the open-endedness of the future and the ongoing relevance of the past in the present moment.

Merleau-Ponty's emphasis upon the co-constitutive relationships among the body, subjectivity, intersubjectivity, the situation and the world anticipates and helps to explain the later Merleau-Ponty's transition away from the terminology of the body (which privileges a particular body-subject) to the more ambiguous notion of the flesh of the world. Before turning to a consideration of the flesh and the related notion of reversibility, I shall first discuss briefly the influence of Merleau-Ponty's earlier formulations of the ambiguity of human existence on his old college classmate and philosophical interlocutor, Simone de Beauvoir, and show how she develops this concept.

Merleau-Ponty's influence on de Beauvoir's ethics of ambiguity

De Beauvoir refers explicitly to ambiguity in the very title of her 1948 volume *The Ethics of Ambiguity* (published three years after *Phenomenology of Perception*). She also notes the importance of the concept:

> From the very beginning, existentialism defined itself as a philosophy of ambiguity. It was by affirming the irreducible character of ambiguity that Kierkegaard opposed himself to Hegel, and it is by ambiguity that, in our own generation, Sartre, in *Being and Nothingness*, fundamentally defined man, that being

whose being is not to be, that engaged freedom, that surging of the for-oneself which is immediately given for others.

(1997: 9–10)

While de Beauvoir does not cite Merleau-Ponty at all here, she had praised his conception of ambiguity a few years earlier in her 1945 review of *Phenomenology of Perception* where, as Sara Heinämaa maintains, she "distances herself from Sartre's ontology and describes Merleau-Ponty's ontology as a fruitful alternative" (2004: 156). Nonetheless, this passage stresses an important point that has a direct bearing on Merleau-Ponty's own understanding of ambiguity, namely, that like de Beauvoir's and Sartre's views of this essentially elusive dimension of human experience, his own account arises out of the larger philosophical tradition in which he is steeped and does not emerge *ex nihilo*.

De Beauvoir begins her analysis with repeated references to the "tragic ambiguity" or "the paradox" of the human condition, and she initially defines it as consisting in human beings' experience of being both the end of all our action and the means by which others achieve their own ends. In her words, people

know themselves to be the supreme end to which all action should be subordinated, but the exigencies of action force them to treat one another as instruments or obstacles, as means. The more widespread their mastery of the world, the more they find themselves crushed by uncontrollable forces. Though they are masters of the atomic bomb, yet it is created only to destroy them. (1997: 9)

Like Merleau-Ponty before her, de Beauvoir slides almost imperceptibly from a description of one type of existential ambiguity to another. She begins with the insurmountable tension between being-for-oneself and being-for-others (which plays out in her account along Sartrean lines, namely as being an end versus serving as a means to others' ends). Then she immediately turns to the paradoxical way in which human creations involve the possibility of destroying the human; that is, we have, through our actions, the means of transforming but also destroying the world of our concern. A few pages later, de Beauvoir defines the "fundamental ambiguity" of human existence in terms of two conflicting desires, which we must continually negotiate without ever reconciling, namely, the "will to be" and the "will to disclose being". Accepting Sartre's account of human being as a lack of being, de Beauvoir maintains that we continually try to "fill" this lack by "making ourselves be", that is, by trying to achieve the density and stability of being that Sartre associates with being-in-itself. On the other hand, she also argues that we can and must at the same time will ourselves to be a disclosure of being, to be the being through which we and other beings gain their significance. This requires that we "be" the very lack of being that the "will to be" tries to overcome.

Rather than becoming frustrated with both de Beauvoir's and Merleau-Ponty's adumbrations of the various types of ambiguity that collectively define human existence, we would do well to keep in mind Langer's admonition:

> We must refrain from trying to clarify ambiguity through explanations or definitions. Explanations assume we can "unfold" ambiguity, "spread it out" in front of us, and analyze it. Definitions assume we can circumscribe, capture, and fix it. Such attempted clarifications miss the very meaning of ambiguity. Ambiguity separated from experience is no longer ambiguity. Beauvoir's and Merleau-Ponty's philosophical method is descriptive, letting us understand ambiguity without destroying it. For Beauvoir and Merleau-Ponty, ambiguity is not ambivalence, equivocation, dualism, or absurdity. Ambiguity characterizes existence and involves an irreducible indeterminacy, and multiple, inseparable significations and aspects.
>
> (Langer 2003: 90)

In her 1945 review of *Phenomenology of Perception*, de Beauvoir depicts this essential indeterminacy of experience described by Merleau-Ponty as a form of incompleteness that is due to the open-ended quality of that experience: specifically, its future-directedness. For Merleau-Ponty, she maintains, "the perceptual synthesis always remains incomplete because the temporal synthesis is never completed" (2004: 163). This temporal ambiguity actively informs all other aspects of our being-in-the-world, including our relations with others. More specifically, it is by emphasizing the future as the omnipresent indeterminate horizon for my current actions which renders the meaning of these latter fluid and open to new interpretations, that de Beauvoir is able to establish the foundation for her own existential ethics. This is because to will to disclose the world is to will to preserve its temporal indeterminacy as opposed to the will to be which seeks to congeal meaning by collapsing the radical alterity of the future and the spontaneity of the present into the haecceity of the past.

Despite the fact that de Beauvoir's account of ethical and existential ambiguity is worked out in an explicitly Sartrean framework
using Sartrean terminology, it is evident that her existential ethics
is also quite heavily indebted to Merleau-Ponty. This latter influence
can be seen especially clearly in the places where de Beauvoir discusses how my freedom is totally and necessarily intertwined with the
freedom of others in such a manner that "To will oneself free is also
to will others free" (1997: 73). While in *Being and Nothingness*
Sartre makes it clear that the other poses the primary obstacle to
the exercise of my freedom – in Garcin's famous words in Sartre's
1944 play *No Exit:* "Hell is – other people" (1976: 47) – and while
he portrays human beings as always experiencing tension between
their existence as beings-for-themselves and as beings-for-others, it
is Merleau-Ponty who successfully breaks through this antinomy
by offering an alternative ontology in which being-for-oneself and
being-for-others are not inherently oppositional but rather *inter-
dependent* aspects of our being in the world. Although, as Margaret
A. Simons (1999) argues, de Beauvoir was cognizant of the inter-
connections between my freedom and the freedom of others long
before she, Sartre and Merleau-Ponty wrote their major philosophical
works, she clearly builds upon Merleau-Ponty's rich understanding
of ambiguity in developing her existential ethics.

Ambiguity, anonymity, reversibility and the flesh

I turn now to consider the close connections between Merleau-
Ponty's appeals to ambiguity, his related conception of anonymity,
and his later concepts of reversibility and the flesh. As mentioned
earlier, for Merleau-Ponty an "atmosphere of generality" or "anonymity" persists in and through the idiosyncratic, subjective, singular
perspective that helps (along with the distinctiveness of each individual body) to distinguish one person from another. This pre-
personal generality also makes perception possible without conscious
direction, helping to orient me from one moment to the next within
my situation. For Merleau-Ponty:

> The senses and one's own body generally present the mystery
> of a collective entity which, without abandoning its thisness
> and its individuality, puts forth beyond itself meanings capable
> of providing a framework for a whole series of thoughts and
> experiences.   (PP: 126)

Some commentators (e.g. Sullivan 1997) claim that this implies a fundamental pre-personal level of experience that is the same for all, thereby privileging a "neutral body" that is unmarked by its race and gender and by its social encounters with others. However, others argue that the anonymity Merleau-Ponty invokes is precisely what intimately connects me to other bodies in all of our particularity (Stoller 2000; Weiss 2002). According to Stoller, "anonymous existence means that I and the other are 'two sides of one and the same phenomenon' (PP: 254), a 'dual being' (PP: 354) or the anonymous collectivity of a 'sorte d'existence à plusieurs', a sort of existence of numerous persons" (Stoller 2000: 176).

This concept of anonymity, along with Merleau-Ponty's ideas of ambiguity, anticipate his later concepts of reversibility and the flesh. The ambiguity of reversibility is particularly interesting because, using Merleau-Ponty's primary example of reversibility in *The Visible and the Invisible*, touching and being touched, it derives from the dynamic interplay between the two experiences, an ongoing process in which the experience of being touched can transition immediately and at any point in time into the experience of touching and vice versa. Describing the similarities between the experiences of touching and being touched on the one hand, and the related relationship between the visible and the tangible on the other hand, Merleau-Ponty argues that what unites these reversible phenomena across their respective differences is that they unfold within one and the same body, and therefore belong to one and the same world. For this reason, he suggests:

> We must habituate ourselves to think that every visible is cut out in the tangible, every tactile being in some manner promised to visibility, and that there is encroachment, infringement, not only between the touched and the touching, but also between the tangible and the visible, which is encrusted in it, as, conversely, the tangible itself is not a nothingness of visibility, is not without visual existence. Since the same body sees and touches, visible and tangible belong to the same world. (VI: 134)

In one of his final Working Notes, dated November 1960, Merleau-Ponty renders the ambiguity of reversibility in more general terms: "The chiasm, reversibility, is the idea that every perception is doubled with a counter-perception (Kant's real opposition), is an act with two faces, one that no longer knows who speaks and who listens . . . Activity = passivity" (VI: 264–5). Rather than viewing this as a totally circular or "bad ambiguity" that is unable to bring together its disparate elements, Merleau-Ponty argues (in another unpublished text now available in *The Primacy of Perception*) for a "good ambiguity" that he claims is manifested "in the phenomenon of expression, a spontaneity which accomplishes what appeared to be impossible when we observed only the separate elements, a spontaneity which gathers together the plurality of monads, the past and the present, nature and culture into a single whole" (PrP: 11).

Although I cannot develop this suggestion here, I would propose that the flesh, as "an ultimate notion", accomplishes this gathering together of all the disparate aspects of experience into a unified, ambiguous, spontaneous and stylized whole (see Chapter 17). In the almost half-century that has elapsed since Merleau-Ponty's untimely death, this "sort of incarnate principle that brings a style of being wherever there is a fragment of being" (VI: 139), which defies any singular interpretation, continues to inspire some of the most creative work being done on his scholarship today. As a "philosopher of the ambiguous", Merleau-Ponty has left behind both a provocative and rich legacy, one that continues to yield new meanings that flow from new ways of giving expression to the ambiguities of our own being-in-the-world.

Further reading

Kruks, S. 1990. *Situation and Human Existence: Freedom, Subjectivity, and Society*. London: Unwin Hyman.

Langer, M. 2003. "Beauvoir and Merleau-Ponty on Ambiguity". In *The Cambridge Companion to Simone de Beauvoir*, C. Card (ed.), 87–106. Cambridge: Cambridge University Press.

Weiss, G. 1995. "Ambiguity, Absurdity, and Reversibility: Responses to Indeterminacy", *Journal of the British Society of Phenomenology* 26(1), 43–51.

Weiss, G. 2002. "The Anonymous Intentions of Transactional Bodies", *Hypatia: A Journal of Feminist Philosophy* 17(4), 187–200.

THIRTEEN

Intersubjectivity and alterity

Michael Sanders

Merleau-Ponty's philosophy provides an important reworking and extension of Edmund Husserl's ideas of intersubjectivity. This reliance on Husserl, however, opens Merleau-Ponty's account of relations with others to criticisms made by Emmanuel Levinas, who claims that phenomenology fails to account for the alterity or absolute otherness that, for him, lies at the heart of intersubjectivity. In this chapter I shall defend Merleau-Ponty against this criticism. The analysis proceeds as follows: first, I provide an overview of Husserl's account of intersubjective experience, the starting point for Merleau-Ponty's early approaches to the question; second, I touch upon the most significant criticisms of this account, notably those of Levinas and his emphasis on the absolute alterity of the Other; and, finally, I examine the evolution of Merleau-Ponty's own theory of intersubjectivity and the extent to which it can avoid these criticisms, as represented by the account he provides in his major uncompleted work, *The Visible and the Invisible*.

Husserl and the problem of intersubjectivity

As Husserl realized, the public nature of the lifeworld and the presence of other subjects within it poses a surprisingly serious problem – some would say, *the* problem – for any phenomenology. Since all consciousness for Husserl is intentional, and all intentional consciousness is "constituting" – i.e. the perceptual world of objects and forms is rendered present due to the subject's synthetic activities alone – there is simply nothing immediately apparent to indicate that experience should possess the public nature that it in fact does. At a transcendental level, the subject's constitutional activities are by definition internal to consciousness and, hence, private. Call it solipsism at its most basic level, the point – and the problem – is this: how and why is the experience of others in subjective awareness at all possible?

Husserl's well-known response to this question is provided in the fifth of his 1929 Sorbonne lectures, published under the title of *Cartesian Meditations*. His account there is analogical in nature. He argues that the consciousness of others as *other* comes about owing to a secondary act of constitution that "modifies" the contents of consciousness's primary, or primordial, acts of constitution. In virtue of this secondary act, constitution *as such* "oversteps itself", making possible an experience in which "not all my own modes of consciousness are modes of my self-consciousness" (Husserl 1967: 135).

Husserl describes this modification in terms of two related ideas, those of "appresentation" and "pairing". Together, they provide consciousness with an empathic recognition, an analogizing intuition, of another subject's existence as alter ego. Appresentation explains the process whereby the direct perceptual presentation of one object mediates or makes possible the indirect perception of certain other aspects of that object that are themselves inaccessible to direct perception. We indirectly perceive the rear sides of a house, for instance, when perceiving the front side. Intersubjectivity is a more complicated case than a house, of course, as the experience of others involves not only an experience of a physical entity (*Körper*), but that of an animate organism (*Leib*) as well. Just as I recognize my own consciousness as embodied in the flesh and blood that comprises my body, so too do I analogically – via "apperceptive transfer" – recognize that the material body now presented before me is not merely one object alongside many, but is itself also a living organism as am I.

This "empathic" presentation of the material body of the other as a living organism provides the grounds on which the other is posited as in fact another person. This positing, in turn, is accomplished via the notion of pairing. Pairing occurs when one object is regularly presented – thereby "associated" – with another (Husserl 1967: 142). In the case of my own awareness of self, I recognize that the animate organism that is my body is always co-presented with my ego. Thus, when I encounter another animate organism like my own, I naturally "pair" this living body with an ego of its own as well. This process forms the basis for Husserl's account of intersubjectivity. Joined in a process in which all other egos are engaged, the individual ego is revealed as the transcendental ego, poised in a moment of absolute flux that marks the upsurge of the living present. From out of this flux, the perceptible world is constituted via a process in which all other egos are likewise engaged. As a result, what is found at the heart of the primordial "now" is no mere isolated ego, but a "transcendental intersubjectivity" or "community of monads" joined together in a moment of absolute coincidence (Husserl 1967: 158). It is in terms of this coincidence that the objective world for Husserl is possible, i.e. that of the lifeworld and, most importantly for Husserl, of a world open to the possibility of science.

Merleau-Ponty's early account of intersubjectivity and Levinas's criticism

For Merleau-Ponty, Husserl's model of relations with others provides the template for much of his early thinking on the question of intersubjectivity, most notably in *Phenomenology of Perception* (PP: xi–xiv, 346–65). The analysis there, while following Husserl closely, nonetheless subtly shifts the focus of discussion away from Husserl's emphasis on the subjective awareness of others towards an account of intersubjective relations arising out of the reciprocity of a shared corporeal existence. Merleau-Ponty begins by recognizing the need to account phenomenologically for the material, concrete situatedness of another consciousness as separate from mine. Other selves, other embodied loci of perception, certainly do exist; only the fact of their existence – as Merleau-Ponty credits Husserl himself with recognizing – is paradoxical for me. As Merleau-Ponty writes, "I must be the exterior that I present to others, and the body of the other must be the other himself" (PP: xii). Phenomenology's chief virtue, according to Merleau-Ponty, lies in its very recognition and refusal to dissolve this distinction between self and other. This is important, Merleau-Ponty adds, for only as truly distinct can the other be recognized as possessing a history all its own. Ultimately, for Merleau-Ponty, the indirect access we have to this separate historicity is what alone ensures that the givenness of the world is not entirely converted by the self into a mere "thought about the world", i.e. what ensures that a viable phenomenological account of intersubjectivity is indeed possible (*ibid.*: xiii).

This recognition of others becomes manifest, according to Merleau-Ponty, in the fact of our shared corporeal presence in a cultural world.

As human subjectivity is first and foremost an embodied subjectivity, the body of the other is "the very first of all cultural objects" (PP: 348). The other person stands out against the "background of nature" that forms the limit of my perception. This background consists of all of that of which I am, but which is nonetheless only partially accessible to me, i.e. the history, the culture, and above all the body that my subjectivity finds itself "thrown into". These pre-objective, pre-personal elements of my being are, strictly speaking, inaccessible to me. As a result, they provide an analogical means of relating to the other. As Merleau-Ponty writes, "The other can be evident to me because I am not transparent for myself . . . because my subjectivity draws its body in its wake" (ibid.: 352). Between my embodied subjectivity and that of the other, there exists then an "internal relation", a correspondence, that brings about in effect the "completion of a system", that of the perceptible, historical and cultural world in which we are situated. So connected are the two, in fact, that Merleau-Ponty goes so far as to state that in the "absolute presence of origins", self and other are "collaborators for each other in consummate reciprocity" (ibid.: 354).

In this manner, Merleau-Ponty's early work on intersubjectivity attempts to impart a sense of dynamism and mutuality to the phenomenological account of relations with others perhaps lacking in previous accounts. Yet the very reciprocity between self and other that Merleau-Ponty so strongly stresses, in addition to his clear reliance upon the foundation provided by Husserl, opens his analysis to what are some of the most radical and far-reaching criticisms of phenomenological approaches to intersubjectivity in general. Emmanuel Levinas, for instance, argues that phenomenology is fundamentally incapable of accounting for intersubjective relations because, despite Merleau-Ponty's early attempts to do otherwise, it never gets beyond the level of subjective experience. To use Levinas's terminology, the phenomenological model inevitably transforms whatever is "other" into what is "the Same", i.e. into one additional item of consciousness among many. For Levinas, on the other hand, the central point of any account of intersubjectivity must be to recognize that the Other (autrui or absolute alterity, which Levinas distinguishes from autre as "other" or otherness in general) always stands in an asymmetrical relationship, one of utter separation and transcendence, with regard to the self.

Intersubjective relations can exhibit no reciprocity, Levinas argues, as subjectivity itself can adequately be understood only on the basis of precisely this separation. According to Levinas, consciousness is something simply posited in an otherwise anonymous field of pure being. This is what accounts for the absolute uniqueness of the "I" or ego. Subjectivity's emergence, therefore, can owe nothing to either past or future. It comes to be solely in what Levinas describes as the "instant" (1969: 226–30; 1978: 57ff; 1987: 51–7). This instant functions as an interruption or break that occurs within, but as distinctly apart from, the ordinary flow of lived experience. Across this "rupture", the subject as an entity defined by its separation emerges. Thus subjectivity, and by extension intersubjectivity as well, is characterized for Levinas by a discontinuity, an interval or "lapse", that guarantees the absolute distinctness of self and other (1998: 51–2). Across such an interval, the Other faces us; through it, the subject in separation is exposed to the infinition of a time – that of fecundity – irreparably removed from, and yet proximal to, the subject's isolation.

By stressing this separation, Levinas means to emphasize the extent to which intersubjectivity for him is not to be determined in any manner by subjective awareness or knowledge of the Other. At the level of concrete existing, i.e. in the face-to-face relation with other human beings, the Other stands out in its very refusal to be reduced merely to an object of my knowing. Instead, in encountering a sense of alterity that cannot be overcome or mastered, the "I" experiences a responsibility and command that strictly speaking precedes the self. This, according to Levinas, is the heart of what he refers to as the ethical relation, the very core of ethics itself. And it is in terms of an inability to account for this very relation that Merleau-Ponty's (along with Husserl's) account of intersubjectivity fails from Levinas's perspective.

Owing to its rootedness in perception, Levinas claims in his essays "On Intersubjectivity: Notes on Merleau-Ponty" and "Meaning and Sense", Merleau-Ponty's account of intersubjectivity never gets beyond Being to the dimension of transcendence crucial to his own understanding of intersubjectivity in general and ethics in particular (Levinas 1993). While praising Merleau-Ponty for his efforts at uniting "the subjectivity of perceiving and the objectivity of expressing", he notes the inability of this same thought to provide Being with the "unique sense", a recognition of the ethical demands (Levinas 1996). This sense can be provided only if an ethical meaning – via the exposure to the radically Other described above – is posited as prior to that of Being and consciousness. Instead of this, Merleau-Ponty's account instead falls back on a notion of constitution, specifically the *re*constitution of a pre-objective, pre-theoretical world, in order for the self to secure an awareness of the other (Levinas 1993: 96–103, 107–15). In other words, according to Levinas, despite the originality of Merleau-Ponty's invocation of the corporeal, his account of intersubjectivity is ultimately determined by a relationship of knowledge between self and other. "The latter [knowledge] remains", Levinas writes, "precisely as *pretheoretical* – already related to the theoretical and already as it were the shadow of that to which it is related" (*ibid.*: 101). Since the self "immediately coincides with whatever might have been foreign to it", there is, simply put, no radical exposure to an Other within the context of Merleau-Ponty's phenomenology (*ibid.*: 102).

Merleau-Ponty's later account of intersubjectivity

What is striking, in coming to terms with Levinas's criticisms of Merleau-Ponty, of course, is the extent to which Levinas restricts his commentary to works in which Merleau-Ponty's relationship to Husserl is at its most complex. Levinas frequently references, for example, Merleau-Ponty's essay "The Philosopher and his Shadow" in *Signs*, a text in which admittedly a good deal of care is needed to separate Merleau-Ponty's own theses from those of Husserl's. Levinas cites Merleau-Ponty's well-known remark from this text, that "I borrow myself from others; I create others from my own thoughts" when explaining Merleau-Ponty's account of intersubjectivity (1993: 111). However, Merleau-Ponty makes this claim immediately after pointing out that Husserl was well aware of the problems involving "communication between 'egos'" (S: 159). The question as to whether Merleau-Ponty takes the claim to be a statement of his own position or merely an account of Husserl's, is then at least to some extent an open one.

With this in mind, it is useful to ask whether Levinas's criticisms of phenomenological accounts of intersubjectivity hold for Merleau-Ponty's later works – especially that of *The Visible and the Invisible* – in which Merleau-Ponty's advances over Husserl are more pronounced. Here, Merleau-Ponty's emphasis on the *reversibility* as opposed to reciprocity inherent in relations with others calls into question the degree to which self and other enter into a relationship of knowledge as defined in Levinas's own terms. Indeed, in *The Visible and the Invisible* Merleau-Ponty claims that no strong coincidence between subject and object ever in fact obtains. At best, there is a "partial coincidence", one Merleau-Ponty characterizes as "always past or always future, an experience that remembers an impossible past, anticipates an impossible future . . . *and therefore is not a coincidence, [not] a real fusion*" (VI: 122–3). Fusion is impossible, as lived experience never proceeds from a situation "where both known and unknown terms belong in advance to the same order" (*ibid.*: 101).

This lack of absolute coincidence demonstrates the extent to which the point of Merleau-Ponty's developing philosophy of interrogation in this text cannot be to enable the reconstitution of a primordial intersubjectivity – corporeally based or not – on the basis of a pre-existing phenomenological or transcendental subjectivity (*ibid.*: 123). Here lies Merleau-Ponty's real advance over Husserl, and a fundamental point Levinas has neglected. For Merleau-Ponty, no perceiver, no *absolute* subject, can be presupposed as anterior to the perceived. Thus, while the guiding question of the philosophy of interrogation may well be, as Merleau-Ponty acknowledges, "what do I know?", this does not mean that interrogation resolves into a *relation* of knowledge between a knower and a known (*ibid.*: 128–9). "These questions", Merleau-Ponty writes, "call not for the exhibiting of something said that would put an end to them, but for the disclosure of a Being that is not posited because it has no need to be, because it is silently behind all our affirmations, negations, and even behind all formulated questions . . ." (*ibid.*: 129).

For Merleau-Ponty, interrogation serves as the basis for a reconception of the philosophical project, as an alternative to those philosophies of reflection or intuition offered by Husserl, Bergson and others. Yet interrogation can provide this basis only if understood as a mode of existence beyond an attitude of mind. The interrogative in fact describes for Merleau-Ponty the mode of existing in a *living* present: not that of linear and abstract clock-time, nor a dirempted temporality exposed to an immemorial past and never-yet future, but the continuity of experience that unfolds as the emplacing of my own and others' corporeal being in a world. In the corporeal richness of this presence, Merleau-Ponty writes, "the visible landscape under my eyes is not exterior to . . . moments of time and the past, but has them really *behind itself* in simultaneity, inside itself and not it and they side by side 'in' time" (VI: 267). The living present is this opening up of space as "compresence", of a corporeity infused with temporal depth, wherein an "overlapping or encroachment" of sensuous being upon itself occurs so as to join "me" to a world and the "world" to me.

Merleau-Ponty terms this sensuous being "flesh". In revealing our engagement with the flesh, interrogation accomplishes its primary role. Far from an "encumbrance" that Levinas viewed as riveting the subject to an "I", Merleau-Ponty's notion of flesh possesses an inherent productivity. As a "general thing" or "'element' of Being", flesh lies "beneath our idealizations" and provides thought, as Merleau-Ponty puts it, with its secret nourishment. This nourishment cannot be reduced to the fulfilment or satisfaction of a Levinasian-style "need"; recognizing the philosophical uniqueness of flesh is not to suggest a return to the anonymity of the "*il y a*" or pure being. Rather, as an "incarnate principle", flesh *produces* sense. Much as with the musical note, whose sonority sweeps over us, vibrating in the air and within our bodies, and which is intelligible despite (or precisely through) the absence of abstraction or concept, flesh subverts the reflective, intentional focus usually given over to thought (VI: 149–53). In being taken up, animated by the flesh, the subject is exposed to an intelligibility that exists as wholly *other* to its constituting capacities, but within which it nonetheless subsists in its entirety. This intelligibility belonging uniquely to the corporeal is not itself to be possessed by thought; rather, to be more precise, flesh in fact is what "possesses us" (*ibid.*: 151).

From the perspective of this fleshly existing, a dimension of otherness is preserved that remains eclipsed in Levinas's own analysis of the ethical–intersubjective relation. Through the flesh, Merleau-Ponty writes, there is "a carnal adherence of the sentient to the sensed and of the sensed to the sentient" (*ibid.*: 142). This corporeal adherence is what is expressed in Merleau-Ponty's well-known thesis of reversibility. Typically read as articulating the "hinge" on which everyday distinctions of inner–outer, exterior–interior, subject–other turn, this thesis is not often sufficiently distinguished from the "consummate reciprocity" highlighted in Merleau-Ponty's earlier works. Yet reversibility should be conceived of along the same lines as that which separates the "instant" from the continuity of time and the self from the Other in Levinas's philosophy. That is, reversibility functions precisely as interval, as rupture, as break in Merleau-Ponty's ontology of the flesh.

According to Levinas, of course, this interval is strictly temporal in nature, arising solely on the basis of an enigmatic "instant" of presence. What fleshly relations and the reversibility they entail reveal, however, is that this interval – occurring across the living present in terms of corporeal thickness and depth – possesses an importantly and previously overlooked spatial dimension as well. In terms of flesh and reversibility, "I" and "Other" exist as temporally proximal, yet across an infinition of space, one always irreducible to the other.

This infinition of space is the permeation of difference and alterity throughout corporeal existence, a permeation that occurs without, importantly, reducing the said relations to the level of what Levinas negatively refers to as the "the Same".

In conclusion, it is worth recognizing how the divergent, though interrelated, approaches taken by both Merleau-Ponty and Levinas (each responding in various ways to Husserl) each have a role to play in understanding the temporal and corporeal dimensions of inter-subjectivity. Considered together, the analyses provided by Levinas and Merleau-Ponty highlight a variety of transcendence particular to lived experience that more traditional philosophical approaches – phenomenological or otherwise – have largely failed to recognize. While Levinas argues for this transcendence through an account of temporality through which subjectivity is opened out on to a radical exteriority, Merleau-Ponty helps us to understand that this very tran-scendence is only ever realized at the level of our corporeal emplace-ment in a world, one that encompasses a movement that continually draws the self ever more deeply and fully into its fleshly existence.

An awareness of the aspects of intersubjective experience addressed here is important, I would argue, especially in terms of developing an account of ethics suitable to the environment of contemporary life. Simply put, in the pluralistic and postmodern milieu in which we find ourselves, not all of ethics can be delineated through the prescrip-tive force of responsibility alone. The perceived "ethicality" of some actions arises, in fact, precisely when considerations of responsibility are put out of play. Elements of a strictly speaking uncountable num-ber of structures maintain an immanent relation in our lives, and in terms of the present as lived, confront us with innumerable, often conflicting, responsibilities. How to manoeuvre amidst such conflicts, without relinquishing the notion of the ethical entirely, requires an ethics that is broader than Levinas's focus upon a univocal respons-ibility whose origin lies precisely outside of time itself.

By demonstrating how a dimension of otherness arises in the lived present owing to the reversibility inherent in our fleshly, corporeal existence, Merleau-Ponty helps to explain how the flesh which per-meates my own body is at the same time the flesh which permeates the world, things and ultimately the other person, without advocating either a pernicious solipsism or an abstract ego that alone enlivens a mute world of sheer substantiality. Our very corporeal existence in the world, in this sense, carries within it a motivating ground for ethical action even in those cases where responsibility is necessarily put out of play. An awareness of this dimension of intersubjectivity could, in particular, highlight the need to alter the bodily styles of our practices in some morally relevant contexts, such as those encompassed by social concerns, institutions and our relations with others, that a focus on normative rules and concepts or an emphasis on discourse alone fails to address. Explicating this range of potentially new spaces for human action, and the net gain in the possibilities open to persons it implies, is but one avenue for research among the many that Merleau-Ponty's analyses of intersubjectivity can provide.

Further reading

Busch, T. W. 1992. "Ethics and Ontology: Levinas and Merleau-Ponty", *Man and World* 25, 195–202.

Johnson, G. & M. B. Smith (eds) 1990. *Ontology and Alterity in Merleau-Ponty*. Evanston, IL: Northwestern University Press.

Levin, D. M. 1997. "Tracework: Myself and Others in the Moral Phenomenology of Merleau-Ponty and Levinas", *International Journal of Philosophical Studies* 6(3), 345–92.

Zahavi, D. 1996. "Husserl's Intersubjective Transformation of Transcendental Philosophy", *Journal of the British Society of Phenomenology* 27(3), 228–45.

FOURTEEN

Expression

Harry Adams

Merleau-Ponty's view of expression should be understood, first, in marked contrast to more traditional and intellectualist views. According to these, expression consists primarily of verbal and written acts and the results of such acts, where one subject uses language to convey certain thoughts s/he has "in mind" to listeners and readers whose job is to interpret these as faithfully as possible. When expression occurs successfully in this context, the subject will use proper verbal signs to accurately express his/her intended meaning; and the propriety and accuracy of these signs will be revealed when no ambiguities obscure the intended meaning, and the recipient consciously interprets the thought without distortion. Similarly, according to what might be called the Cartesian dream of ideal expression, disembodied minds or transcendental egos are invoked – whereby these minds and egos struggle through stutters and stammers, lips and bodies, emotions, obscure circumstances and personal backgrounds, to try to express themselves in semantically pure or intellectually aseptic ways. Merleau-Ponty is radically opposed to such views, which to him represent the death and sterility, rather than preservation or invigoration, of meaning and expression. "There can be no question of making language rest upon pure thought . . . 'Language is not an external accompaniment to intellectual processes'" (PP: 192–3). In what follows, then, I shall consider some of the salient ways he reacted against such views and, especially, some of the most striking and fertile innovations he introduced to the concept of expression.

The body-subject and expression

For Merleau-Ponty, expression is not the intentional activity of dis-embodied minds or consciousnesses; rather, the body (and, in his later work, "the flesh of the world") becomes the medium of expression. "Our body is comparable to a work of art [and as such] is a nexus of living meanings"; it makes no more sense to talk of expression with-out bodies than it would to talk of poetry without words or paper, music without sounds or notes, or paintings without paint or brush or canvas (PP: 150–51). Certainly, without mouths, vocal cords, hands, limbs and brains, expression would be strangely mute if not impos-sible. But Merleau-Ponty is claiming more than this. He insists that bodies are not mere vessels of minds or vehicles of intellectual messages, but also actively evoke, interpret and transform meaning. Often with a flick of the wrist, a gesture, a nod, glance or stance, we spontaneously comport a meaning that is itself the message, a message that was not preconceived in our mind and then merely translated out – as if the body were always only the passive servant or mouthpiece of the mind.

Merleau-Ponty uses insights from children and child development to convey some of these points. Contrary to a Cartesian model of development, he notes that children do not "learn the [un-] truths of rationalism until about the age of twelve" (PP: 355). They spend the first decade or so of their life communicating more directly and immediately through their bodies and body language. It is not until around twelve that they appear to gain the Cartesian ability to diseng-age from their body and the world in forming inner thoughts and reflectively pondering how they might "best" express their thoughts through language (cf. CAL). In lieu of these observations, Merleau-Ponty suggests that our bodies are what anchor us to the world and make us contiguous and continuous with it. It is only through our bodies – functioning as what he calls "essentially expressive spaces" – that we communicate with the world and let it express itself to and through us (PP: 144–6). Merleau-Ponty insists:

> My body is the seat or rather the very actuality of the phenom-enon of expression (*Ausdruck*), and there the visual and audi-tory experiences, for example, are pregnant one with the other, and their expressive value is the ground of the antipredicative unity of the perceived world, and through it, of verbal expres-sion (*Darstellung*) and intellectual significance (*Bedeutung*). My body is the fabric into which all objects are woven. [So] my

body is not only an object among objects, [but] is that strange object which uses its own parts as a general system of symbols for the world, and through which we can consequently "be at home in" that world, "understand" it and find significance in it.

(*Ibid.*: 235)

The body is not merely an inert housing of some Cartesian ego, which receives and transmits meaning. Rather, the body already communicates with a material and meaningful world prior to, and as a condition of, thought and linguistic expression. Further, as this nexus of material significances, the body "actualizes" meaning at a pre-reflective level and this corporeal expression is creative.

To explain what Merleau-Ponty means when claiming that the body actualizes expression pre-reflectively in a way that is also creative, it helps to contrast his view with what he calls "intellectualism" and "empiricism". As discussed elsewhere in this volume, both intellectualists and empiricists assume that the subject is located in consciousness and separate from the objective world. Merleau-Ponty claims that intellectualists hold that expression involves imposing meaning on the world – the subject is actively creative in the sense of giving meaning to a world (whether through thought or action) in a process that Merleau-Ponty describes as "centrifugal" (PP: 111). Empiricists take the opposite view: expression is "centripetal" in that the subject passively receives meaning from the outside world to which it then "adheres". Merleau-Ponty's model of expression falls between these two. As the body is the "fabric" of the world, there is no clear distinction between inside and outside, self and world, nor, therefore, between meaning that may come from me and meaning that comes from the world. For Merleau-Ponty, expression is both centripetal and centrifugal. The world already "has a meaning" (*ibid.*: 177). As with Heidegger, Merleau-Ponty accepts that we are thrown into a significant social and material world that we did not create. However, I only express and "understand" this meaning in so far as it has been taken up into my corporeal "style" of being (*ibid.*: 182) by inhabiting a world through action and "by taking part in communal life" (*ibid.*: 179). Moreover, in thereby appropriating "significant cores which transcend and transfigure" the body's powers, the body also "opens itself to some new kind of conduct" (*ibid.*: 193). That is, whether acting, thinking or speaking, the body is dispersed into a world: its signifying powers are thereby "decentralized, broken up and reorganized" (*ibid.*: 194) and the meaning it is expressing is transformed.

In his later writings, especially *The Visible and the Invisible*, Merleau-Ponty speaks less of individual body-subjects as the loci of expression, and more in terms of the "flesh of the world". Here language, the social world (including the worlds of art, of science and of politics), human corporeality and the natural world are more obviously intertwined. In these broader contexts, expression occurs across a vast and holistic *expressive field*, not only when any body or collective body speaks or interprets some message but, just as much or more, when language itself or the "whole wild world" speaks to and through us (VI: 155). "The whole of nature is the setting of our life, or our interlocutor in a sort of dialogue" (PP: 320). In almost Heideggerian fashion, Merleau-Ponty notes:

> From the very start I am in communication with one being, and one only, a vast individual from which my own experiences are taken, and which persists on the horizon of my life as the distant roar of a great city provides the background to everything we do in it.   (*Ibid.*: 328)

Throughout his work Merleau-Ponty remains consistent regarding the idea that expression is fundamentally ambiguous, since it is never quite clear who or what is doing the expressing. It is not simply the case that we try to express ourselves through language, given that language, or even being itself, may be seen as expressing itself through us. He also increasingly refers to this fundamental ambiguity in terms of the "paradox of expression" to explain the creative dimension of expression (e.g. PP: 389; PW: 35; PrP: 163; VI: 144). It is to this idea that I now turn.

For Merleau-Ponty, expression operates somewhere between the two extreme views mentioned above ("empiricism" and "intellectualism"), both of which, he insisted, are simplistic and fail to capture accurately the essence of expression. Both views assume that some being (be it a person, a past, a text, a thing, a fact, or being itself) can express itself, mean what it says, or transmit its meaning undistorted to some passive listener. While he accepts that meaning can appear to be fixed, sedimented and unambiguous in its expression, this is a secondary phenomenon – what he sometimes refers to as "secondary expression" or "empirical language". However, "[e]mpirical language can only be the result of creative language" (S: 44) or creative expression. It is in the context of this idea that all expression has a creative dimension (PP: 391) that Merleau-Ponty finds a fundamental paradox.

As Bernhard Waldenfels explains, the paradox of expression lies in a tension between the idea that expression must draw on sedimented meanings that have already been expressed and the view that expression is purely creative of new meaning (2000: 92). Merleau-Ponty cautioned us not to view expression merely as a creative process, as if expression could spontaneously generate a wholly new meaning. Rather, expression must lie between the reproduction of the already expressed and the creation of new meaning. Somehow, that is, expression must occur in the transition between old and new, between text and interpreter, between past and present, between the already spoken and the speaking of the yet to be expressed. For if expression involved only the perfectly faithful transmission of some original meaning, this would not constitute real expression, only repetition and reproduction. On the other hand, if expression involved a wholly new meaning, created just in and for the present, this also could not constitute real expression, only a kind of mute utterance or private language.

For Merleau-Ponty, then, it is precisely this ambiguity, the operation of expression between the transmission and generation of meaning, that constitutes the fundamental paradox of expression. This paradox cannot be eradicated, as if we could get to the true, original meaning by attending to it more carefully, or by being more acute listeners or scholars. Rather, this paradox is ontological and irreducible in so far as it inheres in the very nature of expression of a world.

Part of the importance of Merleau-Ponty's ideas here is their relevance across a wide range of fields of life. As he tried to show in his writings, this paradox of expression manifests not only through written texts or linguistic contexts, but also through artistic, political, social and scientific enterprises. Within these fields, actors are continuously engaged not only in the responsive process of interpreting what is already expressed but, simultaneously, in the active process of transforming meaning and so contributing to what is expressed. To further understand these dynamics of expression, we must examine more closely his views of speech and language – starting with dialogue.

Expression in speech and language

In *Phenomenology of Perception*, Merleau-Ponty describes the ambiguous paradoxical expression of meaning in face-to-face conversation in the following terms:

In the experience of dialogue, there is constituted between the other person and myself a common ground; my thought and his are interwoven into a single fabric, my words and those of my interlocutor are called forth by the state of the discussion, and they are inserted into a shared operation of which neither of us is the creator. We have here one dual being, where the other is for me no longer a mere bit of behavior in my transcendental field, nor I in his; we are collaborators for each other in consummate reciprocity. Our perspectives merge into each other, and we coexist through a common world. In the present dialogue, I am freed from myself, for the other person's thoughts are certainly his; they are not of my making, though I do grasp them the moment they come into being, or even anticipate them. And indeed, the objection which my interlocutor raises to what I say draws from me thoughts which I had no idea that I possessed, so that at the same time that I lend him thoughts, he reciprocates by making me think too. (PP: 354)

As Merleau-Ponty suggests here, the meaning that emerges from such "consummate reciprocity" is not limited merely to whatever thoughts two subjects consciously or explicitly bring to bear. Beyond this, a vast intersubjective expressive field of already-expressed, shared and sedimented meanings is always at play in the background, so that at one point a long-forgotten thought or quote from a family member may surprisingly emerge through me; at another point, ideas from some friends may express themselves through me. At other times, I will even misinterpret what my interlocutor (or friend or family) has said to me, so as to introduce new or "mutated" elements into our discourse.

We should especially note the way that *new* meaning emerges here. It is not the case that dialoguers merely interpret, conceive and articulate old thoughts or already-expressed messages. If this were the case, nothing new would ever be conceived or expressed. Rather, an excess of meaning is always insinuated in linguistic interaction. New ideas and insights emerge through our speech-acts – even when we did not intend them and "had no idea we possessed them" – through hidden or ambiguous channels that introduce novel and surprising elements into our discourse.

From 1947, Merleau-Ponty increasingly elaborated this "miraculous advent of meaning" by an idiosyncratic appropriation of a number of concepts and distinctions from the linguistic theory of Ferdinand de Saussure (see, for example, "Indirect Language and the Voices of Silence" and "On the Phenomenology of Language" in *Signs*). Saussure's initial insight was to elaborate the linguistic sign in terms of two distinct elements: the signifier and the signified. The signifier is the auditory element of the sign as a speech-sound or in visible form as a written word, whereas the signified is the concept or mental image that is signified. While the signifier and signified are inseparable (there are no concepts without signifiers), the bond between the signifier and signified is arbitrary, for Saussure, in that there is no natural or intrinsic relationship between them. For instance, it is by mere convention and not by any natural resemblance or analogy that the English word "cat" or the Spanish "*gata*" come to stand for a small, furry carnivore that purrs, sheds hair and rubs against our legs. For both Saussure and Merleau-Ponty, meaning arises not through concepts that pre-exist language but through language as a system of differences: "What we have learned from Saussure is that, taken singly, signs do not signify anything, and that each one of them does not so much express a meaning as mark a divergence of meaning between itself ands other signs" (S: 39). For example, while the English word "knowledge" may trigger a vague meaning for us, the three German words for knowledge may be said to trigger more specific meanings, in so far as "*wissen*" (to know facts), "*kennen*" (to know people) and "*können*" (to know languages) all become clearer through the differences between them. In turn, Saussure distinguishes language (*la langue*) as the systematic repository of signs and grammar rules that are built up over time by communities of language users, from speech (*parole*), as specific "speech-acts" that individuals utter.

While Saussure focuses on what he takes to be a stable structure of language at a particular point in time (synchronic linguistics) when elaborating how meaning is expressed, Merleau-Ponty elucidates the creative aspect, the way that new meaning emerges over time, in new eras and social situations (the diachronic dimension of language). Meaning emerges through a dynamic process, whereby linguistic signs of the past (whose meanings have become sedimented and whose differential relations have become systematized) metamorphose anew through current and spontaneous speech-acts:

It might be said, restating a celebrated distinction, that languages (*la langue*) – or constituted systems of vocabulary and syntax, empirically existing "means of expression" – are both the repository and the residue of acts of speech (*parole*), in which unformulated significance not only finds the means of being conveyed outwardly, but moreover acquires existence for itself, and is genuinely created as significance.   (PP: 197)

On the one hand, then, meaning is not merely found or tapped, as if it were permanently fixed in a static language that the speaker holds in their mind above or beyond speech. "Speech in the speaker does not translate ready-made thought, but accomplishes it" (ibid.: 178). On the other hand, just as a melody cannot be conveyed in a vacuum or appreciated apart from other notes and songs, so meaning is not simply created ex nihilo, out of nothing. Speech cannot say anything new or meaningful without operating within the structure, and using the components, of an inherited frame of reference. This explains "the operation through which a certain arrangement of already available signs and significations alters and then transfigures each of them, so that in the end a new signification is secreted" (PW: 13). Meaning is thus neither determined by an external, stable language, nor created anew in a speech-act; rather, it emerges in that paradoxical relation between existing and not-yet-expressed meaning, through the expressive field situated between speakers, signs, and prior language use and current speech.

Thus Merleau-Ponty explains the creative element of linguistic expression by refuting Saussure's privileging of synchronic linguistics over diachronic linguistics. For Merleau-Ponty, meaning emerges from a kind of interpenetration between the synchronic and diachronic registers of speech – with the synchronic providing the structure and inherited resources of meaningful speech, and the diachronic providing the creative, spontaneous and innovative elements for this speech, including changes that occur between two or more successive speech patterns or utterances. As Merleau-Ponty explains in "On the Phenomenology of Language":

[S]ynchrony envelops diachrony. The past of language began by being present . . . In another connection, diachrony envelops synchrony. If language allows random elements when it is considered according to a longitudinal section, the system of synchrony must at every moment allow fissures where brute events can insert themselves.
Thus a double task is imposed on us:

(a) We have to find a meaning in the development of language, and conceive of language as a moving equilibrium . . .

(b) But correlatively, we must understand that since synchrony is only a cross-section of diachrony, the system
realized in it never exists wholly in act but always involves
latent or incubating changes.   (S: 86–7)

All the while the body remains the "seat" of this dynamic expression
between the synchronic and diachronic dimensions of language (*ibid.*:
88–9). Although he first mentioned Saussure in 1947, the distinction
and relation between the synchronic and diachronic registers came
increasingly to pervade not only Merleau-Ponty's understanding of
language and expression but also of art, politics, history, ontology,
and human action and freedom.

With the development of the ideas of "flesh" and the "chiasm"
towards the end of his career, Merleau-Ponty came to understand the
creative expression of meaning as emerging less in terms of the interplay between these synchronic and diachronic registers of language,
and more in terms of a fundamentally ambiguous nexus of hidden,
reversible and intertwining forces. This presents us with a more complex, even perplexing picture of decentred subjects who call and
respond to messages whose origins and meanings are never altogether
clear and whose truth is never absolute. The chiasm becomes the
nexus around which all meanings, significations, and material forces
revolve and intertwine, akin to a tornado that gathers up things in its
spiral only to scatter them again (see Chapter 17). "The chiasm is not
only a me–other exchange, it is also an exchange between me and
the world, between the phenomenal body and the 'objective' body,
between the perceiving and the perceived" (VI: 215). Our words and
acts are clearest or most "pregnant with meaning", then, when we are
not trying to impose an artificial order on things in a detached way, as
some Cartesian ego might try to construct the external world or tame
the wildness of bodies and being. Rather, Merleau-Ponty thinks that
our words and acts will often be most meaningful when we acknowledge our physical intertwining with the world, when we serve as
muses and let the world and its "wild meaning" speak through us:

If we were to make completely explicit the architectonics of the
human body, its ontological framework . . . we would see that
the structure of its mute world is such that all the possibilities
of language are already given in it . . . The whole of philosophy,
as Husserl says, consists in restoring a power to signify, a birth
of meaning, or a wild meaning, an expression of experience by
experience, which in particular clarifies the special domain of

language. As Valéry said, language is everything, since it is the voice of no one, since it is the very voice of the things, the waves, and the forests.   (VI: 154–5)

Our calling, as communicative beings, seems to be to get in tune with the world, rather than try to make the world get in tune with us or to impose "our own" meanings on it. Further, it is as corporeal beings that we speak with and through each other, and act as conduits of this "universal world-flesh". We are to communicate neither as "dictators" nor as mere stenographers of meaning, but as muses and choral singers, or midwives – who on the one hand allow meaningful discourse to come through our lips but who, on the other hand, have a significantly active and creative role to play, by giving birth to whatever meaning or beauty does emerges through us. This ambiguous communicative ideal is exemplified, for Merleau-Ponty, by painting, and painters such as Cézanne:

It is not enough for a painter like Cézanne, an artist, or a philosopher, to create and express an idea: they must also awaken the experiences that will make their idea take root in the consciousness of others. A successful work has this strange power to teach its own lesson . . . The meaning Cézanne gave to objects and faces in his paintings presented itself to him in the world as it appeared to him. Cézanne simply released this meaning: it was the objects and the faces themselves as he saw them that demanded to be painted, and Cézanne simply expressed what *they wanted* to say!   (SNS: 18–19, 21)

If a distinctive virtue of great painters and philosophers is to function as creative oracles of the world's meaning, allowing us to "see" things we never saw before, it seems that Merleau-Ponty, the phenomenologist, was gripped by the self-same ambition he attributed to Cézanne, the painter: "He wanted to put intelligence, ideas, sciences, perspective, and tradition back in touch with the world of nature which they must comprehend. He wished, as he said, to confront [people] with the nature 'from which they came'" (*ibid*.: 14). In this light, perhaps Merleau-Ponty and his view of expression offer us an opportunity, once again and as Husserl would have hoped, to draw closer "to the things themselves".

Further reading

Adams, H. 2001. "From Consummate Reciprocity to Ambiguous Reversibility: Merleau-Ponty and the Advent of Meaning", *Continental Philosophy Review* 34, 203–24.

Lawlor, L. 1998. "The End of Phenomenology: Expressionism in Deleuze and Merleau-Ponty", *Continental Philosophy Review* 31(1), 15–34.

O'Neill, J. 1970. *Perception, Expression, and History: The Social Phenomenology of Merleau-Ponty*. Evanston, IL: Northwestern University Press.

Risser, J. 1993. "Communication and the Prose of the World: The Question of Language in Merleau-Ponty and Gadamer". In *Merleau-Ponty in Contemporary Perspective*, P. Burke & J. Van der Veken (eds), 131–44. Dordrecht: Kluwer.

Waldenfels, B. 2000. "The Paradox of Expression". In *Chiasms: Merleau-Ponty's Notion of Flesh*, F. Evans & L. Lawlor (eds), 89–102. Albany, NY: SUNY Press.

FIFTEEN

Affect and sensibility

Suzanne L. Cataldi

It is curious that a thinker as interested in embodiment, psychology and sense-perception as Merleau-Ponty did not explicitly develop a philosophical account of the emotions or devote at least one of his several essays entirely to the subject. While keen observations concerning emotional phenomena appear throughout his writings, affectivity is typically taken up only in relation to one or another of his more explicit themes or interests – for example, art, childhood development, relations with others, erotic or expressive embodiment. Indeed, affectivity is so interfused with sense-perception in the living experience Merleau-Ponty tries philosophically to capture that it is somewhat difficult to imagine how he might have thought them apart. Perceived objects are simultaneously evocative. "The body which possesses senses is also a body which has desires" (EP: 197). Together they comprise our sensibility, our means or manner of opening on to a world we are already "in" or "of" (*l'en-être*).

Before positioning Merleau-Ponty relative to certain mainstream theories and existential thinkers on affectivity, some terminological clarifications are in order. Merleau-Ponty did not draw distinctions between affective phenomena. Recognizing that it may be impossible to sharply differentiate emotions from motives, attitudes, behaviour or character traits and that it is difficult to categorize affects because their manifestations are complex and elusive, the following provisional distinctions, some from psychoanalytic terminology, can serve our purposes.

"Affectivity" is a comprehensive, generic term for psychological experiences that are felt and fluctuate with respect to each other.

These include emotions, outwardly observable and sometimes turbulent feelings that may "diminish our sense of control over what is happening" (Corradi Fiumara 2001: 63); atmospheric moods, relatively durable and dynamic constellations of affects that may not appear to be about anything in particular but nevertheless may "colour" our outlook or infiltrate our surroundings with a certain emotional "tone" or weight; passions, "intensified moods which are polarized by some specific object" (*ibid.*); feelings, which are subjectively experienced, inwardly directed, and relatively short-lived states of bodily consciousness such as an exhilarating surge of joy or a searing pang of jealousy.

Because Merleau-Ponty was apt to situate his own position somewhere between intellectualism and empiricism, he would subscribe neither to a purely cognitivist nor a purely behavioural (in the sense of non-cognitive) account of emotional experience. So, for example, he would not identify fear with a belief that one is in danger, but neither would he identify fear with, or as a "raw feel" triggering, a bodily "mechanism" of running away. Human behaviour is meaningful and purposive, in his view, an aspect of living embodiment. Fleeing from a perceived threat is sensible behaviour and incomprehensible apart from the situation occasioning it. On the other hand, although for Merleau-Ponty affective behaviour and expression contain cognitive or intelligent aspects (since they are meaningful or comprehensible), the meaning of a threatening gesture "is not perceived as the colour of the carpet, for example, is perceived". Its sense is "not given, but understood, that is, recaptured by an act on the spectator's part". The "whole difficulty", in Merleau-Ponty's view, is "to conceive this [kind of affectively lived, bodily] act clearly without confusing it with a cognitive operation" (PP: 184–5).

I shall track Merleau-Ponty through some of his key texts to acquire a sense of how his approach to affective sensibility developed over time. By considering emotion initially as a structure of behaviour and then as a "living" embodied meaning in his perceptual phenomenology, and relating it through his notion of an affective space to descriptions of "carnal essences" in his later ontology of flesh, we can begin to appreciate, where perhaps he failed to underscore, the novelty of his view of affectivity and its import to his project of thinking beyond mind–body, subject–object and inner–outer, emotion–reason, and affective–cognitive polarities.

Emotion as a structure of behaviour

Merleau-Ponty begins elaborating his "doctrine of the [emotionally] involved consciousness" in *The Structure of Behavior*, an early work influenced by the "new" Gestalt psychology. In this text he articulates a middle position between Freudian psychology as "a science of the facts of consciousness" and the "psychology without consciousness of Watson" (SB: 182). In place of their causal analyses, which reduce behaviour to a sum of conditioned reflexes on the one hand or a product of unconscious forces on the other, Merleau-Ponty analyses behaviour as a form or Gestalt, a relationship of significance or meaning. In his view, the relationship between stimulus and response is not causal, but that of sign to signified.

As a dialectical process or circulation of meaning between intentional actions and phenomenal objects, human behaviour sets up an "internal relation between the goal and acquired responses", intermingling the subjective and the objective in a way that forms indecomposable or unified "wholes" that impart momentary significance. Considered in their human meaning, these significative wholes cut across the mental–material divide: the structure "properly belongs neither to the external world nor to internal life" (SB: 182).

Emotions, as structures of behaviour, are types of adaptive movements. In responding emotionally to a complex situation, our bodies try to attain or regain a situation of momentary stability, a state of equilibrium (SB: 36–7) with respect to an ever-changing and flexible field of meaning. Because our possibilities of sensing and of moving function as parts of a single organism, they can be coordinated with respect to each other. Over time, preferred responses become rooted in behaviour as emotional habits or dispositions, and these confer integrity or coherence, a personal emotional style, to our interactions or outlooks. An activity such as dressing might reveal a "new attitude toward oneself and others" – modesty, for example, or rebellion. In caring for one's appearance, like a house one builds for oneself, one "projects and realizes . . . preferred values" (SB: 174).

Behaviour is "ordered or disordered, significant or insignificant with respect to" objective values of the organism (*ibid.*: 38). Normally structured behaviour is dialectically assimilated or "perfectly integrated" (*ibid.*: 177), developmentally and circumstantially. Failures to conform or adapt to altered circumstances, staying stuck in an emotional tendency or earlier developmental stage or persisting in a "stereotyped attitude . . . with regard to a category of stimuli" are constitutive of emotional disorders, in Merleau-Ponty's view. He reinterprets Freudian complexes (e.g. repression, regression, resistance) as disorders in emotionally structured behaviour. An example is that of a child, jealous at the arrival of a new brother, who remains rigidly attached "to the situation of the 'latest born' which was hitherto his own" (PrP: 110).

Merleau-Ponty recognizes that relational vicissitudes are characteristic of affective experiences and that emotions involve some disorganization, but the sense of this must be distinguished from the disorders discussed above. In "The Film and the New Psychology", he asserts his agreement with Janet's depiction of emotion as "a disorganizing reaction which comes into play whenever we are stuck" (SNS: 53). He would also agree with John Dewey's definition of emotion as "the conscious sign of a break" (1958: 15), for the movements of emotions involve positioning and repositioning (organizing and reorganizing) ourselves in relation to different life-stages and to changes in some aspect of a personally significant situation (or, more deeply, to changes in one's entire situation). Emotion is "a variation in our relations with others and the world which is expressed in our bodily attitude . . . the body incarnates a manner of behavior" as a word bears its meaning. To create a psychology of a particular emotion is to try to ascertain its meaning, "to ask oneself how it functions in human life and what purpose it serves" (SNS: 53). In so far as an emotional experience concerns the structure rather than a content of behaviour, it is "understood" rather than observed. Physical stimuli "play the role of occasions rather than cause; the reaction depends on their vital significance rather than on the material properties of the stimuli" (SB: 161).

This understanding is a bodily grasp. Emotional experiences "touch" and "move" us. We feel their *sens*. For example, I sense the significance of the loss of a cherished loved one through the emotion of grief it occasions. Weeping signifies my struggle to adapt myself to it. The experience "moves" or repositions me with respect to a treasured relationship, to a "place" where it/I break down, where I can no longer experience it. Sobbing symbolizes this disintegration in my own relational or communicative capacities; through it I realize the impossibility of any future interactions with this loved one. My behaviour of mourning is also intentional inasmuch as I try, as I work my way through it, to reorient or reintegrate myself with/in a transformed *sens* of my future/life, one that may initially appear as bleak, empty and bereft as I am feeling but will eventually afford me some stability and other occasions for happiness. For the time being, however, while I am in the process of accepting the fact of a loved one's demise, I may feel myself to be entirely "at a loss", and this deprivation is felt as occupying two different places at once, a place "inside" and "outside" of me, but neither here nor there.

Because, in Merleau-Ponty's view, emotions are not entirely private, my sorrow is not confined to me. Others can see it in my facial expressions or hear it in the sound of my cry. "Anger, shame, hate and love are not psychic facts hidden at the bottom of another's consciousness: they are types of behavior or styles of conduct which are visible from the outside. They exist *on* this face or *in* those gestures, not hidden behind them" (SNS: 52–3). Although I may "perceive the grief or the anger of the other in his conduct . . . without recourse to any 'inner' experience of suffering or anger", they "have never quite the same significance for him as they have for me. For him these situations are lived through, for me they are displayed" (PP: 356).

In Merleau-Ponty's view, "higher" forms of behaviour are perceived as meaningful wholes, "moments" of a global dynamic structure, figures on a background. Emotional structures, "moulded by situations which evoke them" (SB: 47), are also (reversibly) traceable in the environs, where they are allusively indicated. He describes the peculiar way they have of appearing by not appearing. In an essay entitled "Indirect Language and the Voices of Silence", he admires Stendhal's skill as a novelist in allusively illustrating a character's passionate desire to kill by appealing to "its nervous and peremptory trace in the surroundings":

> Consulting his own sensitivity to others, Stendhal suddenly found an imaginary body for Julien which was more agile than his own body. As if in a second life, he made the trip to Verrières according to a cadence of cold passion which itself decided what was visible and what was invisible, what was to be said and what was to remain unspoken. The desire to kill is thus not in the words at all. It is between them, in the hollows of space, time and signification they mark out . . . (S: 76)

Artistic expressions, like emotional ones, speak through their silences, "as though the secrecy wherein they lie and whence the literary expression draws them were their proper mode of existence" (VI: 149).

Merleau-Ponty's focus on the way Stendhal unites disparate elements through rhythmic breaks or pauses (cadences, caesuras) anticipates his later notions of affective or aesthetic ideas as circumscribed absences, "open vortexes" or "living movements" of meaning as well as his notion of *l'écart*, a "between-space" of differentiation that holds different (e.g. perceiving and perceptible; evocative and emotional) and incompletely reversible "sides" of flesh open to each other in an intermingled "distant-contact". Our relationship to flesh or the field of perceptibility is that of being "in" or "of" it, and the point of its chiasmic blind spots is that there must be some imperceptible non-sensing taking place for the sense of the perceptible to be "in".

It is also instructive to note the metaphorical use Merleau-Ponty makes of musical and other aesthetic forms throughout his writing as he searches for new ways to think beyond traditional philosophical binaries. Melody is his favourite image for behaviour as a dynamic "ensemble" or constellation of inner and external stimuli (PP: 186). Musical images also help connect his later work on affectivity with its earlier, structural origins. The "felt movements" of the performer, dashing on his violin bow and feeling himself to be "at the service of the sonata" in *The Visible and the Invisible* (151), are still "linked together by a practical intention which animates them, which makes them a directed melody; and it [still] becomes impossible to distinguish the goal and the means as separable elements" (SB: 173).

Human behaviour is motivated by desire. Human perception, and hence knowledge, have affectual roots. An originary intention, affectivity conditions perception, relationally binding sensing subjects to their sensible worlds. In *The Structure of Behavior*, "nascent perception is an emotional contact . . . much more than a cognitive and disinterested operation" and "the advent of human action and human perception . . . are irreducible to the vital dialectic of the organism and its milieu" (SB: 176).

Emotional body language

Phenomenology of Perception preserves the insight from *The Structure of Behavior* that human behaviour is meaningful and develops it in connection with the notion of a lived or phenomenal body. The *Phenomenology* is existential in its orientation. Body and existence presuppose each other; neither "can be regarded as the original of the human being". Transcendence consists in the act of "taking up" and transforming "a de facto situation" and existence is the "very process whereby the hitherto meaningless takes on meaning" (PP: 167). We must look to our affective life, Merleau-Ponty says, "if we want to bring to life the birth of being for us" (*ibid.*: 154).

Bodies incarnate significance, but human existence is indeterminate and ambiguous; "everything we live or think always has several meanings" (*ibid.*: 169). Just as he does not conceive of existence as reducible to a set of psychic or physiological "facts" but as consisting instead in the "the ambiguous setting of their inter-communication, the point at which their boundaries run into each other" (*ibid.*: 166), he does not conceive of affectivity as a "mosaic of . . . mutually incomprehensible pleasures and pains each sealed within itself . . . and explicable only in terms of the bodily system" (*ibid.*: 154).

Synaesthetic perception, the intercommunication of the senses (e.g. seeing that a fabric is soft) is the rule in Merleau-Ponty's phenomenology of perception. The structure of objects, which is "not their geometrical shape", appeals to all our senses (*ibid.*: 229). The sensory and the affective overlap just as sensory modalities do. They are, in the language of *The Visible and the Invisible*, "intertwined". These chiasmic interminglings help explain how sights and sound have the power to touch us emotionally, move us to laughter or tears. They account for why we might describe ourselves as freezing in terror or having "blue" moods, or how words and phrases can also have their emotional tones or content, how even verbal expressions can be colourful, or cutting.

Emotions are existential significations. We live (rather than know) them. They are a way of establishing embodied relations with the world:

> The love which worked out its dialectic through me . . . was not, from the start, a thing hidden in my unconscious, nor was it an object before my consciousness, but the impulse carrying me towards someone, the transmutation of my thoughts and behavior. (PP: 381)

The body experiences (subject–object; autonomous–dependent; self–other) ambiguity "pre-eminently in sexual experience" (PP: 167). Erotic "comprehension" serves as a model for the way we apprehend emotional or evocative significance generally: "desire comprehends blindly by linking body to body" (*ibid.*: 157).

These "blind" bodily "links" reappear as "chiasms" in Merleau-Ponty's later ontology, obscure(d) spaces of differentiation where passive and active, or perceptual and affective, "sides" of flesh can be conceived as "crossing over" each other. A sight that has me (passively) frightened may itself appear (actively) frightening, just as my frightened countenance can frighten an onlooker. According to the ontology's reversibility thesis, every perception "is doubled with a counter-perception . . . is an act with two faces . . . seeing–being seen, perceiving–being perceived circularity . . . *Activity* = *passivity*" (VI: 264–5).

Merleau-Ponty uses the example of love to discuss how it is possible (*contra* Sartre and Gide) to differentiate true from false or illusory feelings, genuine emotion from imaginary sentiments. Some have more depth, more reality, than others. They concern us in our "entire being" (PP: 378–81). There are degrees of reality within as well as outside us, and feelings differ correspondingly; that is, in terms of their depth as well as qualitatively (see Cataldi 1993 and Scheler 1973: 328ff).

Although he may have less to say about emotions than some of his existential contemporaries, Merleau-Ponty would not disagree with Heidegger that we always find ourselves in a certain mood or affective state of attunement, or that we are concernfully related to our surroundings. But we find little privileging in Merleau-Ponty, as we do in Heidegger, of special emotions such as dread or anxiety, a reflection perhaps of his being more interested in beginnings rather than the endings of things, as well as tending generally speaking to be less individualistic and "nihilistic" in his philosophical orientation than some of his existential contemporaries.

So then again, while Merleau-Ponty agrees with Sartre that emotional experience is a distinct form of consciousness and although he, like Sartre, would reject a view of the "the passions" that considers them only as passive "affects", he would not accept Sartre's thesis that the overall purpose of our emotional life is to magically transform a world we cannot effectively change by transforming (only) what we can, i.e., our attitudes towards it (1971: 60). While Merleau-Ponty recognizes that emotions have an active, voluntary aspect (a role to play in deciding what matters or is important to us) and may open on to (indeed have a real affinity with) the imaginary, "decisions do not arise *ex nihilo*" (PP: 447), and he faults Sartre for failing to "recognize a sort of sedimentation of our life", and that "an attitude toward the world, when it has received frequent confirmation", does not transform itself so easily or magically (*ibid.*: 441). The body cannot be relieved of its heaviness, its density, its flesh, its emotional "baggage".

The active–passive polarity is in any case problematically dualistic for Merleau-Ponty and too oversimplified a structure for his intermingled view of affect and sensibility, an intermingling that seems to me to illustrate "the passivity of our activity" described in his later work. As his example of the frenetic violinist is intended to show, it seems to be, in the reversible terms of the flesh ontology, that we do not possess emotions (as carnal or sensible ideas) "precisely because they are negativity or absence circumscribed; they possess us" (VI: 151). So some magical absences appear in Merleau-Ponty's descriptions of emotional meaning too. The carnal texture of a musical phrase (interpreted as an intermingling of joy and sorrow – "the essence of love") is "a furrow that traces itself out magically under our eyes without a tracer, . . . a negativity that is not nothing, being limited very precisely to these five notes" (*ibid.*).

Merleau-Ponty invents a category for quasi-perceptible affective (and aesthetic) meanings that he calls "living" or carnal meanings. These "open" meanings cannot be abstracted out of bodily or perceptual sensibility. They exist in the heart of the sensible, as its invisible "lining" and depth. The sense of these circumscribed absences, which only appear "behind" sensible screens, can only be grasped through the body and are communicated through a reciprocity of intentions and gestures discernible in conduct. Their sense is "secreted" in bodily gestures and in the activity of "lending ourselves" to sights or sounds we "join in a kind of blind recognition which precedes the intellectual working out and clarification of . . . meaning" (PP: 185).

Consider, for example, my typical reaction when approaching the site/sight of a steep cliff. My sense of the danger posed to my body is evident in the curtailing of my stride and the small, deliberate, tentative steps I take as I proceed towards the edge. I go slow. I'm careful. In fact, I walk as I walk when I am not on terra firma or as though I am (already) descending a slope. Thus, in an attitude of caution, my body "joins" the spectacle of a cliff by conformatively overlapping with it in my "blind recognition" of it as a "falling-off place".

A similar process takes place in the conveyance of emotional meaning between people. It is, Merleau-Ponty says, "as if the other person's intention inhabited my body and mine his" (PP: 185). We blindly apprehend another's emotional gesture by adapting our own bodily conduct or expressivity to it. We might, for example, apprehend a look of contempt or loathing directed at us through a desire to burst into tears or by wanting to stick out our tongue – just as we might apprehend a gesture of generosity extended our way in an attitude of resentment or through a desire to embrace our benefactors. Notice that if we do embrace, they in turn can be said to feel or sense our appreciation. The significance of generosity or appreciation is something that we can share.

Experience is transitive in Merleau-Ponty's view. "What happens in me can pass over into the other." Out of an early, affective "spatiality of adherence" that precedes imaginary and idealized space, he derives a notion of syncretic or sympathetic sociability. Sympathy appears to Merleau-Ponty on a foundation of mimesis (introjection) through an "internal linkage" between a child's body and the (m)other's expression (PrP: 121). He believed that an early sympathetic state of indistinction – "the mark of childish affective situations" (*ibid.*: 142) is never entirely eliminated. The experience of being without boundaries may reappear in adult love relationships; it grounds his discussion of jealousy, for example. ("I would not covet what others have if I did not sympathize with them" (*ibid.*: 143).) It may also be brought to bear on Merleau-Ponty's discussion of racial and other forms of prejudice, where one attributes or projects on to others "those personality traits they do not themselves want to have" (*ibid.*: 104). Along with the notion of an adaptive space "bound up with the animal's own body as part of its flesh" (Buytindijk in SB: 30), this spatial syncretism provides some develop-mental basis for the possibility of intentional encroachments or overlaps between oneself and others that figure so prominently into his view of emotional apprehension.

In the flesh ontology, "affectivity arises through the ambiguity and generosity of intercorporeality, a generosity that transforms exist-ence" (Diprose 2002: 95). Merleau-Ponty's philosophical accom-modation of "an affectivity where I am given to the field of the other" (*ibid.*: 96) can be construed as opening a way to the construction of ethical and politically sensitive accounts of relations between different kinds of bodies (Gatens 1996: 40). By calling attention to traces of the other in me and to the "solidarity and unity" of affective and expressive phenomena in early childhood development, Merleau-Ponty's views on affect and sensibility help to show how "the intel-lectual elaboration of our experience of the world is constantly supported by the affective elaboration of our inter-human relations" (PrP: 112–13).

Further reading

Barbaras, R. 2006. *Desire and Distance: Introduction to a Phenomenology of Perception*, P. B. Milan (trans.). Stanford, CA: Stanford University Press.

Cataldi, S. L. 1993. *Emotion, Depth and Flesh: A Study of Sensitive Space. Reflec-tions on Merleau-Ponty's Philosophy of Embodiment*. Albany, NY: SUNY Press.

Cataldi, S. L. 2000. "Embodying Perceptions of Death: Emotional Apprehension and Reversibilities of Flesh". In *Chiasms: Merleau-Ponty's Notion of Flesh*, F. Evans & L. Lawlor (eds), 189–202. Albany, NY: SUNY Press.

Haar, M. 1996. "Painting, Perception, Affectivity". In *Merleau-Ponty: Difference, Materiality, Painting*, V. Fóti (trans. and ed.), 177–93. Atlantic Highlands, NJ: Humanities Press.

Mazis, G. 1993. *Emotion and Embodiment: Fragile Ontology*. New York: Peter Lang.

SIXTEEN

Nature and animality

Scott Churchill

Merleau-Ponty's interest in nature in general and animality in particular was first made known in his *The Structure of Behavior*, which was an effort to explore the relationship of consciousness and nature by establishing the "founding" of consciousness in nature itself. At the same time, he wanted to explore how nature was in turn "given" to consciousness, and this in fact is the question raised on the first page of *The Structure of Behavior*. One can already observe here the ambiguity at play within Merleau-Ponty's thought, in this case his alternating between *the givenness of nature to consciousness* and *the "foundedness" of consciousness in nature*. Alphonse de Waelhens observed that for Merleau-Ponty "the natural experience of man situates him from the beginning in a world of things and consists for him in orienting himself among them and taking a stand" (SB: xxiv). While his *Phenomenology of Perception* is situated mostly at the level of this "natural [pre-scientific] experience", *The Structure of Behavior* took scientific experience as its point of departure. His aim was to show that "the facts and the materials gathered together by this science are sufficient to contradict each of the interpretive doctrines to which behaviourism and Gestalt psychology have implicitly or explicitly resorted" (*ibid.*: xxv). His examination of the scientific experience of nature was first approached through a critique of the behaviourists' efforts to observe behaviour as reducible to antecedent events and contingencies of reinforcement. Merleau-Ponty was interested, however, in deeper issues: what is the "being" of nature and the "being" of consciousness such that an understanding of one by the other is possible? This enquiry drew Merleau-Ponty into a discussion of Gestalt psychology's notion of isomorphism – the thesis that there is a corresponding kinship between consciousness and nature such that "in a given case the organization of experience and the underlying physiological facts have the same structure" (Köhler 1947: 177) – and eventually into a critique of its intellectualist bias (in so far as isomorphism names but neither explains nor clarifies the ontological relation of consciousness and nature). Within Merleau-Ponty's critique of existing psychological theories, the intellectualist bias of the Gestalt psychologists became the counterpart to the realist bias found in the behaviourists' untenable epistemological stance (empiricism).

Eventually, in the third part of *The Structure of Behavior*, Merleau-Ponty had begun to take another approach, examining nature through a consideration of the physical and vital orders, and consciousness (as an extension of nature) through an examination of the human order. The result of this explication was to place consciousness and nature into a structural relation, where, in so far as consciousness is a distinctive characteristic of the human order (which, in turn, both transcends and subsumes the orders below it), consciousness must accordingly incorporate the order of nature within itself. The relationship between consciousness and nature was referred to by Merleau-Ponty as a "structure" because of the double implication of this term in so far as it refers both to the order of knowing (the perceptual relation of the knower to the known) and to the order of being (the ontological kinship of knower and known). Thus Merleau-Ponty could say, "I am able, *being connatural with the world*, to discover a sense in certain aspects of being without having myself endowed them with it through any constituting operation" (PP: 217, emphasis added). It is because the world of nature and my own lived consciousness are of the same "flesh" (as he would later refer to it in *The Visible and the Invisible*) that consciousness is able to enter into a relationship of knowing through *kinship* with the world. Genuinely scientific knowledge of nature would ultimately be a "knowledge by acquaintance" rather than a merely theoretical "knowledge about" nature.

Indeed, this experientially grounded way of knowing led Merleau-Ponty to articulate the structural connection between consciousness and nature on the basis of a relational bond. Merleau-Ponty was interested in showing "how a higher order is founded on a lower and in a sense contains it, but at the same time takes it over and integrates it into new structures which cannot be explained by those that are taken over" (John Wild, Foreword SB: xiii). In this dialectical play of "parts" within a "whole", human existence is viewed as emerging from nature. It was Merleau-Ponty's aim to show how the human order is founded upon, while taking up and transforming, the vital order (which in turn is a taking up and transforming of its own foundation in the physical order). It is interesting to note that this follows a similar train of thought in Husserl's *Ideas II*, which moved from Material Nature to Animal Nature to the Spiritual World, in order to show how the "constitution" of each level both leads to and is surpassed by the succeeding level.

Merleau-Ponty would return to this general theme in his lecture courses at the Collège de France during the mid- to late 1950s, where he was developing a philosophy that would dialectically weave together and transcend the existing conceptions of nature represented by the Cartesian and Kantian traditions. These modern philosophies had effectively positioned consciousness (as a self-reflective agent, a for-itself that is always anchored in the concrete) against nature (as the sum total of all material objects, the in-itself, which is in turn transformed by human history). In these lecture courses he presented nature as "an object from which we have arisen, in which our beginnings have been posited little by little until the very moment of tying themselves to an existence which they continue to sustain and aliment" (TL: 64). One hears in this an echo of the way in which he had earlier posited the relation between existence and carnality, both in *The Structure of Behavior* and *Phenomenology of Perception*. In his assessment of mechanistic physiology, Merleau-Ponty had been struck by the fundamental contingency of our freedom: "The question is . . . Why our being in the world, which provides all our reflexes with their meaning, and which is thus their basis, nevertheless delivers itself over to them and is finally based upon them" (PP: 86). Such a dilemma exists only when we allow ourselves to dwell within the alternatives posed by a materialist conception of the body and an intellectualist conception of the soul. That is, when the body is brought into the discussion merely as a system of reflexes, and when the soul is conceived as an ethereal subject that presides over the world, we then have no way of bringing these two realms together into a true synthesis. It is not, however, the ideas of body and soul that need to be overhauled, but rather the perspectives of naturalism and intellectualism (which have distorted our conceptions of them). What is required to undercut the horns of this dilemma is more than just the "common middle term" proposed in *Phenomenology of Perception* (77) as a tentative solution to the dualistic opposition of mind and body (see especially his discussion there of the problem of the phantom limb: 76–82). The question for Merleau-Ponty was how to integrate impersonal physiological processes and personal acts into a singular conception of the human subject; and, to point the way to such a synthesis, he appealed to Heidegger's notion of "Being-in-the-world" (*ibid.*: 77–81) as a unifying concept. Just as "isomorphism" for the Gestaltists alluded to a solution to the problem of how consciousness can know the world, without their having succeeded in working this solution out completely, there was something lacking in Merleau-Ponty's treatment of the same problem in *Phenomenology of Perception* where he appropriated the expression "being-in-the-world" as a "middle term" without fully liberating himself from the dilemmas posed by Descartes's dualism of "body and mind". Perhaps this is why he returned to the problem of the body-subject in his later reflections on nature and animality.

In the lectures he gave at the Collège de France from 1952 to 1960, Merleau-Ponty was in the process of finding a new direction for understanding the meaning of nature, consciousness, existence and being-in-the-world. He was determined in these courses to address the "fundamental problems" of a philosophy of nature (N). His goal was to lay the ground for a solution to these problems, which would (a) avoid the tendency to go merely in the opposite direction from materialism, thereby evoking a purely spiritualist conception of nature that would be both "incorporeal" and "fantastic"; and (b) result in an ontology that gave place to nature, man, spirit and history without reducing one to the other. In the first lecture course his effort took the form of indicating the direction for subsequent development. There he observed that "However surcharged with historical significations man's perception may be, it borrows from the primordial at least its manner of presenting the object and its ambiguous evidence" (TL: 65). This "borrowing from the primordial" means more than a simple "receiving" of nature's objects by means of our senses. It also implies a "borrowing" or appropriating of the primordial perceptual apparatus within ourselves, an apparatus that transcends mere anatomy and suggests a carnal *presence to* the world. This carnal presence that we *are* – this is the primordial "always already" constituting schema of *all* our perceptions, including our perception of nature, as well as ourselves, others, art and history. Hence the body in its "natural" state is for Merleau-Ponty no longer just an object of perception, but a constituting (*noetic*) presence as well.

Following a path similar to that of Husserl in his *Crisis*, Merleau-Ponty first critiqued the Cartesian idea of nature for reducing the facticity of nature to its bare existence (TL: 67) – because such a conception would mean that nature contained no latent meanings within itself, "no hidden possibilities" (outside of the being given to it by God) (*ibid.*: 68–9). If Descartes's concept of nature as the mere "effect" of an ultimate cause did not satisfy Merleau-Ponty, then neither did Kant's humanistic view of "a nature that is nature *for us*", constituted under the rational functions of human understanding (*ibid.*: 71, emphasis added). The problem for Merleau-Ponty with these views was that nature remains in both cases a mere *object*. Merleau-Ponty's originality enters the picture when he tells us that we must find a way of articulating the "interior" of nature itself:

> It seems that within an entity that is in the world one encounters a *mode of liaison* which is not the connection of external causality, that is, an "interior" unlike the interior of consciousness, and thus nature must be something other than an object.
>
> (*Ibid.*, emphasis added)

What is, then, this "mode of liaison" which is an "interior" that can be reduced neither to what philosophy conceives as the interiority of consciousness nor to the external relationships which for science govern physical objects? To arrive at an improved conception of nature, Merleau-Ponty considered some of the paths taken by others, most notably Schelling (representing philosophy) and von Uexküll (representing biology). Merleau-Ponty observed that "Schelling tries to think, or rather live (*leben*) and experience (*erleben*)" (*ibid.*: 75) his way through the issues, and thus Schelling's thought might avoid some of the limitations of the empiricist–intellectualist alternatives. What he found in Schelling was an "intellectual intuition" in which nature was regarded as though it were an object in a mirror – and for Merleau-Ponty, "consciousness cannot be a detached spiritual or intellectual mirror or reflection. It is intertwined with the body, which is intertwined with the world" (Low 2000: 41). Reflecting on our pre-reflective access to nature, Merleau-Ponty, following Fichte and Schelling, observed that human beings represent a development of consciousness within the natural order, and yet, "he who becomes nature is distancing himself from nature in order to learn about it" (TL: 76). It is for this reason that he turned his attention, with renewed interest, to our perception of the lives of animals: "For they bring to light the movement by which all living things, ourselves included, endeavor to give shape to a world that has not been pre-ordained to accommodate our attempts to think it and act upon it"

(WP: 73–4). Merleau-Ponty called for a "rehabilitation of the animal world" (*ibid*.: 77) in which we might see the ways that other living beings "proceed to trace in their environment, by the way they act or behave, their very own vision of things" (*ibid*.: 75). What a wonderful expression – a "rehabilitation" of the animal world, implying both our capacity to "inhabit" and "share" in the animal world and perhaps even an ethical commitment to "restoring" it to its proper place in our relations with the environment.

Merleau-Ponty was inspired by the work of the early ethologists who, rather than distancing themselves from nature in order to learn about it, plunged themselves into a direct perceptual experience of it. Merleau-Ponty observed, on the basis of their studies, "all zoology assumes from our side a methodical *Einfühlung* into animal behaviour, with the participation of the animal in our perceptive life and the participation of our perceptive life in animality" (TL: 97–8). Among those from whom he drew inspiration, Köhler is cited for his early efforts (in *The Mentality of Apes*) "to sketch the structure of the chimpanzee's universe" (WP: 75). From Köhler, Merleau-Ponty learned the importance of lending our attention to the spectacle of the animal world, of being prepared to "live alongside" the world of animals, and of holding in abeyance our tendency of "rashly denying it any kind of interiority" (*ibid*.). In his "Second Course on Nature", Merleau-Ponty observed, in relation to his reading of von Uexküll, that an organism's "behavioural activity oriented toward an *Umwelt* begins well before the invention of consciousness" (N: 167). Here, following his early studies in *The Structure of Behavior*, Merleau-Ponty recognized that even before the advent of reflective consciousness, there is evidence of an *interior presence to the world* revealed in animal behaviour.

Von Uexküll's contribution to the history of animal psychology, Gestalt biology, and semiotics – with which he has been variously identified – was his professed interest in how living beings subjectively perceive their environment and how this perception determines their behaviour. Von Uexküll's (1909/1932) *Umwelt theory* has sometimes been described as a form of neo-vitalism and therefore considered a "romantic philosophy of nature" (von Uexküll 1992: preface). According to von Uexküll's position, what we call the reality of the individual organism "is not to be found 'outside' ... And is not to be found 'inside'. Rather it manifests itself in *Umwelten* (subjective-self-worlds) like a bubble: 'subjective-self-world-bubbles'" (*ibid*.: 281). The ultimate reality – Nature – which lies "beyond and behind" the nature conceived by science – reveals itself only through signs. These signs therefore comprised the only true empirically given reality for von Uexküll – and the laws of signs thus became for him the only true laws of nature. Within this overall system of nature, "the *mind* – in the final analysis – is an organ created by nature to perceive nature" – and hence cultivation of our own minds provides proper methodological access to the world of nature. Von Uexküll asserted in his classic essay *A Stroll through the Worlds of Animals and Men: A Picture Book of Invisible Worlds*, the rudiments of an approach to the world of others that would later be taken up by Merleau-Ponty:

> We no longer regard animals as mere machines, but as subjects whose essential activity consists of perceiving and acting . . . Perceptual and effector worlds together form a closed unit, the *Umwelt*. These different worlds, which are as manifold as the animals themselves, present to all nature lovers new lands of such wealth and beauty that a walk through them is well worth while, *even though they unfold not to the physical but only to the spiritual eye*. So, reader, join us as we ramble through these worlds of wonder. (Von Uexküll 1957: 6, emphasis added)

> To do so, we must first blow, in fancy, a soap bubble around each creature to represent its own world, filled with the perceptions which it alone knows. When we ourselves then step into one of these bubbles, the familiar meadow is transformed . . . A new world comes into being . . . This we may call the *phenomenal world* or the *self-world* of the animal. (*Ibid.*: 5)

Note that what comes into view does so only in the presence of our own perceptual apparatus which, itself being a part of nature, enables us to "resonate" with the *Umwelten* of the species we are attempting to know. Such an approach to the world of animals would eventually inspire a new generation of phenomenological psychiatrists to build their own approaches to understanding the "worlds" of their patients upon von Uexküll's *Umwelt* research (see May *et al.* 1958).

What we learn from von Uexküll – as well as from the existential psychiatrists – is that it is through the lived experience of identification with the behaviour of another that we discover our common ground, which is the body gifted with intentions. When I enter into a playful exchange with an ape at the zoo, I find myself living in this shared moment of experience in which his expressions belong not to him alone but to the two of us. This is how we as phenomenologists

might elaborate and expand upon von Uexküll's more rudiment-
ary conceptualization of "participatory observation" (see Churchill
2007). It is not surprising, then, that Heidegger and Merleau-Ponty
saw in von Uexküll a point of departure, if not a foundation, for
phenomenological considerations of animality.

In his first lecture course on *Nature*, Merleau-Ponty called attention to the definition of nature given in *Ideas II* in which Husserl
referred to a "domain of common primal presence for all communicating subjects" as the first and original sense of "nature"
and thereby of intersubjectivity (N: 78). Husserl's thesis was that
we "originally" experience (that is, in primordial experience, or
"*Ur-präsenz*") both our bodies and the bodies of others – including
both animals and humans – as expressive. In *Ideas II* he wrote: "Each
movement of the Body is full of soul, the coming and going, the standing and sitting, the walking and dancing, etc." (1989: 252). Furthermore, for Husserl empathy (*Einfühlung*) or "feeling-one's-way into"
the expressive body of an other was the means of my entering into a
consciousness of the other. Taking this a step further, Merleau-Ponty
observed: "*Einfühlung* is a corporeal operation . . . to perceive the
other is to perceive not only that I shake hands, but that he shakes
my hand" (N: 76). This would mark the move from first-person to
second-person perception, in so far as it involves a recognition of
the subjectivity – and not merely the objectivity – of the other (see
Churchill 2006, 2007 and Thompson 2001 for elaboration of the
"second-person" perspective). Note that in Merleau-Ponty's working
out of the perception of others, it is his notion of the positing of an
aesthesiological (that is, a perceiving but not yet a thinking/speaking)
subject that will enable him to provide a basis for understanding
our experience of the animal's comportment toward us. He says:
"I apperceive the body as perceiving before apperceiving it as
thinking . . . The look that gropes the objects is what I see at first"
(N: 76).

Merleau-Ponty states that this carnal relation with the world
brings with it the possibility for a radical "reversal" that we might
also characterize as a reflexivity. We might understand this reversal to
consist in the fact that our body orients us to the behaviour of the
other, of the animal, of ourselves in the mirror, rather than to his, her
or our consciousness. The "reversibility of the flesh" is a "reflexive"
(gestural) and not a "reflective" (intellectual) phenomenon. When we
visit the zoo and stand face to face with a great ape, we discover – if
we give time to the encounter – that the ape's gestures do seem to fur-
nish our own intentions with a visible realization. There are different

"layers" of experience, in which the personal, volitional body that smiles and gestures to a friend can be seen to presuppose an underlying "anonymous" body whose "operative intentionality" delivers us to the raw perceptual encounter with others, animal others and even things (Heinämaa 2003).

Inspired by her reading of Merleau-Ponty's *Nature*, Elizabeth Behnke has proposed a descriptive phenomenology that speaks from a style of improvisational comportment characterized by a thoroughly bodily reflexivity. Behnke writes: "I want to move, within lived experiencing itself, from a separative, subject-facing-object type of experiencing to a more inclusive, connective mode" (1999: 96). "[F]or Merleau-Ponty the human–animal relation is not a 'hierarchic' one characterized by the 'addition' of rationality to a mechanistically conceived animal body, but a lateral relation of kinship, *Einfühlung*, and *Ineinander* among living beings" (*ibid*.: 99). In an effort to move towards what we might call a phenomenological ethology, Behnke suggests that "we speak from within our life among animals – from shared situations in which we and the animals co-participate, from the lived experience of interspecies sociality where it is not just I who looks at the animal, but the animal who looks at me" (*ibid*.: 100). In his book *Corporal Compassion: Animal Ethics and Philosophy of Body*, Ralph Acampora likewise takes as his philosophical starting point a "background of relatedness and interconnectivity" (2006: 5). Rejecting the positions of those (including Heidegger) who would presume that an ontological gulf exists between ourselves and other creatures, Acampora draws from his readings of Nietzsche and Merleau-Ponty the position that we are "always already caught up in the experience of being a live body with other living beings in a plethora of ecological and social interrelationships with other living bodies and people" (*ibid*.). What is being expressed here in both the work of Behnke and Acampora is, I believe, a realization of the vision of Merleau-Ponty when, in the resumption of his studies on nature in the third and final course "Nature and Logos: The Human Body" (1959–60), he speaks of an "Ontology that defines being from within and not from without" (N: 220).

In light of the work of the early ethologists and of a new breed of phenomenological ethologists, it may be that Merleau-Ponty's incorporation of reflections upon animality into his more general working out of a philosophy of nature is more than just an arbitrary starting point for a deepening of our understanding of nature. Philosophers have tended to look only at human reality – individual behaviour, artistic expression and historical accomplishments – when studying such things as consciousness, carnality and symbolic representation. It might be that a closer examination of the world of animality, accomplished through our own experiences of interspecies communication (Churchill 2001, 2003, 2007) as well as through our observations of the fascinating forms of animal expression throughout the animal kingdom (Portman 1967), will turn out to be the next step for a revitalized philosophy of nature. To quote Merleau-Ponty at the conclusion of his second lecture course on nature,

> We may already say that the ontology of life, as well that of "physical nature," can only escape its troubles by resorting, apart from all artificialism, to brute being as revealed to us in our perceptual contact with the world. It is only within the perceived world that we can understand that all corporeality is already symbolism. (N: 98)

What this challenging statement seems to be saying is that we must abandon the troubles ensuing from both scientific materialism (which strips nature of its inner *anima* as well as its inner beauty) and philosophical idealism (which makes of nature a construction of our consciousness), and revert to that primordial experience that we know through our own bodies when we come into contact with others, with things, with the world. We must learn to "tune back in" to what we have left behind when we have philosophically taken leave of our senses; we must learn to be spellbound once again, and to recognize our status as participant-observers within that mysterious world of nature that delivers us to ourselves.

Further reading

Abram, D. 1996. *The Spell of the Sensuous: Perception and Language in a More-Than-Human World*. New York: Random House.

Behnke, E. A. 1999. "From Merleau-Ponty's Concept of Nature to an Interspecies Practice of Peace". In *Animal Others: On Ethics, Ontology, and Animal Life*, H. P. Steeves (ed.), 93–116. Albany, NY: SUNY Press.

Lingis, A. 1994. *Foreign Bodies*. New York: Routledge.

Lingis, A. 2000. *Dangerous Emotions*. Berkeley, CA: University of California Press.

SEVENTEEN

Chiasm and flesh
Fred Evans

The relation between us and our surroundings is paradoxical. On the one hand, we sometimes feel that we and the things around us are part of a seamless whole. Thus mystics speak of experiences in which they meld into the background. On the other hand, things often resist our efforts to assimilate them to our purposes. We then experience them as separate from us and sometimes even as alien. Indeed, some thinkers have claimed to be overcome by nausea in the face of a landscape's muteness and seeming utter disregard for them. These ontological postures involve epistemological stances. Some thinkers emphasize the immediate accessibility of things to us; they postulate that we are internally related to these things and thereby already have an at least implicit knowledge of them in advance of any empirical learning. In contrast, those thinkers who stress the separateness between us and things hold that we are only causally or otherwise externally related to them and must therefore build up our knowledge of these things from scratch.

Phenomenologists have found each of these positions one-sided. They suspect that each of them involves an imposition of preconceived ideas on to the relationship between selves and the world. They think that both rationalists and empiricists have ignored the testimony of immediate experience in favour of ideas that have other sources. In order to escape this dilemma, phenomenologists perform their famous *epoché* and put aside common-sense or science-based conceptions of reality. This manoeuvre, they hope, will allow them to return to and better understand the original paradoxical presence of objects – of their simultaneous belonging to and separation from us.

From almost the very beginning of his career, Merleau-Ponty joined phenomenologists in the endeavour to bridge the apparent divide between subjects and objects, self and world, without effacing the difference between these two poles of perception and knowledge. Many thought he had achieved this goal in his book, *Phenomenology of Perception*. But Merleau-Ponty felt otherwise. In the "Working Notes" to his incomplete and posthumously published manuscript, *The Visible and the Invisible*, he declared, "The problems posed in [*Phenomenology of Perception*] are insoluble because I start there from the 'consciousness' – 'object' distinction" (VI: 200). In order to cross the divide imposed by this distinction and to overcome the problems associated with it, Merleau-Ponty proposed a novel idea that he called "flesh". So new did he feel this notion to be that he claimed there was "no name in traditional philosophy to designate it" (*ibid*.: 139). We shall first see how Merleau-Ponty characterized the relation between subjects and objects in *Phenomenology of Perception*, then examine the notion of flesh in detail and ask what it adds to the account given in his earlier book.

The intertwining of self and world in *Phenomenology of Perception*

In *Phenomenology of Perception*, Merleau-Ponty presents to his readers a passage that encapsulates his phenomenologically based view of the subject–object relationship:

> This subject–object dialogue, this drawing together, by the subject, of the meaning diffused through the object, and, by the object, of the subject's intentions – a process which is physiognomic perception – arranges round the subject a world which speaks to him of himself, and gives his own thoughts their place in the world. (PP: 132)

This account of perception depicts subjects as neither reacting to nor constituting an object. Instead, subjects participate in a dialogic or bilateral rather than unilateral relation with objects. We are not first subjects who *then* play a role in rendering an object more determinate than it first appeared to them; nor do objects first exist for us as mute, as already fully determinate things, that only *then* impose themselves upon us. Rather, we exist from the beginning, and "all the way down", as this creative type of engagement with objects ("this drawing together . . . of the meaning diffused through the object"); at the same time, the objects exist as soliciting our attention and our momentary completion of them ("this drawing together . . . of the subject's intentions"). This simultaneous entwinement is the only way we and these objects exist for one another.

Moreover, the dialogue in which the object becomes something definite for us, and we become a specific way of being in relation to it, occurs in a world. This world is immanent in relation to us ("speaks to us of ourselves"); it reflects our hold on it, it is "our" world, one brought down to our size and the embrace of our bodies. We are our bodies, and our bodies are a schema whose parts or organs already symbolize the objects that could possibly appear to us through them; the objects in turn are woven into the "fabric" of our bodies. Subjects and objects are like the two sides of a coin. Thus our hands are not lifeless objects on the anatomy table; they are, as part of the opening on to or engagement with the world that we are, that which grasps things; simultaneously, things are present to us as that which can be grasped, as that which either solicit or abjure this response to them. Neither one, neither the hand nor the object, can be understood without reference to the other.

But the world is transcendent as well as immanent in relation to us: we do not constitute or insert ourselves into the world; we find ourselves already situated there. Rather than the collection of an infinite number of entities, the world is the setting for us and the objects with which we are engaged; it is the "horizon" within which objects are present to us and which recedes when we try to convert it into an object of perception or thought, that is, when we try to treat it as if it were something already fully determinate rather than letting it be what it is, a merely "presumptive" or incomplete, if guiding, unity (PP: 327).

This description of the subject–object dialogue clarifies the unity of subjects and objects as well as their difference from each other. Objects solicit our bodies, that is, ourselves, and we complete their meaning within the setting where they appear to us: they beckon to us, we render them more definite, and each, from the very beginning, requires the other in order to be that invitation and that response. So intertwined are we with what we encounter that Merleau-Ponty says "the world is wholly inside [me] and I am wholly outside myself", and "I understand the world because there are for me things near and far, foregrounds and horizons, and because in this way it forms a picture and acquires significance before me, and this finally because I am situated in it *and it understands me*" (PP: 408, emphasis added). In expressing the unity of subject and object, self and world, Merleau-Ponty finds himself compelled to speak of the world as "understanding us" and of us as "projecting it". Yet he does not intend to say that the world and objects are sentient subjects like us. It is clear, moreover, that his description of the subject–object dialogue does give the meaning-granting, as opposed to the invitational, role to the subject or "consciousness" and not to the objects. Merleau-Ponty must have felt, therefore, that he still needed to come closer to the idea of a bond between subjects and objects, between ourselves and the world, that would *almost* allow us to speak of the world understanding us. For this reason, then, the working note to *The Visible and the Invisible* quoted above claims that *Phenomenology of Perception* is still mired in the "consciousness–object" distinction.

Intertwining of self and world in *The Visible and the Invisible*

Flesh and "narcissism"

In order to overcome the "consciousness–object" distinction and in order to capture the "intimacy" between the "visible" and ourselves that is "as close as [that] between the sea and the strand" (VI: 130–31), Merleau-Ponty develops the idea that our bodies and the world are two aspects of a single reality: "flesh". Despite the univocity of this flesh, Merleau-Ponty is quick to point out that it means neither that we "blend into" the "visible", that is, into the things as they are present to us in perception, nor that the visible "passes into us". If either of these two alternatives came to be, then either the seer or the visible would disappear and, as a result, vision also (*ibid.*: 131). Nonetheless, Merleau-Ponty wants to arrive at a formulation that comes as close as possible to this passing of the seer into the visible and of the visible into the seer. He therefore speaks of the "fundamental *narcissism* of all vision" (*ibid.*: 139). According to this formulation, seers and what they see form a "couple" in the "commerce" between them, "a couple more real than either of them", a "Visibility in itself" (*ibid.*). Since both the seers and the visible are "so caught up in" this encompassing couple, it makes sense to say that seers are seeing themselves when they see things, and that the things "see" the seers, "such that, as many painters have said, I feel myself looked at by the things, [and] my activity is equally passivity" (*ibid.*). Indeed, "the seer and the visible reciprocate one another and we no longer know which sees and which is seen" (*ibid.*).

Flesh and "reversibility"

This narcissistic intertwinement of subject and object is what Merleau-Ponty calls flesh: "the thickness of flesh between the seer and the thing is constitutive for the thing of its visibility as for the seer of his corporeity" (VI: 135). Besides the anonymity of the flesh, besides the erasure of strict boundaries between us and the things with which we are engaged, Merleau-Ponty says that the flesh is neither spiritual nor material, neither mind nor matter, neither an idea nor a spatio-temporal thing – it is like a "general thing", an "element" in the sense that the ancients used to speak of water, air, earth, and fire (*ibid.*: 139, 147). Moreover, the crossing over that takes place between the seers and the things seen suggests that Merleau-Ponty equates "flesh" with his notions of "chiasm" and "reversibility". This definition of "chiasm", including its anatomical variant, the criss-crossing of the optic nerves in the brain, is discussed in more detail in Evans (1998) and Evans & Lawlor (2000). The rhetorical meaning of chiasm (*"chiasme"* in French) captures the notion of reversibility: in a phrase such as "To stop too fearful, and too faint to go", the second phrase inverts the grammatical order of the first. This formally mimics the way in which our seeing objects can change into their seeing us.

The notion of reversibility allows Merleau-Ponty to characterize flesh in a manner more precise than the inability to know where seeing ends and being seen begins. He says that the relation of the visible with itself – here the visible in itself or flesh – "traverses me and constitutes me as a seer" (VI: 140). The flesh "coils back upon itself" (*ibid.*), sees itself or touches itself, by dividing itself into "the flesh of the world" and the "flesh of the body", into the "sensible" and the "self-sensing" or "sentient" (*ibid.*: 250). What we call perception *is* this "dehiscence" or division of the flesh into the visible as seen, on the one hand, and the visible as embodied seers or sensible sentients, on the other (*ibid.*: 154). From the advent of the flesh, this division and perceiving is ongoing: it is the flesh's very being.

Because it is this dehiscence, the flesh cannot see itself seeing, cannot become fully one with itself. The closest flesh can come to seeing itself is in our sensible bodies seeing it; but just at the moment we see flesh it becomes pure visible, the sort of objects that we see, rather than a sensible sentient throughout. Flesh also comes close to unity with itself when objects are on the verge of seeing us. But here again that total unity is thwarted: the flesh of the world and the flesh of our bodies are part of the one self-dividing flesh, and our status as

sensible sentient beings lends the flesh of the world a power of sensing that it *would* have had if just at that moment – the moment when
we begin to feel that things are sensing us – we did not convert the
things (rocks, trees, etc.) that make up the flesh of the world back
into the pure visibles they end up being for us. Thus Merleau-Ponty
says that the coincidence, the becoming one, between the flesh of
the world and the flesh of the body is always, but only, *imminent*:
"[The reversibility of the seeing and the visible, of the touching and
the touched] is a reversibility always imminent and never realized in
fact" (VI: 147).

In order to render this idea of flesh's reversibility more concrete,
Merleau-Ponty makes an analogy with the sentient body's ability to
touch itself touching something:

> [The body's flesh] is the coiling over of the visible upon the
> seeing body, of the tangible upon the touching body, which is
> attested in particular when the body sees itself, touches itself
> seeing and touching the things, such that, simultaneously, *as*
> tangible it descends among them, *as* touching it dominates them
> all and draws this relationship and even this double relation-
> ship from itself, by dehiscence or fission of its own mass.
>
> (VI: 146)

This "dehiscence" and its implied reversibility are most obvious when
one of our hands touches the other. In this case, my single body is the
flesh that touches itself by distributing itself into the two hands that
touch one another. But this touching is reversible to the core: the one
hand becomes an object under the pressure of the other, and when
our body reverses the direction of the two, the pressure of the second
hand now sends the first into the realm of the things or the tangible (VI: 133–4, 138, 141, 147–8). Thus Merleau-Ponty says of this
exemplar of reversibility what he says of reversibility in general: the
one hand, attempting to touch the other touching it, is a "being to"
(*être à*), that is, a directedness toward the other hand (just as the body
is always already directed toward the visible), but the unity it seeks
never goes "beyond a sort of *imminence*" (*ibid*.: 249/302–3). Just as
we cannot fulfil our attempt to touch ourselves as the ones touching,
so the flesh cannot see itself seeing or touch itself touching, though
it exists as always on the verge of doing just that, of becoming one
with the being that it always divides, as if to accomplish just that
unity.

Flesh and truth

Merleau-Ponty's reference to our bodies as a "being to" highlights another dimension of flesh's relation to itself. He says that because the seer and the visible are caught up in one and the same flesh, a "cohesion, [or] visibility by principle, prevails over every momentary discordance" (VI: 140). In accordance with this principle of cohesion, Merleau-Ponty develops two notions related to the idea of truth. The first of these notions is the "invisible". Merleau-Ponty speaks of an "*intuitus mentis*", that is, a thought or idea, which he describes as a "sublimation of the flesh" (*ibid.*: 145). This idea is not primarily in our minds; rather, it is "the invisible *of* this world" – that which renders the world visible – the "Being of this being" (*ibid.*: 151). The invisible renders the world visible because it is, in any particular case, a "dimension" or "level" of the visible "in terms of which every other experience [we have of the visible] will henceforth be situated" (*ibid.*). The flesh traverses us and establishes us as its means of exploring the invisible side of itself through the visible things that are present to us. For example, in understanding a piece of music we are taken over by a presence or meaning that "can never be closed" (*ibid.*). We will recognize that presence and its inexhaustibility in all its future repetitions. Our bodies are the "measurant" of things and necessary for the emergence of their invisible dimension (*ibid.*: 152). Our bodies, to repeat, are the means by which the flesh makes itself visible to itself, but always falls short and thus leaves us and the visible intact and open to the endless recurrence of perception and the other modes of encounter between subjects and objects.

The invisible is closely related to Merleau-Ponty's second notion concerning truth: a continuous "crossing-out" of current visibles in light of others that are fuller realizations of their inexhaustible "invisible side". Thus Merleau-Ponty claims that all less "exact" vision or visibles are replaced in perception by more exact versions of them. Thus neither of these two is ever nullified or "erased" but instead only "crossed out" and brought to a greater degree of exactitude. More generally, this principle "already invokes the true vision and the true visible, not only as substitutes for their errors, but also as their explanations" (*ibid.*, see also *ibid.*: 140). In other words, Merleau-Ponty accepts a type of teleology or inherent directedness of the body towards the invisible side of the visible. Because the flesh is only ever imminently one with itself, however, this teleology is at most a quasi-teleology, one that can never in principle or practice be completed nor have a fully determinate entity (e.g. God or atoms) as its end. In *Phenomenology of Perception*, Merleau-Ponty also spoke of perception as in league with our body to achieve as complete or secure a hold on things as possible. He said that such a hold expressed itself as the optimal balance between maximum richness and maximum clarity of the object's presence to us. For example, we always find ourselves bringing something small closer to us, or straightening up a tilted picture, when we want to see these things better (PP: 318, 251). Our bodies, in their dialogue with objects, operate in accordance with this embodied principle of optimality. For this reason, too, we can come to agree on the most propitious presence of something to us within a particular context, be that something an object or each other as members of a social and political group.

The above portrayal of reversibility and this discussion of the direction of perception towards truth make clear that Merleau-Ponty's view of being differs from the two traditional alternatives: a duality of substances (subject and object, mind and body) or a single substance completely at one with itself. What he offers us is something closer to what we might call a "unity composed of difference" rather than a collection of separate, merely externally related entities or a unity formed through domination by one of the elements of that unity – he eschews, in other words, both pluralism and monism. The flesh holds seers and the visible together (they are of the same flesh), while still respecting their difference and keeping them apart (as, respectively, the flesh of the body and the flesh of the world). But the direction of truth Merleau-Ponty speaks of, even if it can never be fulfilled in principle, does seem to put a premium on perceptual and epistemological convergence rather than divergence: "The flesh (of the world or my own) is not contingency, chaos, but a texture that returns to itself and conforms to itself" (VI: 147). Whether Merleau-Ponty actually tilts more to convergence and modernism's penchant for unity, or instead in the direction of postmodernism's valorization of divergence (*écart*, *ibid.*: 22, 270), is, however, a matter of continuing debate (cf. Evans 1998; Evans & Lawlor 2000).

Other forms of reversibility

Merleau-Ponty's notion of flesh also serves to capture the closeness we experience between our different sense modalities, each other, and language and perception. For example, the single object that we both see and touch reflects the intimacy of these two sense modalities. They are united and criss-cross one another in our body's orientation towards the object in question. Indeed, their mutual encroachment is also expressed in the synaesthesia of the qualities of their objects, for example, the cold look of an icicle or the silence of a frozen sky. But we seem to absorb ourselves completely in only one modality at a time, switching back and forth between touching, hearing and seeing an object. This reversibility marks the imminent, but never accomplished, coincidence of these modalities with one another (VI: 134, 143).

In the same vein, Merleau-Ponty speaks of other human bodies as the reverse side of our own. The same visible that traverses oneself animates other bodies as well, thus establishing an "intercorporeity" (*ibid.*: 141). Merleau-Ponty uses the body analogy again in order to clarify this intercorporeity: just as my two hands touch the same object because they are the hands of the same body, and yet each of them has its own tactile experiences, so the anonymous visible inhabits each of us, though each of us has it in his or her own way (*ibid.*: 140–42). Because we are established by the dehiscence of the same flesh, we can *almost* see through each other's eyes. But no sooner do I take up your perspective than it becomes mine and no longer yours. Our unification, like that of the flesh with itself, can therefore only be imminent and never achieved. We can only be the "outside" of each other's "inside", and not the inside for each other. But for this reason we have the richness of our different perspectives upon the same visible, and thus something special to offer one another. Reversibility, the mere imminence of unity, is not a lack but a gift.

Merleau-Ponty goes on to speak of further forms of reversibility, for example the reversibility of hearing and what produces phonation, that is, the throat's and mouth's articulations of speech (VI: 144–5). But the most important of these other forms is the reversibility between language and perception. Merleau-Ponty says that the invisible or "ideal" dimension of the flesh is made visible to us by its "emigrat[ion] . . . into another less heavy, more transparent body, as though it were to change flesh, abandoning the flesh of the body for that of language . . ." (*ibid.*: 153). As the invisible of the visible emigrates into language, "the whole landscape is overrun with words as with an invasion" and "is henceforth but a variant of speech before our eyes" – language "is the very voice of the things" (*ibid.*). This emigration of the invisible of the visible into language, and the corresponding overrunning of the visible by words, is the reversibility of language and perception, words and things. In other words, the flesh sees its invisible dimension – becomes an *intuitus mentis* – by allowing that dimension to enter the "less heavy body" of language; but this linguistic embodiment is also a metamorphosis of the invisible dimension of the visible, and so the uniting of flesh with itself still retains its purely imminent status. Thus language and perception, like the seer and the seeable, "are two aspects of the reversibility which is the ultimate truth" (*ibid.*: 155). Indeed, we could say that the relation between seer and seen is a relation of "horizontal" reversibility, and that it is mediated by the relation of "vertical" reversibility between perception and language: flesh sees itself by traversing our bodies and directing them towards itself as the visible, the invisible of this visible emigrating into a linguistic body the better to be seen, but thereby unable to be seen "in itself".

In sum, Merleau-Ponty's notion of flesh is an attempt to capture the unity we share with the other beings that make up our surroundings. But it does so by simultaneously preserving and indeed valorizing the difference between the two types of flesh, the sensible sentient and the sensible. The same reversible relation holds for language and what is said in it as well as for us and others and for our sense modalities. Merleau-Ponty has given us a novel way of understanding our relation to the world and a new name for it as well: flesh.

Further reading

Barbaras, R. 2004. *The Being of the Phenomenon: Merleau-Ponty's Ontology*, T. Toadvine & L. Lawlor (trans.). Bloomington, IN: Indiana University Press.

Dillon, M. C. 1997. *Merleau-Ponty's Ontology*, 2nd edn. Evanston, IL: North-western University Press.

Madison, G. B. 1981. *The Phenomenology of Merleau-Ponty: A Search for the Limits of Consciousness*. Athens, OH: Ohio University Press.

PART IV

Extensions

EIGHTEEN

Feminism and race theory

Ann Murphy

One of the more abiding criticisms of phenomenology is that it is grounded in a fundamental effacement of difference, and that its retreat to the basic structures of experience all too often occurs at the expense of those differences that mark bodies in ways that are ethically and politically meaningful. In relation to Merleau-Ponty's thought in particular, feminists and race theorists have argued that his descriptions of the anonymous body are tacitly male and white, although they present themselves as universal and general. There is little doubt that this is indeed true, but theorists interested in giving voice to gender- and race-specific experiences have nonetheless drawn widely on Merleau-Ponty's phenomenology. Merleau-Ponty's legacy has been a provocative one in critical discourses on race and gender, and writers in both feminist theory and the philosophy of race have extensively engaged his writings. While Merleau-Ponty has been criticized for his neglect of racial and sexual specificity in his descriptions of the lived body, his work has also been enthusiastically appropriated by those interested in giving voice to experiences of raced and sexed embodiment that have been notably neglected in the history of philosophy.

Merleau-Ponty, feminism and the body

An appropriate place to begin an analysis of Merleau-Ponty's influence on feminist theory would be his relationship with Simone de Beauvoir, who is considered the founding figure of French feminism.

When de Beauvoir famously claims that one is not born, but rather becomes, a woman, she makes tacit reference to the existential phenomenological belief that existence precedes essence, or that identity is an expressive and temporal unfolding, and not an essential or objective "truth". De Beauvoir's appeal to the notion of "becoming" in *The Second Sex* is made with reference to Merleau-Ponty, who understood identity was a historical, contingent and mutable accomplishment, not as a static entity. As Merleau-Ponty claims in *Phenomenology of Perception*, "neither body nor existence can be regarded as the original of the human being, since they presuppose each other, and because the body is solidified or generalized existence and existence a perpetual incarnation" (PP: 166). Merleau-Ponty's claim that identity is a "perpetual incarnation" thus clearly informs de Beauvoir's own attempt, in *The Second Sex*, to explicitly gender this account of identity in order to free women from oppressive stereotypes that rely on the assumption that women share an immutable and objective essence. Needless to say, this kind of essentialism is pernicious to the degree that it justifies the treatment of women as the lesser "other" of man. Through his rendering of identity as a culturally situated becoming, Merleau-Ponty provides a means by which gender identity may be thought in a different way, one that avoids the dangers of essentialism.

There is undeniable symmetry between the respective philosophies of the body that emerge in de Beauvoir and Merleau-Ponty. Both projects take aim at the Cartesian notion of a *cogito* that is somehow suspended apart from the flesh. Both likewise recognize the importance of the lived ambiguity of human embodiment, its simultaneous existence as both subject and object. While the provocation of de Beauvoir's work lies in her bending this analysis in an explicitly feminist direction through her exploration of the ways in which women's status as the other contributes to the objectification of women through their identification with the body, her descriptions of women's lived experience importantly echo Merleau-Ponty's own elaborations of embodiment and ambiguity.

Indeed, Merleau-Ponty consistently renders the binary polarization of mind and body, consciousness and world, problematic, and for this reason his own project accords quite well with a feminist agenda that would seek to make explicit the denigration of materiality and corporeality that has marked the history of philosophy. This dimension of Merleau-Ponty's project points to a symmetry between his own philosophical aims and those of Luce Irigaray, who argued that philosophy's renunciation of the body is consonant with a renunciation and dismissal of the feminine. Despite the apparent proximity between Irigaray and Merleau-Ponty in this regard, Irigaray expresses a fair degree of trepidation when it comes to Merleau-Ponty's claim that human existence is characterized by an intertwining, a reversibility that pertains between subject and world. In her *Ethics of Sexual Difference* (1993), Irigaray draws on Merleau-Ponty's notion of the flesh to ask how a philosophy of reversibility might ever accommodate a the theorization of two sexes, each irreducible to the other. On Irigaray's account, the "lived body" in Merleau-Ponty is always already a male body, and there is a certain masculine bias that pervades his work. While she shares with Merleau-Ponty a belief in phenomenology's promise to return to prediscursive experience, Irigaray argues that Merleau-Ponty's descriptions of this experience as a kind of intertwining of the visible and the invisible privilege sight over touch. This priority that Merleau-Ponty affords to vision is symptomatic of a devaluation of the tactile that Irigaray understands as being synonymous with a devaluation of the feminine. Irigaray uses the example of intrauterine life to illustrate her point, claiming that these very first experiences are fully tactile, while vision is not yet constituted. On Irigaray's account, this tactile, intrauterine experience would be the precondition of vision, and so the priority that Merleau-Ponty affords to sight is unjustified on her account. Whether or not Merleau-Ponty is actually guilty of this hierarchical ordering of the visible and the tactile is subject to debate, however, as is the claim that Irigaray is an antivisual theorist. Cathryn Vasseleu argues, in *Textures of Light* (1998), that Irigaray is not so much arguing for the priority of the tactile as she is suggesting that touch is conceived in terms of vision in Merleau-Ponty's philosophy. In effect, Irigaray is suggesting that there is a dimension of touch that is irreducible to the economy of the visible. Still, Irigaray does find that Merleau-Ponty's theorization of the lived body may provide a window into a new sexual ontology where both sexes are represented, even if he fell short of this ideal himself.

Drawing some inspiration from the Heideggerian notion of being-in-the-world, the lived body is meant to connote the body's thrownness into a world in which it always already finds itself situated, which lends this body its intelligibility and a horizon for its actions. For Merleau-Ponty, the "corporeal schema" is the figure of the lived body as it is subjectively experienced. The lived body is not conceived through an exercise of cognition or intellect; nor is it understood as one object among others in the world. Human embodiment is defined by a fundamental ambiguity: it exists neither as pure ideality nor as mechanistic object. The very merit of Merleau-Ponty's phenomeno-logical approach is that it refuses both of these options, and lets the lived experience of the body serve as a guide.

As the fundamental locus of intentionality, the body is undeniably responsible for the constitution of a world in some sense, yet it is also bound by the laws of this world, and subject to its influence in myriad ways. Merleau-Ponty favours the example of habit in demonstrating the inadequacy of various philosophies of the body that would appeal solely to claims about the consciousness of one's body (intellectual-ism) or to mechanistic and material conceptions of the body as a thing. Habits testify to the body's being given over to a world which it constitutes and by which it is in turn constituted: "The world is already constituted, but also never completely constituted; in the first case we are acted upon, in the second we are open to an infinite number of possibilities" (PP: 453). The interest in habit is one that feminists have been particularly keen to engage; feminist philoso-phers such as Iris Marion Young and Gail Weiss have used Merleau-Ponty's philosophy as a resource to speak to the specificity of female body experience manifest in a wide range of phenomena, from shame, to anorexia, to "throwing like a girl".

Iris Marion Young, in her seminal essay "Throwing Like a Girl" (reprinted in 2005), draws on Merleau-Ponty's analysis of embodied ambiguity to argue that women often experience their bodies as things, and to this extent remain rooted in immanence, always at a distance from their transcendent possibilities. This is obvious, accord-ing to Young, should one observe the many ways in which women's embodied habits seem more hesitant, unsure and confined than those of men. Femininity is announced in a particular comportment, style or embodied orientation towards the world. While largely in sympathy with Young's analysis, Gail Weiss argues that many feminist appropriations of Merleau-Ponty's philosophy tend tacitly to redeploy a dualistic understanding of human experience that is grounded in the distinction between immanence and transcendence. In *Body Images* (1999), Weiss argues for a non-dualistic understand-ing of corporeal agency. Weiss furthers this insight to the sexual specificity of embodied experience through her analysis of the body image, or the corporeal schema that endows existence with a pre-reflective sense of its orientation and possibility. Using the example of anorexia, Weiss demonstrates the manner in which sexism and misogyny can engender a distorted body image. The starving anorexic who is convinced she is overweight would serve as a good example of this. Young and Weiss are among those feminists who have found Merleau-Ponty's account of the ways in which identity is sedimented in embodied comportment and habit to be a productive means by which one might examine gender-specific corporeal patterns.

Indeed, Merleau-Ponty's influence can be strongly felt in the body of literature known as "corporeal feminism", a designation that was born in the 1990s to designate a burgeoning body of feminist theory that took corporeality to be central in the figuring of experience. The authors who would fall into this camp include, but are not limited to, Judith Butler (1990), Moira Gatens (1996) and Elizabeth Grosz (1994). While these authors explore the themes of embodiment and sexuality in different ways and with different aims, they all employ phenomenological and existential resources (albeit in more or less acknowledged ways) in their attempts to give voice to sexually specific experiences of the body. Corporeal feminism is that subset of feminist theory that emphasizes the importance of lived, sexed, embodiment, and takes corporeality as its starting point for any consideration of sexual difference. As such, Merleau-Ponty figures as a resource for many in this group. Since the body is central in the figuring of subjectivity, corporeal feminism can be read as an implicit critique of the undue accord that has been afforded to rationality and consciousness (over and above the body) in the history of philosophy. Hence corporeal feminism is markedly anti-Cartesian, as it criticizes the dissociation of mind and body, consciousness and corporeity. Merleau-Ponty's own critique of Descartes, as well as his theory of the relationship between language and embodiment, both figure as central resources in corporeal feminism.

Performativity, sexuality and embodiment

Merleau-Ponty's account of identity as a becoming anticipates the contemporary paradigm of gender performativity, where "performativity" is meant to connote a model wherein gender identity is accomplished in time as a series of performances. The notion that gender is performative is deeply existentialist, honing in on the claim that existence precedes essence, as well as the truism that the accomplishment of an identity is a project undertaken in the eyes of others. Indeed, there is no making sense of a performative elaboration of gender apart from some understanding of the inherent other-directedness of our actions. As Rosalyn Diprose argues in *Corporeal Generosity* (2002), identity is an ambiguous accomplishment, always open to change, not simply because our performances of necessity change over time, but because the performance is vulnerable from the start to the recognition and misrecognition of others. Indeed it is others who solicit this performance, and who call it to existence in the first place. The body is constituted only in and through this exposure. I can feel and perceive only because I am sensible in the world of the other, and while I am always given as corporeal difference, this difference opens me, and renders me vulnerable. For Diprose, this corporeal generosity should imply an ethics and a politics that welcomes the other and resists violence.

The notion that identity only exists as such by the grace of others, and also the notion that this identity is fluid and mutable, both point to a likeness between Merleau-Ponty's account and the performative account of gender identity advanced by Judith Butler. Butler's engagement with Merleau-Ponty begins in an early article, "Sexual Ideology and Phenomenological Description" (1989), in which she expresses some reservations about the heterosexist tenor of Merleau-Ponty's discussion of sexual being in *Phenomenology of Perception*. Butler argues here that while Merleau-Ponty's discussion of sexuality is a resource for those interested in arguing against naturalistic accounts of sexuality, his phenomenological account of sexed embodiment nonetheless imports "tacit normative assumptions about the heterosexual character of sexuality" (1989: 86). These assumptions are two-pronged, according to Butler. Not only does Merleau-Ponty assume that all sexual relations are heterosexual; he also identifies male sexuality with a disembodied gaze that reduces its others to pure objects. As evidence for this claim, Butler cites Merleau-Ponty's discussion of Schneider, who provides for Merleau-Ponty a model of sexual disinterestedness. As Butler notes, Merleau-Ponty's judgement of Schneider's disinterest as pathological is based on the assumption that a normal man would be aroused upon viewing "obscene images". According to Butler, Merleau-Ponty's assessment of Schneider's sexuality betrays the fact that Merleau-Ponty's masculine subject is a "strangely disembodied voyeur" whose own sexuality is rendered in a markedly non-corporeal light.

Notwithstanding this early critique, Butler's account of gender performativity resonates with existentialism (as discussed by Schrift 2001) and with Merleau-Ponty's phenomenology in obvious ways. In *Gender Trouble* (1990), Butler argues that there are regulatory gender norms that both legitimate and undermine the appearance of certain gender identities. Moreover, the norms themselves, as well as the gendered performances that they circumscribe, are legitimated only by virtue of their repeatability. Hence Butler argues that there is no discrete "truth" to sex or gender; rather one's gender is accomplished in time as an effect of certain performances that are deemed intelligible by virtue of their conformity with sexual norms.

> In this sense, gender is always a doing, though not a doing by a subject that might be said to pre-exist the deed . . . There is no gender identity behind the expressions of gender; that identity is performatively constituted by the very "expressions" that are said to be its results.   (1990: 25)

The performative account of gender does not rely on the claim that there is a volitional agent free to adopt, or cast off at will, one gender identity or another. On the contrary, gender performances are in many ways coerced and called forth by gender norms, although these norms themselves remain vulnerable to subversion, as their existence is entirely contingent upon their iteration. Clearly this account is anticipated in many ways by de Beauvoir's understanding of gender identity as a becoming, and Merleau-Ponty's understanding of identity as a temporal and expressive undertaking. Moreover, in so far as Merleau-Ponty is also concerned to elaborate the manner in which the body both maintains and disrupts habit, the temporal dimension of his philosophy of existence is not unlike the one that comes to inform the model of gender as performativity. According to the performative account, the accomplishment of gender is a forward-looking temporal unfolding. It is not in the realization of isolated acts that one's gender comes to be, but rather through the repetition or iteration of certain acts that gender is instantiated.

The proximity between a performative account of gender and the phenomenological and existential approach is evident when one recalls Merleau-Ponty's discussion of the body in the chapter on "The Body as Expression, and Speech" from *Phenomenology of Perception*. Expression, for Merleau-Ponty, is the simultaneous constitution of language and thought; this account of expression is meant to undermine the intellectualist pretence that language and expression exist only as thought's superficial outside. For Merleau-Ponty, thought does not exist for itself prior to expression (PP: 183). The expressive powers of the body themselves give rise to reason and thought; priority is afforded to the expressive and corporeal dimension of language and not to an abstract and disembodied *cogito*. Merleau-Ponty argues for the simultaneous constitution of thought and language, such that there is no thought apart from its expression in the flesh. So, too, when he writes of a particular "corporeal style" with which one approaches the world, he provides a resource for thinking through the relationship between materiality and language that does not reduce each to the other, but forces an examination of their ambiguous relationship. When he claims that speech does not translate thought, but accomplishes it (PP: 178), he aims to under- mine the belief that language encapsulates or conveys thoughts that were already pre-formed. For Merleau-Ponty, thought was "accom- plished" in language and expression, meaning that consciousness is realized in an embodied and animate subject and does not exist apart from its corporeal instantiation and expression.

In the chapter on "The Body and its Sexual Being", Merleau-Ponty productively describes sexual life as "one more form of original inten- tionality" (PP: 157). In this respect, sexuality would be an influence that bends us towards the world and towards others in ways that are largely unreflective. Thus sexuality in an important sense engenders our world: it lies at the very origin of experience, knowledge and expression. On this account, sexuality pervades experience through and through and is not a discrete dimension of existence: "Sexuality, without being the object of any intended act of consciousness, can underlie and guide specified forms of my experience. Taken in this way, as an ambiguous atmosphere, sexuality is coextensive with life" (*ibid.*: 169). Put differently, sexuality could never be accurately rendered as the discrete and occasional *content* of experience, but is instead understood as a fundamental influence at the origin of experi- ence itself.

Merleau-Ponty, Fanon and the philosophy of race

While Merleau-Ponty's influence on the philosophy of race is not as substantial as his influence on feminist theory, his insight into embodied experience has been productively employed by several philosophers working in this area. Most notable among these is Merleau-Ponty's contemporary Frantz Fanon, who significantly engages with Merleau-Ponty's philosophy in his text *Black Skin White Masks* (1967), especially in the chapter entitled "The Lived Experience of the Black". *Black Skin White Masks* is devoted to the lived experience of the Black man under colonialism. While Fanon references Merleau-Ponty's phenomenology in his work, the en- gagement is largely critical. Fanon claims that under colonialism a "historico-racial schema" comes to replace what Merleau-Ponty names a corporeal schema. The corporeal schema is a pre-reflective sense of location and possibility that lies between the body and the world, and sketches for us a possible horizon of our actions. Fanon claims that "in the white world, the man of colour encounters difficulties in the development of his bodily schema" (1967: 110). Fanon's criticism of Merleau-Ponty, and of phenomenology more generally, is that this pre-reflective sense of the body's integrity and intelligibility is irrevocably ruptured by the experience of a racialized encounter with the colonizer. This encounter is an experience of brute objectification and of one's possibilities for transcendence being radically undermined. Objectified by a racist gaze, one is reduced to the racist mythology that rests on the skin, and is deprived of agency. Fanon is unequivocal in his insistence that this experience is one of overdetermination: "I am overdetermined from without. I am the slave not of the 'idea' that others have of me, but of my own appearance" (*ibid*.: 116). Fanon claims that the experience of racism is one wherein one's body is returned to oneself "sprawled out" and "distorted". His criticism of Merleau-Ponty relates to the claim that where Merleau-Ponty posited an ambiguous corporeal schema that was realized in a dialectic between body and world, the experience of racialized oppression stalls this dialectic, and reifies one's status as an object. The consequent deprivation of freedom and agency is the result of the historico-racial schema supervening on the fluidity and malleability of Merleau-Ponty's corporeal schema. The implicit critique here is that Merleau-Ponty's phenomenology is not anonymous and universal, and that it assumes a certain racial privilege. Nonetheless, Merleau-Ponty remains useful to Fanon in describing what racialized lived experience under colonialism entails, if only in so far as it enables one to think through how phenomenology and ontology are "broken" when applied in the instance of colonialism. As Jeremy Weate (2001) has argued, it is Fanon's attempt to repair what is broken that leads him to consider the birth of a new humanism wherein the violence of racism is undone, and the oppressed are able to accomplish a corporeal "disalienation" that frees them from the racist stereotypes of the colonizer.

More recently, Nigel Gibson (2003) and Linda Alcoff (2006) have both employed Merleau-Ponty's philosophy in an attempt to give voice to those experiences of racialization that can impair the development of coherent body images. Alcoff reiterates the fact that one of the greatest merits of Merleau-Ponty's approach is his attention to the role of habit, and the way in which our largely unconscious, habitual bodily mannerisms are constituted through historically and culturally specific practices and institutions that are deeply racialized. One of the great political strengths of an analysis that utilizes Merleau-Ponty's phenomenology is that it can account for the ways in which racism does much of its damage at the pre-reflective, unconscious level, thus undermining the naive belief that all racism is explicit and easily recognized.

Further reading

Bartky, S. L. 1990. *Femininity and Domination: Studies in the Phenomenology of Oppression*. London: Routledge.

Diprose, R. 1994. *The Bodies of Women: Ethics, Embodiment and Sexual Difference*. London: Routledge.

Heinämaa, S. 2003. *Toward a Phenomenology of Sexual Difference: Husserl, Merleau-Ponty, Beauvoir*. Lanham, MD: Rowman & Littlefield.

Kruks, S. 2001. *Retrieving Experience: Subjectivity and Recognition in Feminist Politics*. Ithaca, NY: Cornell University Press.

Olkowski, D. & G. Weiss (eds) 2006. *Feminist Interpretations of Merleau-Ponty*. University Park, PA: Pennsylvania University Press.

NINETEEN

Cognitive science

Shaun Gallagher

Merleau-Ponty can have only a posthumous relation to cognitive science given that at the time of his death the idea of an interdisciplinary, scientific study of the mind was only at its start. In some cases, however, it is not difficult for a philosopher to have a posthumous relation to some idea, to the extent that those who continue to read his texts and to write in a way that continues and extends his thought do so in relation to that particular idea. And this has certainly been the case with Merleau-Ponty and cognitive science. In this essay I shall suggest that the relation is two-sided, and that it involves a double movement, or if you prefer a key term associated with the later Merleau-Ponty, a theoretical reversibility. My primary focus, however, is on the early Merleau-Ponty, and I first want to say something about Merleau-Ponty's philosophical practice in that early period.

Simply put, the kind of investigations that engaged Merleau-Ponty in his first books, *The Structure of Behavior* and *Phenomenology of Perception*, would today easily fit under the title "cognitive science". Easily, *today*; but not so easily at the advent of cognitive science. This has more to do with the history of cognitive science than it has to do with Merleau-Ponty, and we shall see some of this in what follows. But if we understand cognitive science in the very general sense of an interdisciplinary scientific enterprise that attempts to explain cognition, where cognition is defined to include not simply higher-order thought, but such things as perception and emotion, then Merleau-Ponty was certainly involved in that kind of enterprise. Trained in psychology and philosophy, he studied and referred to neurological studies, neuropsychology, developmental psychology and psychopathology. Although he did not engage in scientific experiments, he took contemporary empirical studies seriously and used science in an interdisciplinary fashion, to motivate his phenomenological investigations. Someone immersed today in the kind of thing that Merleau-Ponty was doing in the 1940s could easily refer to themselves as a cognitive scientist. Moreover, not only do philosophers and scientists who work in and around cognitive science make explicit reference to Merleau-Ponty – including philosophers such as Hubert Dreyfus and Andy Clark, neuroscientists such as Vittorio Gallese and Francisco Varela, developmental psychologists such as Andrew Meltzoff and roboticists such as Kerstin Dautenhahn – but the general trend today in cognitive science involves precisely the kind of embodied, environmentally embedded and enactive approach for which Merleau-Ponty is well known. In this regard Merleau-Ponty's work is now being recognized as a resource that can play a significant role in areas such as neuroscience and robotics.

A critical resource

The relevance of Merleau-Ponty's work for cognitive science is, as I indicated, twofold. To understand this, however, one needs to understand that cognitive science has been undergoing a profound change. If one thinks of cognitive science as it was first formulated, in terms of computational analysis and unconscious information processing, it is difficult to see how Merleau-Ponty would play any kind of positive role. On this formulation, the scientific study of cognition was concerned with the sub-personal manipulation of discrete symbols according to a set of syntactical procedures, and it involved some attempt to cash this out in neuroscientific terms. This approach, which treats cognition as the product of a mechanical mind, is, in fact, explicitly criticized by Merleau-Ponty.

> When one attempts, as I have in *The Structure of Behavior*, to trace out, on the basis of modern psychology and physiology, the relationships which obtain between the perceiving organism and its milieu one clearly finds that they are not those of an automatic machine which needs an outside agent to set off its pre-established mechanisms. (PrP: 4)

Merleau-Ponty, appealing to the science of the 1930s and 1940s, and especially to biology, had already worked out an analysis that not only rejected behaviourism, but that also undermined the behaviour-istic aspects of computationalism and functionalism as they were developed in the 1950s. The basis of his critique was not a return to the Cartesian mind or, as he put it, to the superimposition of "a pure, contemplative consciousness on a thing-like body" (*ibid.*). Rather it involved recognizing the profound contribution of embodiment to perception and cognition.

The approach that Merleau-Ponty took in *Phenomenology of Per-ception* is fully informed by a profound but also critical knowledge of the phenomenological works of Husserl, Scheler, Gurwitsch and others. It is equally informed by neurology, experimental psychology, and psychopathological studies. In his account of perception he gives central place to the body, not merely as a biological organism, but as an experiencing subject. "For contemporary psychology and psycho-pathology the body is no longer merely *an object in the world* . . . It is on the side of the subject; it is our *point of view on the world*, the place where the spirit takes on a certain physical and historical situa-tion" (PrP: 5). This is a statement that simply could not be made by the theorists who were developing the early functionalist conception of the mind, a conception that bestows a causal role to syntactical operations, but rules out significant contributions from embodied experience.

A number of authors have thus recognized in Merleau-Ponty's work the basis for a thoroughgoing critique of cognitive science. Primary among them is Hubert Dreyfus. In his now classic *What Computers Still Can't Do* (1992) he uses Merleau-Ponty's analysis of skill acquisition and object recognition to show how embodied experience can by-pass the formal and explicit analyses that com-putational machines would have to do to accomplish the same thing. The complexity of cross-modal perception, for example, which still remains a problem for artificial intelligence (AI), is a natural accom-plishment of the body: "Thus I can recognize the resistance of a rough surface with my hands, with my feet, or even with my gaze. My body is thus what Merleau-Ponty calls a 'synergistic system', a ready-made system of equivalents and transpositions from one sense to another" (Dreyfus 1992: 249).

Furthermore, in action, as Merleau-Ponty points out, I do not have to explicitly represent my body or the tools taken up by my body in order to accomplish a particular goal, and this contrasts so completely with the possibilities that one can build into a robotic design that, in Dreyfus's view, robots that are run as computational machines will never come close to human performance. In his most recent statement of this view, Dreyfus contends: "Merleau-Ponty has turned out to be right. Neither computer programs abstracting more and more sophisticated rules nor those classifying and storing more and more cases have produced intelligent behavior" (Dreyfus 2005: 130). We find quick and easy echoes of the Merleau-Ponty/ Dreyfus critique in many phenomenologically inclined authors. Gary Madison, for example, presents a definitive dismissal of cognitive science in the name of Merleau-Ponty.

> If anything can make plausible Merleau-Ponty's seemingly paradoxical thesis that human understanding necessarily tends to misunderstand itself, it is, surely, those two particularly rampant forms of logocentric objectivism that today go under the heading of Cognitive Science and Artificial Intelligence . . . In their search for the universal algorithm, they represent a kind of innate, genetically programmed disease of the human mind, or, at least, of modernist, Western logocentric consciousness.
>
> (Madison 1991: 131)

Of course artificial intelligence is not simply repeating the same algorithm, and since the beginning of the 1990s some things have changed. Thus, in his continuing critique, Dreyfus considers the more advanced connectionist or neural net technology. A neural network provides a model that comes closer to human performance; it can learn so that its past experience is built into its system and it does not need to find a representation or a stored memory or a rule in its system to deal with the world. It simulates the same kind of intentional arc that allows us to do what we do. Yet a neural net that is not embodied faces problems. For example, disembodied neural nets are without resources for solving the problem of generalization, which Dreyfus defines as the problem of not being able to recognize and cope with things that are in some ways the same and in some ways different, in differing degrees. A system that will cope with the diversity of the world will need to classify things in very nuanced ways, and this requires very specific kinds of constraints that gear us into the world in the right way. Merleau-Ponty's continuing relevance is apparent here. He shows that embodiment provides just those constraints for being-in-the-world in a way that allows the system to recognize and cope with things. And if his account explains how humans are capable of discriminating situations and affordances because of their specific style of embodiment, this has to be a lesson for cognitive science. It remains an open question whether more contemporary attempts to embody neural nets in robots that move around and learn from the world will be able to close in on the kind of performance that we associate with human beings.

Changing fortunes

There is an important signal here in the way that artificial intelligence has moved on, because in some ways it has moved on precisely by appropriating the critical insights offered by Merleau-Ponty's work. That is, artificial intelligence has become more embodied: specifically, the more exciting and advancing aspects of AI are to be found in robotics. And robotics today is not your father's robotics. Marvin Minsky has been replaced by Rodney Brooks and by those contemporary theorists and robot builders who champion an *embodied* (and even more recent *social*) robotics. Importantly, the change in our understanding of computation has also been informed by advances in our understanding of the brain. And with such changes there comes a required reversal of the role played by Merleau-Ponty's work. Where it played an important part in developing a critique of GOFAI (good old-fashioned artificial intelligence) in the 1970s, it is now operating as a positive and supportive resource for the continuing advance of cognitive science.

The change in cognitive science corresponds to a new emphasis on neuroscience and connectionism, in approaches that challenge what had been the prevailing computational orthodoxy by introducing an approach based on non-linear dynamical systems. This turn in the fortunes of cognitive science involved a shift away from reductionistic approaches to notions of emergence and self-organization, and at the same time motivated a new interest in consciousness. Just when many phenomenologists were converting to the historically later forms of continental poststructuralist thought, which involved the deconstruction of the very concept of consciousness, philosophers of mind, who had cut their teeth on Gilbert Ryle's behaviouristic dismissal of consciousness, were beginning to invade territory left behind by the phenomenologists.

It is not certain that Merleau-Ponty, even the later Merleau-Ponty, would have gone the way of the continentalists. Consider, for example, his comments on a paper given by Ryle at a meeting in 1960 at Royaumont that put Ryle, A. J. Ayer and W. Quine into conversation with R. P. Van Breda (the original founder of the Husserl Archives) and Merleau-Ponty. After some favourable comments by Ayer about

Husserl, Merleau-Ponty responded: "I have also had the impression, while listening to Mr. Ryle, that what he was saying was not so strange to us [phenomenologists], and that the distance, if there is a distance, is one that he puts between us rather than one I find there" (TD: 65). Although Ryle would have no part of this assessment, thirty years later his student Daniel Dennett would seriously entertain the possibilities offered by phenomenology, although he too rejects them (1994, 2007). While you can find fleeting reference to Husserl in Dennett's work, however, you never find reference to Merleau-Ponty. But this is not the case more generally in the cognitive sciences. Indeed, more generally, and more recently, there has been not only a serious consideration of phenomenology, but a continuing exploration of what phenomenology might have to offer cognitive science. Specifically, in this regard, Merleau-Ponty has been viewed as a positive resource by a variety of contemporary theorists.

The current situation in the cognitive sciences is characterized by a growing interest in the embodied–ecological–enactive. This approach takes up the connectionist emphasis on dynamical mechanisms and self-organizing emergence, but it further insists that cognition is best characterized as belonging to embodied, situated agents – agents who are *in-the-world*. On this understanding of the cognitive sciences, the task is to develop a fuller and more holistic view of cognitive life – a life that is not just the life of the mind, but of an embodied, ecologically situated, enactive agent.

To understand phenomenology's role in this recently redefined cognitive science requires that we conceive of phenomenology in a different way. In this respect, Merleau-Ponty again offers a model. His work suggests that there is a place for phenomenology if we are willing to think of it as something other than strict transcendental analysis. The idea of *naturalizing phenomenology*, for many phenomenologists, will seem self-contradictory. Phenomenology just is, by definition, non-naturalistic. For others, the difficult question is how it might be accomplished without losing the specificity of phenomenology. Everything, however, depends on what one means by naturalization. Naturalization in the minimal sense means "not being committed to a dualistic kind of ontology" (Roy *et al.* 2000: 19) and certainly Merleau-Ponty's approach meets this criterion. In contrast to a Husserlian escape from the naturalistic framework (the natural attitude), which depends on a change of attitude achieved through a methodical practice (the phenomenological reduction), it seems that it is also possible to move in the opposite direction by effecting a second change of attitude that follows on the first. Indeed, what Merleau-Ponty acknowledges as the incompleteness of the phenomenological reduction (PP: xiv) does not entail abandoning phenomenological methods, but taking what we learn within the phenomenological attitude and applying it in the development of naturalistic explanation. Although Husserl defined phenomenology as a non-naturalistic discipline, the idea that the results of his transcendental science might inform the natural sciences is not inconsistent with his own intent. He suggested, quite clearly, that "every analysis or theory of transcendental phenomenology – including . . . the theory of transcendental constitution of an Objective world – can be produced in the natural realm, when we give up the transcendental attitude" (1970: 131).

A number of ways to naturalize phenomenology have been proposed. One involves a mathematical formalization that would re-categorize phenomena at a level of abstraction sufficient to allow for the recognition of common properties between first-person and third-person data (Roy *et al.* 2000; Marbach 1993, 2007). Other approaches, such as neurophenomenology (Varela 1996) and front-loaded phenomenology (Gallagher 2003; Gallagher & Sørensen 2006) are less formalistic and more oriented towards incorporating phenomenological methods or insights into empirical experiments. Despite the variations involved in these approaches, however, there is one issue on which there is good consensus, and this is clearly expressed by Merleau-Ponty.

> Psychology, like physics and the other sciences of nature, uses the method of induction, which starts from facts and then assembles them. But it is very evident that this induction will remain blind if we do not know in some other way, and indeed from the inside of consciousness itself, what this induction is dealing with. (PrP: 58)

Phenomenology is certainly positioned to play the important role of saying precisely what it is that cognitive science is trying to explain, certainly when it is trying to explain human experience. More than this, with Merleau-Ponty's work in mind, it seems intuitively right to think that the analysis of the body is the natural place for phenomenology and natural science to meet. The lived body, so insightfully captured in Merleau-Ponty's phenomenology, is always at the same time a biological entity. We live our biology; we live our neurophysiology – and that is precisely what accounts for our lived bodily experience. What the phenomenology of embodied experience describes is what cognitive science attempts to explain. The fact that one vocabulary is not easily translatable into the other is precisely a tension that should not be dismissed; rather it is precisely the challenge that should keep these differences in play in the ongoing research agendas of both phenomenology and the cognitive sciences.

Intercorporeity and intersubjectivity

Let me conclude with a concrete example of where I think the kind of phenomenology that Merleau-Ponty offers can both benefit and contribute to research and debate that is ongoing in cognitive neuroscience. More specifically, in the relatively new area defined as cognitive social neuroscience, researchers are exploring the neural underpinnings of social cognition or intersubjectivity. When they look to psychology and philosophy of mind for models of intersubjectivity to help them explain what they are discovering, they find that two approaches dominate.

The first model is referred to as theory of mind or "theory theory" (TT) and it claims that our relations to others are based on our proclivity to use a folk-psychological theory to infer the other person's mental states. To understand your behaviour, according to this view, I consult a common-sense psychology and from your behaviour I "mind-read"; that is, I infer your beliefs and desires, mental states to which I have no direct access. I then use these inferred mental states to explain and predict your behaviour. This kind of mentalistic operation is frequently claimed to be pervasive in our social relations.

This approach is subject to a number of criticisms, many of them based on phenomenological analysis (Gallagher 2005). The simplest and most straightforward criticism is that this approach construes intersubjectivity as something based on a third-person observational stance, in contrast to our own everyday experience of intersubjectivity as a second-person interaction. Furthermore, the appeal to theory is an appeal to general explanatory principles or rules, when in our everyday encounters the real task involves particular interpretations of specific individuals, in specific contexts.

The second model, simulation theory (ST), also criticizes "theory theory", and argues that to understand others we do not need a theory because we have something more immediate that we can use, namely, our own mind. Using the model of our own mind we can simulate the mind of the other person. Alvin Goldman has defended an explicit version of ST, describing it as when a mindreader tries to predict or retrodict someone else's mental state by simulation, and the use of pretence or imagination. This enables the mindreader to put themselves in the target's "shoes" and generate the target state.

> First, the attributor creates in herself pretend states intended to match those of the target. In other words, the attributor attempts to put herself in the target's "mental shoes". The second step is to feed these initial pretend states [e.g. beliefs] into some mechanism of the attributor's own psychology . . . and allow that mechanism to operate on the pretend states so as to generate one or more new states [e.g. decisions]. Third, the attributor assigns the output state to the target . . . [e.g. we infer or project the decision on to the other's mind].
>
> (Goldman 2005: 80–81)

There are both logical and phenomenological objections to ST (and indeed, Scheler, Gurwitsch and others worked out these objections in response to an older version of ST called the argument by inference from analogy). Gilbert Ryle, for example, echoing an objection made by Scheler, argued that the logic of simulation isn't correct because imputing to a variety of others what is true of my simulated action ignores the diversity of their actions. As Ryle put it, "the observed appearances and actions of people differ very markedly, so the imputation to them of inner processes closely matching [one's own or] one another would be actually contrary to the evidence" (Ryle 1949: 54). Furthermore, as with TT, we can say that there is no phenomenological evidence that in everyday circumstances, when I understand another person, I use such conscious (imaginative, introspective) simulation routines.

One strategy that the simulation theorist can take is to turn to the concept of implicit simulation, and this possibility has been made more attractive by recent research in cognitive neuroscience. Neuroscientists have recently discovered a specific set of neurons ("mirror neurons") located in the premotor, and possibly other brain areas, that are activated under two conditions: (1) when I perform certain intentional actions, such as reaching and grasping something; and (2) when I see you perform the same kind of action (Rizzolatti *et al.* 1996). That is, the very same neurons activated for my action are also activated for my perception of your action.

As it turns out, it is not only the case that the discovery of mirror neurons offers a way to explain implicit simulation for the simulation theorists, but it is also the case that ST offers a model to the neuro-scientists by which they can explain their discovery. Thus Gallese, one of the neuroscientists who discovered mirror neurons, as well as Goldman, argue that mirror-neuron activation during observation of another person represents an implicit simulation of that person's action in my own motor system, and that this facilitates my empathic understanding of the other (Gallese 2001; Gallese & Goldman 1998; Goldman 2006).

First, let me note that no clear-cut phenomenological objections can be made against implicit ST, since implicit simulations are non-conscious and don't show up in experience as such. Nonetheless, there are several objections that can still be made against this implicit version of ST (Gallagher 2007). Here, I'll mention just one. There is no reason to conceive of our experience of others, as it is considered within this theory, as anything more than a perceptual experience. Activation of the mirror-neuron system is not something extra-perceptual if we understand perception to be non-momentary (as Husserl's analysis of time-consciousness demonstrates, for example) and enactive (i.e. perception is a sensory-motor process, and not just a passive sensing of the world).

Of course it is not sufficient simply to offer objections to other theories without offering an alternative. The alternative is based on both phenomenological considerations and the science of develop-mental psychology, and it makes good sense out of the neuroscientific evidence for mirror neurons. One important part of this alternative theory cites both phenomenological and scientific evidence that in our encounters with others our perception of their embodied movements, gestures, facial expressions and intentional actions richly inform our understanding of them without the need to make inference to a set of mental states. Moreover, even our perceptions of others are inter-actional rather than just observational, in so far as the actions of others elicit the activation of our own motor systems. At a very basic level, in my perception of you, my motor system resonates with your actions. What is at stake here is precisely what Merleau-Ponty calls intercorporeity (VI: 141). What holds for one's own mirror image, thanks to the mirror system in the brain, holds also for our perception of others. As Merleau-Ponty suggests, this is a "reflexivity of the sen-sible", a reversibility that I have with others: "The mirror arises upon the open circuit [that goes] from seeing body to visible body . . . My own body's 'invisibility' can invest the other bodies I see" (PrP: 168). In effect, the alternative and phenomenologically cogent account of intersubjectivity, which offers the best interpretation of the neuroscience of mirror neurons, can find in Merleau-Ponty's concept of intercorporeity an important resource. I offer this as just one example of how Merleau-Ponty's work continues to resonate in contemporary cognitive science research.

Further reading

Dreyfus, H. 1992. *What Computers Still Can't Do*. Cambridge, MA: MIT Press.

Dreyfus, H. 2005. "Merleau-Ponty and Recent Cognitive Science". In *The Cambridge Companion to Merleau-Ponty*, T. Carman & M. Hansen (eds), 129–50. Cambridge: Cambridge University Press.

Gallagher, S. 2005. *How the Body Shapes the Mind*. Oxford: Oxford University Press.

Roy, J. M., J. Petitot, B. Pachoud & F. Varela 2000. "Beyond the Gap: An Introduction to Naturalizing Phenomenology". In *Naturalizing Phenomenology: Issues in Contemporary Phenomenology and Cognitive Science*, J. Petitot *et al.* (eds), 1–80. Stanford, CA: Stanford University Press.

Varela, F., E. Thompson & E. Rosch 1991. *The Embodied Mind*. Cambridge, MA: MIT Press.

TWENTY

Living well and health studies

Philipa Rothfield

Existential phenomenological approaches to questions of health and medicine highlight the patient's experience of illness as key to understanding the medical encounter. Merleau-Ponty's philosophy has been central to this project. Whilst medical science is concerned with the manifestation of physical symptoms, phenomenologists focus on the subjective aspects of ill health. The distinction between *Körper* (physical body/matter) and *Leib* (living body/organism) can and has been used to articulate the difference (Leder 1992). According to these accounts, medicine tends to focus on people in terms of their physical bodies, bodies that can be diagnosed, manipulated, technically managed and cured. Sartre uses this distinction to formulate how the medical gaze transforms *Leib* (in his terms, body-for-itself) into *Körper* (body-for-others). For Sartre, the subjective experience of illness becomes something else when apprehended by another:

> [A]t times it is revealed to the Other by the "twinges" of pain, by the "crises" of my Illness, but the rest of the time it remains out of reach without disappearing. It is then objectively discernible *for Others*. Others have informed me of it, Others can diagnose it; it is present for Others even though I am not conscious of it . . . If I have hepatitis, I avoid drinking wine so as not to arouse pains in my liver. But my precise goal – not to arouse pains in my liver – is in no way distinct from that other goal – to obey the prohibitions of the physician who revealed the pain to me. Thus another is responsible for *my* disease.
>
> (Sartre 1993: 356)

Inasmuch as bodies are treated apart from their existential, lived, felt dimension, they resemble *Körper*, that is, objects or things. If, however, illness cannot be reduced to the compromised workings of a body, narrowly conceived, then *Leib* comes to signify that which resists reduction. *Leib* exceeds the medical conception of the body, for it suggests that, however ill, however close to death, bodies are nevertheless lived. While Merleau-Ponty takes up this idea of the lived body, he also provides the basis for a more nuanced account of health and illness that challenges the absoluteness of this distinction between *Leib* and *Körper*.

Rethinking corporeality

If existential phenomenological accounts of illness concern themselves with questions of experience and perspective – the lifeworld of illness, the priority of the patient's experience, and its implications for the medical understanding of disease – Merleau-Ponty's work invites a deeper consideration of its corporeal dimension. Although *Phenomenology of Perception* is clearly a phenomenological enterprise, its focus moves it beyond phenomenology's characteristic preoccupation with consciousness to give priority to the "incarnate subject" (PP: 57).

His project is to give a richer account of the relation between the embodied subject and the perceived object, between self and world. Like other phenomenologists, Merleau-Ponty begins with subjectivity at a "pre-objective" level, that is, before any assumption is made regarding the existence of a world of objects. But, as discussed elsewhere in this volume, Merleau-Ponty's focus is to specify the kind of body that stands in relation to the world, to capture the way in which I corporeally experience the perceptual object. My body which is key to my perceiving – I touch this pen, feel my seat, taste this mango – is not simply an object. Rather, this "incarnate body" is the site, the source and means of my perceptual experience. That body is me.

In laying claim to the existential situatedness of the lived body, Merleau-Ponty notes two problems with Cartesian dualism of relevance to health studies and illness. First, mechanistic physiology ("empiricism") treats the body as an object like other objects (as *Körper*). Yet my body is not experienced by me as an objectivity. We come to the idea of the body as an object when we apprehend our bodies from what Merleau-Ponty calls the third-person perspective (PP: 55). The "body-as-object" view fails to acknowledge that the perceiving bodily subject engages the world through the "medium" of his/her body, that my lived body is that which makes *possible* the achievement of the objective approach (e.g. *ibid.*: 58–9). Secondly, a similar problem dogs psychological (that is, "intellectualist") approaches towards the experience of the body. Inasmuch as these adopt the impersonal attitude of science, they fail to appreciate the body in perceptual, lived terms (*ibid.*: 95). Instead, the experience of the living subject becomes an object (of psychological science), "not a phenomenon but a fact of the psyche" (*ibid.*: 94). Psychology transforms subjective experience into the point of view of universal, impersonal thought – into an idea or mental representation dissociated from its corporeal dimension. Merleau-Ponty is critical of both approaches to the body and subjectivity (and the distinction between *Körper* and *Leib* they imply). Instead of assuming that the subject oscillates between one and the other way of being-in-the-world, Merleau-Ponty responds by positing his idea of lived corporeal subjectivity found in the "corporeal schema" of the "incarnated subject": "The union of soul and body is not an amalgam between two mutually external terms, subject and object, brought about by arbitrary degree. It is enacted at every instant in the movement of existence" (*ibid.*: 89). Merleau-Ponty's subsequent analysis of the body aims to take account of the fundamental way in which it is the means by which we experience the world. His approach to "the problem" of the body is able to enhance phenomenological approaches to illness. In particular, his critique of the Cartesian separation of mind and body has been applied to medical practice to rethink the manner in which the medical body is "modeled upon a lifeless machine" (Leder 1992: 23). Merleau-Ponty fills out the existential phenomenological conception of the patient's experience with a commitment to a sense of lived corporeality coincident with perception. This has a number of consequences for understanding the impact and nature of illness, health and everyday life.

The unwell body

Existential phenomenological approaches towards illness vary as to how they conceive of its corporeal dimension. In *The Meaning of Illness*, Kay Toombs utilizes the Sartrean idea that both the medical gaze and illness itself objectify the body, so that illness is not so much lived as objectified. Toombs claims that the experience of illness always involves some kind of "alien body sensation" which disrupts everyday life. In such cases: "[t]he body can no longer be taken for granted and ignored. Rather, the bodily disruption must be attended to and interpreted" (Toombs 1992: 35). Attention to bodily disruption converts alien sensations into objects of reflection. For example, reading a book can be disrupted by a headache, which demands a focus upon the pain, its location, duration and the like. Toombs takes this notion of disruption to illustrate Sartre's view that at "the level of 'disease' the patient experiences his or her body as an object" (*ibid.*).

If the lived body becomes objectified through illness, emerging as a malfunctioning organism, there is a sense in which it becomes a "threat to the self" (*ibid.*: 73). Toombs writes of the body as an "oppositional force" in illness (*ibid.*: 72). Here, the weak, stiff or shaking body is an encumbrance, an impediment, a source of frustration or alienation. Language also has an objectifying effect: "I have MS"; "My kidney is not working". Corporeal malfunction is thereby conceived in opposition to the lived body. Toombs puts it thus: "The disruption of lived body causes the patient explicitly to attend to his or her body *as* body, rather than simply living it unreflectively. The body is thus transformed from lived body to object-body" (1992: 71).

Drew Leder's analysis follows a different path, more indebted to Merleau-Ponty than to Sartre. Leder draws upon Merleau-Ponty's view that the body is an implicit third term in Gestalt psychology's notion of the figure/background (PP: 101). To that end, he depicts a body that is typically absent from experience. As I sit here writing, holding this pen, watching the words shape themselves on this paper, I am not thinking about the role my body plays in all this. I am not aware of how my body moulds the chair, the grip of my fingers on the pen. I *could* become aware of my body within all these activities but, in general, the body is not explicitly felt. It is when pain occurs that the body comes to the fore. Like Toombs, Leder sees the body in pain or illness as a distinct mode of experience. But rather than relying on the notion of objectification to explain the transformations incurred by the body in pain, Leder coins the term "dys-appearance" (1990: ch. 3). Whilst the body in pain is apparent – it makes an appearance – it does so in an uncomfortable manner. Hence the "dys" in dys-appearance. Leder's point is that pain or illness involves a *disturbed* bodily attention in which the body comes to the fore as a threatening kind of presence – alien, disruptive, dysfunctional. The dys-appearance of the body in pain is different from the body's usual absence: "No longer absent *from* experience, the body may yet surface as an absence, as being-away *within* experience" (*ibid.*: 91).

Leder's account of dys-appearance, "being-away within experience", is similar to Toomb's notion of objectification, inasmuch as "being-away" is a *kind* of objectification, an alienation felt with respect to subjectivity itself. Merleau-Ponty discusses illness in a slightly different way:

> Let us therefore say rather, borrowing a term from other works, that the life of consciousness – cognitive life, the life of desire or perceptual life – is subtended by an "intentional arc" which projects round about us our past, our future, our human setting, our physical, ideological and moral situation, or rather which results in our being situated in all these respects. It is this intentional arc which brings about the unity of the senses, of intelligence, of sensibility and motility. And it is this which "goes limp" in illness. (PP: 136)

Rather than posing a threat to the lived body (via objectification or "being-away"), pathological conditions provoke Merleau-Ponty to probe the particulars of lived corporeality. Pathology does not take on the mantle of objectification. It is, instead, a lived corporeal phenomenon, engendering a certain kind of lived body. His discussion of the First World War veteran, Schneider, explores the way in which pathology *qualifies* the lived body (rather than objectifying (Toombs) or alienating it (Leder)). Although Schneider allows Merleau-Ponty to make some general claims about the body in space, Schneider is not to be thought of as "normal" minus some capacity: "Illness, like childhood and primitive mentality, is a complete form of existence . . . It is impossible to deduce the normal from the pathological" (PP: 107).

One cannot infer what the ill person "lacks" from knowing the "normal" protocols of movement (*ibid.*). This is illustrated by Oliver Sacks's discussion of a woman who lost all proprioceptive feeling in her limbs (Sacks 1985: ch. 3). Despite having no feeling in her body at all, Christina trained herself to move. She found she could move if she watched, instead of felt, the position of her limbs. To do so, she had to track her hands holding the fork, monitor her fingers tapping the keyboard. Sean Gallagher refers to a similar condition experienced by Ian Waterman, who also lost all proprioceptive sensation (2005: 43). Like Christina, Waterman found he could move by visually tracking, rather than feeling, the pathway of his limbs. Merleau-Ponty's view is that adaptations like this differ from everyday forms of movement;

that pathological conditions through which corporeal intentionality "goes limp" call for extraordinary *modus operandi* (PP: 107).

Consequences and applications

Ethics of the clinical encounter

Existential phenomenological bioethics posits the subject's perspective as an antidote to the dominance of the medical framework. Kay Toombs's (1992) depiction of living with multiple sclerosis, and Vivian Sobchack's (2005) account of moving with and without a prosthesis, are worthy exponents of phenomenology's patient focus. Toombs describes her experience of using a wheelchair, both in terms of her own purchase on the world and as an influence upon others' perceptions, showing that the meaning of illness resides in its day-to-day experience, the way in which symptoms colour and condition everyday life (1992: 65). She also makes a case for the difference in perspective between patient and doctor, arguing that the patient/subject's experience of illness differs from the doctor's because it is lived by the patient. She, like Leder, claims that physicians regard bodies in objectified terms because they access the patient's condition from the outside, through observing or hearing about (rather than experiencing) symptoms (Leder 1990: 77). Suffering drives an experiential, and therefore epistemological, wedge between the patient and doctor, leading Toombs to conclude that "[t]he phenomenological analysis of the 'worlds' of physician and patient reveals a fundamental distinction between the lived experience of illness and its conceptualization as a disease state" (1992: 31).

Existential phenomenological bioethics seeks to redress the occlusion of the patient's perspective according to the instrumental, objectivist tendencies of medical science. It is allied with medical approaches to the clinical encounter that highlight the importance of the patient's world (see, e.g., Baron 1992; Cassell 1985; Frank 1995; Purtilo & Haddad 2002; Thomas 2005 and Zaner 1988). Toombs endeavours to bridge this divide between patient and doctor through a notion of their common humanity. Although the medical encounter engenders a divergence of perspective, both patient and doctor are said to have "lifeworld experiences which provide the basis for a shared world of meaning between them" (1992: 102). In other words, doctors also fall ill. They experience symptoms, disruptions and frustrations that enable them to approach patients more empathically and thus effectively. Hence Eric Cassell appeals to an intercorporeal sameness that allows the doctor to understand the patient:

> Because all of us have bowel movements, we all have a framework of reference to help us understand her. Persons taking histories should use themselves and their own experiences with their bodies and the world as a reference for what they hear.
>
> (1985: 46)

Rosalyn Diprose's (2002) approach to the clinical encounter draws upon an intercorporeal sense of indeterminacy and ambiguity that hails from Merleau-Ponty's work (see also Toombs 1999 for a discussion of intersubjectivity in relation to the corporeal ethics of organ donation). Rather than claim that a common humanity exists between doctor and patient, Diprose uses Merleau-Ponty's work on embodiment to insist upon the corporeality of the doctor as a site of difference rather than sameness. As the clinical encounter is "an encounter between bodies" the patient's and doctor's perception of the situation may well differ irrespective of any obvious objectification (2002: 117). Since doctors cannot assume an experiential basis for understanding the breadth of patient backgrounds, there is an epistemological gap that cannot be bridged: "It is unrealistic to expect that a particular clinician could be open to every possible body history and every experience of a particular patient, unless we assume that the clinician is a god without a body at all" (*ibid.*: 119). Difference according to this account cannot be effaced. Rather, medical practitioners need to acknowledge that their lived corporeality will influence their diagnosis while patients do their best to find practitioners with whom they feel comfortable (*ibid.*).

Difference and illness

There has been some debate over whether Merleau-Ponty's approach to the lived body allows for the discernment of difference between bodies (see Chapter 13; Chapter 18; and Rothfield 2005). Whatever the upshot of these debates, his work has been used by cultural phenomenologists such as Thomas Csordas as a springboard for investigating differences between lived bodies, posed as a nexus between culture and embodiment (1994: 7; see also Csordas 1993, 1997, 1999). Csordas has extended Merleau-Ponty's notion of the lived body to account for the manner in which sensibility is culturally configured and deployed. He utilizes Merleau-Ponty's concept of indeterminacy to suggest that corporeal encounters are always some-what ambiguous, that understanding is always filtered through a body, which is "always already" culturally configured. Cultural phenomenology thereby reminds us that health has multiple inflexions and that these are made manifest at the level of the lived body.

Anne Becker's work on the significance of community for Fijian notions of the body is an illustration of the cultural dimension in the way health and illness are lived. According to Becker, the "fundamental orientation of the Fijian is to the community" (1994: 104). Corporeal experience is not confined to the one body but may be discerned across bodies through the appearance of lived bodily signs. This shows itself in social relations around feeding and food sharing, according to which an underfed person makes the household and community look bad (*ibid.*: 105). The community orientation of lived corporeality explains why individual bodily conditions need to be made public: they are everybody's concern. Pregnancies kept secret, for example, oppose the interests of the community, and are thus liable to cause problems in others' bodies (spoiling the milk in nearby mothers' breasts) (*ibid.*: 110).

Differences between kinds of lived corporeal experience are also to be found within the hospital setting. These may shape the perceptions of doctors, which include apprehensions of racial or ethnic difference. Yasmin Gunaratnam (1997) has documented the manner in which different cultures grieve, and whether this fits in with protocols of hospital, palliative care (see also Jon Willis's (1999) work on culturally specific ways of dying among central desert peoples of Australia). According to Gunaratnam, ethnic groups who grieve vocally are perceived through the norms of an English hospice as disruptive and undisciplined, undermining hospital notions of order. Order might seem a neutral term, but Gunaratnam shows that it is predicated upon an Anglo-Celtic preference for muted expressions of suffering and loss. This is an illustration of the way in which institutions themselves embody perceptual norms which are themselves culturally configured.

These examples show not only that people of different cultures experiences their bodies in particular ways, but also that medical perception is both culturally specific and potentially hegemonic. In contrast to Cassell's assertion that "all of us have bowel movements", and Toombs's notion of a "shared lifeworld", cultural phenomenology suggests that illness is not a universal experience. In a multicultural society, it cannot be assumed that one person's corporeality corresponds to another's, including that of the doctor. The extension of Merleau-Ponty's work on the lived body within intersubjectivity and illness into the domain of cultural difference has the potential to provoke phenomenological bioethics to adopt a more culturally sensitive and differentiated stance. Equally, extension of his work to consider sexuality and sexual difference, disability and age affects medical ethics (see Shildrick 2004). It is not simply a question of how people experience illness but of the way in which day-to-day activities are conducted, for these qualify the manner in which health and illness are lived.

This is illustrated in the work of Robert Desjarlais, who studied healing among the Yolmo Sherpa people of Nepal, while apprenticed to a shamanic healer, Meme. Desjarlais links Yolmo notions of health to their everyday manner of living:

> [E]veryday actions are rooted in local sensibilities; this rooted-ness forces us to rethink how we talk of moralities, bodies, pain, healing and politics. For Yolmo wa, the aesthetic values that govern how a person dresses in the morning or talks with a neighbour constitute a tacit moral code, such that ethics and aesthetics are one. In Helambu, values of presence, balance and harmony are embodied, sensible ones, and thus contribute to the force and tenor of human sentience. Yolmo sensibilities influence how and why villagers fall ill, how they heal, and what moments of pain and comfort feel like.   (1992: 248–9)

Desjarlais is very clear that illness and well-being are connected to local forms of sensibility and moral value. Morality is not a set of abstract principles so much as a field of lived corporeal relationships among a people. It concerns how to "eat a bowl of rice" with style or greet an elder with grace (*ibid.*: 251). Ethics and aesthetics there-by come together through corporeal interaction. The way in which people conduct everyday matters reveals their understanding of health and illness. For example, Desjarlais describes Yolmo men smoking cigarettes in muddy fields, crouching on their haunches, and cupping burning embers with their hands. For Desjarlais, this prac-tice and its postures resonate with Yolmo's views about the body as a compact system of energies. Similarly, Yolmo people value what Desjarlais calls "kinaesthetic attentiveness", being in the sensible present, rather than dwelling in the past or future (*ibid.*: 78). The importance of corporeal attentiveness is reflected in the way in which people feel themselves to be unwell through its absence. This is in contrast to Leder's formulation of the lived body and illness, where "absence" of corporeal attentiveness is a sign of everyday well-being.

Phenomenological bioethics draws attention to the patient's experience of illness in the context of medical treatment. Merleau-Ponty's work asks us to think more carefully about the corporeal dimensions of that experience, especially in perceptual terms. In a healthcare setting, this leads to a focus upon the lived body within illness. Merleau-Ponty's own discussion of pathology manifests an interest in the specificity of lived conditions. His work informs the efforts of cultural phenomenologists to trace the ways in which culture, situation and corporeality interact. Their intercorporeal focus leads to the view that the nuances of everyday life espouse values concerning the body, health, illness, ethics and aesthetics. Sickness is inextricable from these socially sedimented nuances; health and illness, expressions of life, are marked by these milieus. Merleau-Ponty highlights the lived dimension of corporeality, the situational "thickness" that attends a richly differentiated conception of illness, one that touches on issues of culture, sensibility, rituals of the everyday, and modes of bodily attention. His work thereby paves the way for an understanding of medical ethics that is sensitive to the perceptual and situational specificities intrinsic to healthcare practice.

Further reading

Csordas, T. 1999. "Embodiment and Cultural Phenomenology". In *Perspectives on Embodiment: The Intersections of Nature and Culture*, G. Weiss & H. F. Haber (eds), 143–62. New York: Routledge.

Leder, D. 1992. "A Tale of Two Bodies, The Cartesian Corpse and the Lived Body". In *The Body in Medical Thought and Practice*, D. Leder (ed.), 17–35. Dordrecht: Kluwer.

Rothfield, P. 2005. "Attending to Difference, Phenomenology and Bioethics". In *Ethics of the Body: Postconventional Challenges*, M. Shildrick & R. Mykituik (eds), 29–48. Cambridge, MA: MIT Press.

Zaner, R. 1988. *Ethics and the Clinical Encounter*. Englewood Cliffs, NJ: Prentice Hall.

TWENTY-ONE

Sociology

Nick Crossley

References to Merleau-Ponty within sociology cluster around four themes. First, he was a central reference point in attempts during the 1970s to develop a phenomenological approach within sociology (e.g. Luckman 1978; Phillipson 1972; Psathas 1973; Roche 1973; O'Neill 1970, 1972; Spurling 1977). Some sociologists sought to re-shape sociology in a phenomenological fashion; some wanted to use phenomenology to advance a longstanding sociological interest in "the actor's point of view"; others were forging their own path but drew inspiration from phenomenology (e.g. Garfinkel 1967). In all cases, however, Merleau-Ponty was deemed important. Secondly, "embodiment" has become important within sociology over the last twenty years, and Merleau-Ponty has been identified as a key theorist of it (e.g. O'Neill 1989; Crossley 2001a). He offers an analysis of em-bodied human agency which allows sociologists to "bring the body back in", challenging a residual dualism which some have identified within the discipline. Furthermore, he offers an alternative concep-tion of "the body" which speaks to the concerns of sociologists much more directly than the mechanistic and objectivist models that other-wise tend to prevail. Thirdly, the resonance between and influence of Merleau-Ponty's thought upon that of Pierre Bourdieu, a (recently deceased) central figure of contemporary sociology, has regenerated interest in the former. Bourdieu seldom mentions Merleau-Ponty directly but his conceptions of embodiment, habit, the pre-reflective domain and reflexivity each resemble Merleau-Ponty's, and most commentators recognize a line of influence (Crossley 2001b). Finally, because both political philosophy and the philosophy of history over-lap with social theory, Merleau-Ponty's interventions in these areas have assumed importance too (O'Neill 1970, 1972; Schmidt 1985; Crossley 1994, 2001b, 2004; Smart 1976). His reflections on Marx-ism formed part of a wider debate that dominated European social theory for much of the 1970s and his attempt to wed Marxism and phenomenology informed sociological attempts to do the same.

The pathway between Merleau-Ponty's work and sociology is not unidirectional, however. Where Husserl and Heidegger attempted to distinguish their work from social science and protect it from scien-tific critique by way of conceptual distinctions (e.g. transcendental/ empirical, ontic/ontological), which, they believed, put phenomeno-logy in a different intellectual dimension, Merleau-Ponty's work dialogues with the social sciences. The social sciences are problematic for Merleau-Ponty if and when they seek to explain human behaviour and consciousness by reference to external mechanical causes. At the very least such accounts are self-defeating because they presuppose, in the form of the social scientist, the very knowing subject that their work either denies or undermines. However, he concedes that social scientists across a variety of disciplines either recognize this or at least circumvent the problem. Gestalt psychology, which treats conscious-ness as an irreducible structure and explains behaviour as a purposive response to events which have conscious meaning, is his key example of this, but he acknowledges that other disciplines too, including certain strands of sociology, are on the right side of the line. Social scientists who have taken this step, he argues, are aligned with phe-nomenology. Their position provides support for phenomenology, and phenomenologists have no basis for rejecting their work. Indeed, phenomenologists can learn from it because the research projects of social scientists reveal aspects of consciousness that are not other-wise available. Stratton's (1896, 1897) experiments with "inverting lenses", which Merleau-Ponty discusses in *Phenomenology of Per-ception*, for example, reveal aspects of perceptual consciousness and its relationship to motor activity which could not be known by philo-sophical meditation alone (PP: 206, 244–54). Likewise with Gelb and Goldstein's case study of the effects of brain injury upon the war casualty, Schneider – a case study that Merleau-Ponty discusses at length, particularly in Part One, "The Body" (see also Hammond *et al.* 1991: 162–77).

Merleau-Ponty does not defer to social science, however, nor does he take social-scientific interpretations at face value. Social-scientific findings become an occasion and resource for phenomenological reflection – reflection that may arrive at different conclusions to those of the author of those findings. Social-scientific research reveals facts about human consciousness and action that philosophy cannot wish away, but philosophy might discern significance in those facts that eludes the scientist. The philosopher can reframe social-scientific findings. Moreover, given this, Merleau-Ponty does not limit himself to a discussion of empirical work from social-scientific allies of phenomenology. Any form of social-scientific work can become a resource for phenomenological reflection.

Much of Merleau-Ponty's engagement with social science is centred upon psychology. He addresses sociology at a number of points, however, and his analyses often border on sociological territory (S: 98–113, 114–25; PrP: 43–95; AD: 2–29). He is constantly bumping up against sociology, often with an explicit awareness of doing so. In what follows I shall explore these "bumps" in an effort to elucidate the sociological assumptions in and significance of his thought. The definition of phenomenology in the Preface to *Phenomenology* provides an interesting way in.

Merleau-Ponty's phenomenology

Phenomenology has been defined in multiple and contradictory ways, according to Merleau-Ponty. He therefore elects to offer his own definition. Phenomenology, he notes, rejects any attempt to explain human behaviour or consciousness by reference to external mechanical causes. It is equally opposed to transcendental idealism, however – that is, to an account that reduces "the world" to human consciousness of it and which seeks to explain the consciously intended world by reference to constitutive acts of the ego alone. Reflective acts of consciousness, such as judgement or interpretation, presuppose perceptual materials that are, in these cases, judged or interpreted, he argues, and phenomenology must dig deeper and explore this primordial, pre-reflective perceptual level. Doing so, he continues, reveals a world that resists and surprises the perceiving subject, thereby casting doubt upon the notion that it is reducible to constitutive acts of consciousness. Phenomenologists know that their only means of access to the world is via consciousness and that, as such, it is impossible to satisfy the sceptic's demand for proof of the world's existence beyond consciousness. Within the bounds of the possible, however, the resistance of the world to one's attempts to know and change it provides a meaningful basis upon which to deem it "always already there" (PP: vii).

The role of the reduction within phenomenological method – that is, the demand that one bracket out reality claims in order to better explore intentional consciousness, can be misleading here because it seems to reduce the world to the subject's consciousness of it. Merleau-Ponty's use of the reduction is different, however. Intentionality, he argues, is connectedness to the world. To say that my consciousness intends a world is to say that it bonds me to the world; indeed, that it *is* a bond with the world. Phenomenology, as an explication of structures of consciousness, therefore, is an exploration of the meaningful bonds that connect us to a world which is always already there. It is, as Heidegger (1962) formulates it, an explication of being-in-the-world. Furthermore, echoing and developing Heidegger's notion of "readiness-to-hand", Merleau-Ponty extends the notion of intentionality to include the "operative intentionality" and embodied understanding involved in our motor activity. Intentionality is not only a matter of the way in which I perceive and think about objects in the world, but also the meaningful and knowledgeable way in which I handle and use them. My feet intend the pedals of my car when I drive, for example. The pedals exist for me by way of my use of them. Intentionality entails practical involvement in the world, in this respect. The purpose of the reduction, for Merleau-Ponty, is to bring to light and analyse these intentional threads, which connect us to the world. Suspending belief in the world, for methodological purposes, is sometimes the only way one can fully recognize and explore one's connection to it. And connection to the world makes us what we are:

> It is because we are through and through compounded of relationships with the world that for us the only way to become aware of that fact is to suspend the resultant activity, to refuse it our complicity . . . put it out of play. (PP: xiii)

> Reflection does not withdraw from the world towards the unity of consciousness as the world's basis; it steps back to watch the forms of transcendence fly up like sparks from a fire; it slackens the intentional threads which connect us to the world and thus brings them to our notice. (*Ibid.*)

Because the world throws up "sparks" of "transcendence", one of the most important lessons we learn from the reduction is "the impossibility of a complete reduction" (*ibid.*: xiv). However, in attempting this impossibility we achieve greater awareness of the intentional threads that characterize our being-in-the-world, and that is the point.

This definition of phenomenology has a twofold significance for sociology. First, the notion that subjects are always already practically involved in the world ("situated") echoes the claims of many sociologists and connects with sociological efforts to investigate such situations. Sociology, as Merleau-Ponty sometimes portrays it, assumes an external perspective on human behaviour and consciousness. This is a skewed perception of sociology (past or present). Even if he is right, however, phenomenology converges with sociology when it explicates being-in-the-world and treats subjectivity as situated. It explores from within what sociology explores from without. The two disciplines become opposite sides of the same coin: different but potentially mutually informative perspectives. Secondly, the theme of relationality is sociologically resonant. Sociologists do not study human beings as isolated atoms but rather as connected nodes. Interactions and relations are the "stuff" of the social world. The phenomenology of intentional consciousness extends wider than inter-human ties, of course, but Merleau-Ponty attaches special signi-ficance to inter-human relations. When, in the closing line of *Phenomenology of Perception*, for example, he claims that "Man is but a network of relationships, and these alone matter to him" (PP: 456), the relationships he has in mind are inter-human. Furthermore, he includes here such institutionalized ("sociological") relations as those between fellow citizens or workers and bosses. In the chapter from which this quotation is drawn, for example, he discusses the historical formation of class consciousness amongst the proletariat (*ibid.*: 442–8) and he argues that the strength that allows prisoners of war to resist torture derives not from "within" but from bonds with comrades, family and collective projects (*ibid.*: 453–4). The meaning, values and identities that give form and direction to our lives, he maintains, derive from our relations with others. On this point he echoes much sociology.

This point is further developed when, on several occasions, Merleau-Ponty challenges the Cartesian assumptions underlying the "problem of other minds" (i.e. how to establish the existence of others). Cartesianism encourages us to regard human behaviour as a mere outward effect of an internal event, he argues, such that shaking my fist might be deemed an effect of the anger I am experiencing internally. This is problematic because it raises the question of how and if I can legitimately infer anger, or indeed any "internal life", from the behaviour of others. How do I know that the behaviour of the other expresses an inner life akin to my own and is not rather a mere mechanical effect? Like Gilbert Ryle (1949), Merleau-Ponty rejects the "doubling up" of inside and outside involved here. Anger is not an inner state, antecedent to and generative of angry behaviour, he argues. It consists in ways of behaving (including speech, comportment and perception) in relation to a context and intended object. There is no inner realm behind or before such behaviour, and even the felt sensations that might accompany it acquire meaning only by reference to it and to its context. As such, anger and other subjective states are not "within" the subject: "The location of my anger . . . is in the space we both share" (WP: 84). They are intersubjective. Pushing the point further, Merleau-Ponty argues that he learns about his own subjective life only by way of a reflection upon his conduct, upon the reactions of others to it and by internalizing the schemas and theories of psychological attribution and description that his peers practice:

> The adult himself will discover in his own life what his culture, education, books and tradition have taught him to find there. The contact I make with myself is always mediated by a particular culture, or at least by a language that we have received from without and which guides us in our self-knowledge.
>
> (*Ibid.*: 86–7)

Others enter into the very reflexive processes constitutive of self, therefore, and the atomism that characterizes certain of Husserl's formulations of phenomenology is replaced by a relational framework. There is no self without the other, no primordial "sphere of ownness", such as Husserl refers to in *Cartesian Meditations*, and our knowledge of the other is not reducible to our knowledge of self. Rather, we achieve knowledge of both self and other by way of interactions with others in the "between space" or "interworld" of our everyday social lives. This rejection of a Cartesian "inner world" and of immediate self-knowledge, combined with his emphasis upon culture and social interaction, constitutes a clear sociological slant in Merleau-Ponty's phenomenology and facilitates a dialogue with sociological theory and research. Self and subjectivity belong and take shape within the public, socio-cultural world that sociology investigates.

Culture and collective consciousness

A phenomenology of social relations and self-hood that sought, building upon these claims, to illuminate their meaning and structure would make an important contribution to sociology. The phenomenologist Alfred Schütz (e.g. 1973) made such a contribution, building upon the work of Max Weber, a founding figure of sociology. Merleau-Ponty, like Schütz, advances much further into sociological territory than this, however. He calls for a phenomenology of collective life and history, or perhaps rather a collective and historical phenomenology. In *The Crisis of the European Sciences* (*Crisis* hereafter), he notes, Husserl recognizes the shared ways of thinking that characterize particular societies at particular times and that can be shown to have developed over extended historical periods. The thought of the average European, for example, evidences concepts and procedures that belong to the history of European culture and science, and one can trace the emergence of those concepts and procedures. Phenomenology, as Merleau-Ponty characterizes it, takes three "sociological" steps here. First, it moves from the individual to the collective. This involves a recognition that concepts and patterns of reasoning are shared and that, to quote a passage from *Crisis* that Merleau-Ponty frequently returns to, "transcendental subjectivity is intersubjectivity". In other words, the underlying architecture of human thought derives not from within human beings but from interactions between them and the sediments of these interactions that crystallize in or rather as culture, albeit sometimes only just long enough for them to be taken up and modified in subsequent interactions. Secondly, it opens up the possibility of what Merleau-Ponty calls "intentional history" – that is, invoking Hegelian phenomenology, an exploration of how particular plot lines emerge within the historical process that those involved in that process are not always fully aware of. Thirdly, it opens up a dialogue with sociologists, historians and anthropologists, since it is these empirical disciplines that provide the data and observations that afford one access to the collective mind *qua* culture.

Merleau-Ponty cites a letter from Husserl to the anthropologist Lévi-Bruhl in this connection, in which the founder of phenomenology concedes that the variations in thought revealed in ethnography exceed those imagined in his own philosophical meditations and pose a serious challenge for philosophy (S: 107–13; PrP: 90–92). They reveal the social relativity of knowledge. *Prima facie* this relativity might seem to privilege the social sciences which have discovered it and to undermine philosophical attempts to ground knowledge and truth, Merleau-Ponty notes, but relativistic claims within social science are self-undermining, and the task of working through the implications of the "fact" of relativism falls to the philosopher. Philosophers need to rethink their conceptions of truth and knowledge in a way that does not exclude history and social inherence. Knowledge and truth must be recognized as historical accomplishments and we should recognize that universals can arise out of particularlity. Moreover, knowledge can never be treated, as a caricatured sociology of knowledge might suggest, as a "thing" to be explained by reference to external causes. Knowledge, because human, is influenced by everything that influences human life, but it has an inside and it is only by approaching it from within, by seeking to grasp it as a part of a continuous intersubjective fabric to which we belong, that the paradox of relativism can be avoided.

Concrete intersubjectivity

Merleau-Ponty's concept of collective life and history overlaps with the sociologist's, creating a pathway between the two. This is a pathway with many twists and turns, however. On Merleau-Ponty's reading, as noted above, sociology is inclined to imagine that it can approach society from the position of an external observer and tends to treat the various "parts" of society as independent elements with a "thing-like" nature whose interrelations are mechanistic and causal. His stereotypical sociologist might, for example, claim that a particular pattern of kinship is the effect of wider social causes or forces. He rejects such objectivism. Social relations and practices are meaningful, he argues. They comprise intersubjective praxes and sociologists only ever have access to them by way of their own intersubjective involvement in them. Kinship patterns are not things caused by other things, such as economies, but rather patterns of meaningful activity that are woven together with other patterns of meaningful activity (e.g. economic activity) in the lives of individuals and collectives. Many sociologists agree with this, so the critique is arguably misplaced. However, it is important because it reveals the value and role that Merleau-Ponty envisages for sociology. He is calling for sociology to become more phenomenological, but also for phenomenology to engage with sociology. Specifically, in arguing that social relations be understood in terms of intersubjectivity, he is pushing that concept far beyond the Husserlian parameters and into sociological territory.

"Concrete intersubjectivity", as he calls it, is a web of meaningful relations, "mediated by things" and involving interdependencies and inequalities that, in turn, generate power, alienation and exploitation. In part this entails a Hegelian conception of the interdependence of human subjectivities affected by the desire for recognition. More centrally, however, it entails the relations of economic and political interdependence identified in Marxist sociology – relations that are mediated by the means of production (which, in turn, are relations to the physical world). It is necessary to reflect briefly upon this dialogue with Marx.

Marx and beyond

Marx had clear ideas about the "plot" of history. Capitalism, he argued, is *en route* to its own destruction by way of workers' revolution. Moreover, he famously inverts Hegel's idealism into a new materialism. These ideas were very important to Merleau-Ponty but he was cautious in his reception of them. Some versions of Marxism proffer an overly reductive view of history, he claimed. Marx is right in his contention, *contra* Hegel, that "history does not walk on its head", but neither does it "think with its feet" (PP: xix). Putting that another way, Merleau-Ponty objects to the primacy afforded to economic relations by some Marxists and the notion that history is propelled and steered, in a law-like manner, by economic dynamics. Everything in human society is affected by everything else, he argues, and there is no good philosophical reason to abstract and prioritize one set of relations within this configuration. However, he concedes that we may grant a priority to economic relations in practice, if they prove to be an effective predictor of historical movement. And in his early work on history and politics he is prepared to accept that they might (HT; SNS).

These arguments are sociologically significant. Many sociologists in the 1960s and 1970s debated the primacy of economic relations. As it happened, Merleau-Ponty had abandoned Marxism in the mid-1950s, not least because of revelations regarding the Gulags, which he felt were becoming institutionalized and self-perpetuating. His post-Marxist reflections on society and history, which tend in two different directions, entail further engagement with sociology, however.

On one hand, he begins to reflect on the work of the sociological pioneer, Max Weber (AD). Weber was a sympathetic critic of Marx, but what most attracted Merleau-Ponty to him were his reflections upon meaning and understanding, and his recognition of contingency and unintended consequences in history. History, for Weber, bears meaning in the sense that it does for Merleau-Ponty, and he emphasizes both the necessity of grasping meaning from within and the location of the interpreter him/herself within history. Moreover, he recognizes that our grasp on this meaning is always tenuous, is reconstructed on the basis of present concerns and that historical plot lines are inclined to fade or shift direction before reaching their projected denouement. These emphases resonate with Merleau-Ponty's own position. Indeed, much that Merleau-Ponty argues regarding the philosophy of history and social science, throughout his career, echoes Weber. These overlaps undermine much of Merleau-Ponty's critique of sociology. Weber (1978) was advocating and practising the type of sociology called for by Merleau-Ponty generations before Merleau-Ponty, and he had a huge influence upon sociology. At the same time, however, the overlaps constitute an important bridge from Merleau-Ponty's phenomenology to sociology.

Merleau-Ponty's second key "post-Marxist" excursion centred on "structure". "Structure" had preoccupied him from his very early reflections upon Gestalt psychology. His later work, however, is rooted in an idiosyncratic reading of Saussure's structural linguistics. He argues that a modified version of Saussure's "structure" could serve as the anchor point for a new and more persuasive philosophy of history and society (EP). This is not the place to examine this claim, but it is important to note that it once again brings Merleau-Ponty into dialogue with sociology. In an important essay in *Signs* he traces a trajectory in French social science running from Durkheim's sociology, to Lévi-Strauss's structural anthropology, via Durkheim's nephew and student, Mauss (S: 114–25). There is, he argues, a break between the old sociology and the new social anthropology, rooted in the fact that the latter recognizes that

> the social, like man [sic] himself, has two poles or facets; it is significant, capable of being understood from within, and at the same time personal intentions within it are generalized, toned down, and tend toward processes, being (as the famous expression has it) mediated by things. (S: 114)

There is a place for sociological "objectivism" according to this quotation. Intersubjective life has another side which is not accessible from within and which requires a different observational vantage point. But this does not negate the intersubjective interior of social life and a thorough sociology should address both. The concept of structure, for Merleau-Ponty, allows us to capture and develop this two-sidedness: to focus upon the fuzzy, messy and imprecise ways in which individuals act and make sense of their world (akin to Saussure's *parole*), but then also to step back and abstract from lived praxis in order to model its externally observable regularities (as Saussure does with *langue*) – regularities that, as in language use, agents reproduce and orient towards without full recognition of doing so.

Much of the force of Merleau-Ponty's discussion of this is focused on its sociological implications. The "social facts", which are so central to Durkheim's sociology, should not be conceived as "things", as Durkheim argued, nor as "ideas", Merleau-Ponty contends, but rather as two-sided structures. Moreover, as such, it is no longer appropriate to treat social institutions as effects of society. Patterns of exchange, *qua* structure, for example, cannot be deemed an effect of society but must rather be conceived as "society itself in act". Society, in other words, is "done" by way of the structured activity of its members. There are philosophical lessons to be learned from the concept of structure too, however. Specifically, it

> points to a way beyond the subject–object correlation that has dominated philosophy from Descartes to Hegel. By showing us that man is eccentric to himself and that structure finds its center only in man, structure enables us to understand how we are in a sort of circuit with the socio-historical world.
>
> (S: 123)

The notions that human beings both make and are made by society, in a "circuit", and that individuals' actions and words draw upon collective conventions for their meaning, making the former "eccentric" to their selves, are present in Durkheim and are not as revolutionary as Merleau-Ponty suggests, therefore. This claim has the effect, however, of opening up a new point of interaction between philosophy and sociology. The sociological exploration of social structures, Merleau-Ponty believes, serves the needs and interests of philosophers by revealing the depth of "our insertion in being" (*ibid.*). It contributes to an explication of our being-in-the-world.

Merleau-Ponty was a profoundly social and even sociological philosopher. Much that he argues overlaps with the claims of sociologists in a manner that facilitates mutual enrichment. His explicit dialogues with sociology were sometimes hampered by the relatively restricted view he had of the discipline, but if we allow for this then we can read his recommendations as a call for sociology to become more phenomenological, a call that resonates with his own desire for phenomenology to engage with the socio-historical world in a concrete and engaged manner. It is doubtless for these reasons that his work has had the impact on sociology noted at this beginning of this chapter.

Further reading

Crossley, N. 2001. "Merleau-Ponty". In *Profiles in Contemporary Social Theory*, B. Turner & A. Elliott (eds), 30–42. London: Sage.

Crossley, N. 2004. "Phenomenology, Structuralism and History: Merleau-Ponty's Social Theory", *Theoria* 103, 88–121.

O'Neill, J. 1970. *Perception, Expression and History: The Social Phenomenology of Merleau-Ponty*. Evanston, IL: Northwestern University Press.

Schmidt, J. 1985. *Maurice Merleau-Ponty: Between Phenomenology and Structuralism*. London: Macmillan.

References

Abram, D. 1996. *The Spell of the Sensuous: Perception and Language in a More-Than-Human World*. New York: Random House.

Acampora, R. R. 2006. *Corporal Compassion: Animal Ethics and Philosophy of Body*. Pittsburgh, PA: University of Pittsburgh Press.

Adams, H. 2001. "Merleau-Ponty and the Advent of Meaning: From Consummate Reciprocity to Ambiguous Reversibility", *Continental Philosophy Review* **34**, 203–24.

Alcoff, L. 2006. *Visible Identities*. Oxford: Oxford University Press.

Archer, M. 2000. *Being Human: The Problem of Agency*. Cambridge: Cambridge University Press.

Barbaras, R. 2004. *The Being of the Phenomenon: Merleau-Ponty's Ontology*, T. Toadvine & L. Lawlor (trans.). Bloomington, IN: Indiana University Press.

Barbaras, R. 2006. *Desire and Distance: Introduction to a Phenomenology of Perception*, P. B. Milan (trans.). Stanford, CA: Stanford University Press.

Baron, R. 1992. "Why Aren't More Doctors Phenomenologists?". In *The Body in Medical Thought and Practice*, D. Leder (ed.), 37–47. Dordrecht: Kluwer.

Bartky, S. L. 1990. *Femininity and Domination: Studies in the Phenomenology of Oppression*. London: Routledge.

Becker, A. E. 1994. "Nurturing and Negligence, Working on Others' Bodies in Fiji". In *Embodiment and Experience: The Existential Ground of Culture and Self*, T. Csordas, (ed.), 100–115. Cambridge: Cambridge University Press.

Behnke, E. A. 1999. "From Merleau-Ponty's Concept of Nature to an Interspecies Practice of Peace". In *Animal Others: On Ethics, Ontology, and Animal Life*, H. P. Steeves (ed.), 93–116. Albany, NY: SUNY Press.

Berkeley, G. 1950. *A Treatise Concerning the Principles of Human Knowledge*. La Salle, IL: Open Court.

Bernet, R., I. Kern & E. Marbach 1993. *An Introduction to Husserlian Phenomenology*. Evanston, IL: Northwestern University Press.

Busch, T. W. 1992. "Ethics and Ontology: Levinas and Merleau-Ponty", *Man and World* 25, 195–202.

Busch, T. & S. Gallagher (eds) 1992. *Merleau-Ponty, Hermeneutics and Post-modernism*. Albany, NY: SUNY Press.

Butler, J. 1989. "Sexual Ideology and Phenomenological Description: A Feminist Critique of Merleau-Ponty's 'Phenomenology of Perception'". In *The Thinking Muse: Feminism and Modern French Philosophy*, J. Allen & I. M. Young (eds), 85–100. Bloomington, IN: Indiana University Press.

Butler, J. 1990. *Gender Trouble*. New York: Routledge.

Carman, T. 2008. *Merleau-Ponty*. London: Routledge.

Carman, T. & M. Hansen (eds) 2005. *The Cambridge Companion to Merleau-Ponty*. Cambridge: Cambridge University Press.

Casey, E. S. 1984. "Habitual Body and Memory in Merleau-Ponty", *Man and World* 17, 279–97.

Cassell, E. 1985. *Talking with Patients*, Vol. 2. Cambridge, MA: MIT Press.

Cataldi, S. L. 1993. *Emotion, Depth, and Flesh: A Study of Sensitive Space: Reflections on Merleau-Ponty's Philosophy of Embodiment*. Albany, NY: SUNY Press.

Cataldi, S. L. 2000. "Embodying Perceptions of Death: Emotional Apprehension and Reversibilities of Flesh". In *Chiasms: Merleau-Ponty's Notion of Flesh*, F. Evans & L. Lawlor (eds), 189–202. Albany, NY: SUNY Press.

Cerbone, D. R. 2006. *Understanding Phenomenology*. Chesham: Acumen.

Churchill, S. D. 2001. "Intercorporeality, Gestural Communication, and the Voices of Silence: Towards a Phenomenological Ethology – Part Two", *Somatics* Spring, 40–45.

Churchill, S. D. 2003. "Gestural Communication with a Bonobo: Empathy, Alterity, and Carnal Intersubjectivity", *Constructivism and the Human Sciences* 8(1), 19–36.

Churchill, S. D. 2006. "Encountering the Animal Other: Reflections on Moments of Empathic Seeing", *The Indo-Pacific Journal of Phenomenology* 6, August, 1–13.

Churchill, S. D. 2007. "Experiencing the Other within the We: Phenomenology with a Bonobo". In *Phenomenology 2005, Vol. IV*, L. Embree & T. Nenon (eds), ch. 6. Bucharest: Zeta E-Books.

Cohen-Solal, A. 2005. *Jean-Paul Sartre: A Life*. New York: The New Press.

Coole, D. 2003. "Philosophy as Political Engagement: Revisiting Merleau-Ponty and Reopening the Communist Question", *Contemporary Political Theory* vol. 2, 327–50.

Coole, D. 2005. "Rethinking Agency: A Phenomenological Approach to Embodiment and Agentic Capacities", *Political Studies* 53(1), 124–42.

Coole, D. 2007a. "Experiencing Discourse: Gendered Styles and the Embodiment of Power", *British Journal of Politics and International Relations* 9(3), 413–33.

Coole, D. 2007b. *Merleau-Ponty and Modern Politics after Anti-Humanism*. Lanham, MD: Rowman & Littlefield.

Cooper, B. 1979. *Merleau-Ponty and Marxism: From Terror to Reform*. Toronto: Toronto University Press.

Corradi Fiumara, G. 2001. *The Mind's Affective Life: A Psychoanalytic and Philosophical Enquiry*. East Sussex: Brunner Routledge.

Crossley, N. 1994. *The Politics of Subjectivity: Between Foucault and Merleau-Ponty*. Aldershot: Ashgate.

Crossley, N. 2001a. *The Social Body: Habit, Identity and Desire*. London: Sage.

Crossley, N. 2001b. "Merleau-Ponty". In *Profiles in Contemporary Social Theory*, B. Turner & A. Elliott (eds), 30–42. London: Sage.

Crossley, N. 2004. "Phenomenology, Structuralism and History: Merleau-Ponty's Social Theory", *Theoria* 103, 88–121.

Csordas, T. 1993. "Somatic Modes of Attention", *Cultural Anthropology* 8, 135–56.

Csordas, T. (ed.) 1994. *Embodiment and Experience: The Existential Ground of Culture and Self*. Cambridge: Cambridge University Press.

Csordas, T. 1997. *The Sacred Self: A Cultural Phenomenology of Charismatic Healing*. Berkeley, CA: University of California Press.

Csordas, T. 1999. "Embodiment and Cultural Phenomenology". In *Perspectives on Embodiment: The Intersections of Nature and Culture*, G. Weiss & H. F. Haber (eds), 143–62. New York: Routledge.

De Beauvoir, S. 1963. *Force of Circumstance*. Harmondsworth: Penguin.

De Beauvoir, S. 1989. *The Second Sex*, H. M. Parshley (trans.). New York: Vintage.

De Beauvoir, S. 1997. *The Ethics of Ambiguity*, B. Frechtman (trans.). New York: Citadel.

De Beauvoir, S. 2004. "A Review of *Phenomenology of Perception* by Merleau-Ponty (1945)". In *Simone de Beauvoir: Philosophical Writings*, M. Timmerman (trans.), 159–64. Urbana, IL: University of Illinois Press.

Dennett, D. 1991. *Consciousness Explained*. Boston, MA: Little, Brown.

Dennett, D. 1994. "Tiptoeing past the Covered Wagons". In "Dennett and Carr Further Explained: An Exchange", *Emory Cognition Project*, Report 28, Department of Psychology, Emory University, April. http://ase.tufts.edu/cogstud/papers/tiptoe.htm

Dennett, D. 2007. "Heterophenomenology reconsidered", *Phenomenology and the Cognitive Sciences* 6, 1–2.

Descartes, R. 1985. *The Philosophical Writings of Descartes*, Vol. II, J. Cottingham *et al.* (eds). Cambridge: Cambridge University Press.

Desjarlais, R. 1992. *Body and Emotion: The Aesthetics of Illness and Healing in the Nepal Himalyas*. Philadelphia, PA: University of Pennsylvania Press.

Dewey, J. 1958. *Art as Experience*. New York: Capricorn Books.

Dillon, M. C. 1997. *Merleau-Ponty's Ontology*, 2nd edn. Evanston, IL: Northwestern University Press.

Dillon, M. (ed.) 1997. *Ecart & Différance: Merleau-Ponty and Derrida on Seeing and Writing*. Amherst, NY: Prometheus.

Diprose, R. 1994. *The Bodies of Women: Ethics, Embodiment and Sexual Difference*. London: Routledge.

Diprose, R. 2002. *Corporeal Generosity: On Giving with Nietzsche, Merleau-Ponty, and Levinas*. New York: SUNY Press.

Dreyfus, H. 1992. *What Computers Still Can't Do*. Cambridge, MA: MIT Press.

Dreyfus, H. 2005. "Merleau-Ponty and Recent Cognitive Science". In *The Cambridge Companion to Merleau-Ponty*, T. Carman & M. Hansen (eds), 129–50. Cambridge: Cambridge University Press.

Evans, F. 1998. "'Solar Love': Nietzsche, Merleau-Ponty, and the Fortunes of Perception", *Continental Philosophy Review* 31, 177–93.

Evans, F. & L. Lawlor (eds) 2000. *Chiasms: Merleau-Ponty's Notion of Flesh.* Albany, NY: SUNY Press.

Fanon, F. 1967. *Black Skin White Masks*, C. L. Markmann (trans.). New York: Grove Press.

Fóti, V. (ed.) 1996. *Merleau-Ponty: Difference, Materiality, Painting.* Atlantic Highlands, NJ: Humanities Press.

Francis, C. & F. Gontier 1988. *Simone de Beauvoir: A Life, A Love Story.* New York: St Martin's Press.

Frank, A. 1995. *The Wounded Storyteller: Body, Illness and Ethics.* Chicago, IL: University of Chicago Press.

Freud, S. 1975. *The Psychopathology of Everyday Life* (SE Vol. VI), Pelican Freud Library Vol. 5, J. Strachey (trans.). Harmondsworth: Penguin.

Freud, S. 1984. "The Unconscious" (SE Vol. XIV) in *On Metapsychology – The Theory of Psychoanalysis*, Pelican Freud Library Vol. 11, J. Strachey (trans.). Harmondsworth: Penguin.

Gallagher, S. 1986. "Lived Body and Environment", *Research in Phenomenology* **16**, 139–70.

Gallagher, S. 1995. "Body Schema and Intentionality". In *The Body and the Self*, J. L. Bermúdez, A. Marcel & N. Eilan (eds), 225–44. Cambridge, MA: MIT Press.

Gallagher, S. 2003. "Phenomenology and Experimental Design", *Journal of Consciousness Studies* **10**, 9–10.

Gallagher, S. 2005. *How the Body Shapes the Mind.* Oxford: Oxford University Press.

Gallagher, S. 2007. "Simulation Trouble", *Social Neuroscience* **2**(1), 1–13.

Gallagher, S. & J. B. Sørensen 2006. "Experimenting with Phenomenology", *Consciousness and Cognition* **15**, 119–34.

Gallese, V. 2001. "The 'Shared Manifold' Hypothesis: From Mirror Neurons to Empathy", *Journal of Consciousness Studies* **8**, 33–50.

Gallese, V. & A. Goldman 1998. "Mirror Neurons and the Simulation Theory of Mindreading", *Trends in Cognitive Sciences* **2**, 493–501.

Garfinkel, H. 1967. *Studies in Ethnomethodology.* Englewood Cliffs, NJ: Prentice Hall.

Gatens, M. 1996. *Imaginary Bodies: Ethics, Power, and Corporeality.* London: Routledge.

Gibson, J. 1979. *The Ecological Approach to Visual Perception.* Boston, MA: Houghton Mifflin.

Gibson, N. 2003. "Losing Sight of the Real: Recasting Merleau-Ponty in Fanon's Critique of Mannoni". In *Race and Racism in Continental Philosophy*, R. Bernasconi (ed.), 129–50. Bloomington, IN: Indiana University Press.

Goehr, L. 2005. "Understanding the Engaged Philosopher: On Politics, Philosophy, and Art". In *The Cambridge Companion to Merleau-Ponty*, T. Carman & M. Hansen (eds), 318–51. Cambridge: Cambridge University Press.

Goldman, A. 2005. "Imitation, Mind Reading, and Simulation". In *Perspectives on Imitation* II, S. Hurley & N. Chater (eds), 79–94. Cambridge, MA: MIT Press.

Goldman, A. 2006. *Simulating Minds: The Philosophy, Psychology and Neuroscience of Mindreading.* Oxford: Oxford University Press.

Grosz, E. 1994. *Volatile Bodies: Toward a Corporeal Feminism.* Bloomington, IN: Indiana University Press.

Gunaratnam, Y. 1997. "Culture Is Not Enough: A Critique of Multi-Culturalism in Palliative Care". In *Death, Gender and Ethnicity*, D. Field, J. Hockey & N. Small (eds), 166–85. London: Routledge.

Haar, M. 1996. "Painting, Perception, Affectivity". In *Merleau-Ponty: Difference, Materiality, Painting*, V. Fóti (trans. and ed.), 177–93. Atlantic Highlands, NJ: Humanities Press.

Hammond, M., J. Howarth & R. Keat 1991. *Understanding Phenomenology*. Oxford: Blackwell.

Hass, L. & D. Olkowski (eds) 2000. *Rereading Merleau-Ponty: Essays Beyond the Continental–Analytical Divide*. Amherst, NY: Humanity Books.

Heidegger, M. 1962. *Being and Time*, J. MacQuarrie & E. Robinson (trans.). New York: Harper & Row.

Heidegger, M. 1976. "Language". In *Poetry, Language, Thought*, A. Hofstadter (trans.). New York: Harper & Row.

Heidegger, M. 1997. *Kant and the Problem of Metaphysics*, R. Taft (trans.). Bloomington, IN: Indiana University Press.

Heidegger, M. 1995. *The Fundamental Concepts of Metaphysics: World, Finitude, Solitude*, W. McNeill & N. Walker (trans.). Bloomington, IN: Indiana University Press.

Heinämaa, S. 2003. *Toward a Phenomenology of Sexual Difference: Husserl, Merleau-Ponty, Beauvoir*. Lanham, MD: Rowman & Littlefield.

Heinämaa, S. 2004. "Introduction to 'A Review of *Phenomenology of Perception* by Merleau-Ponty'". In *Simone de Beauvoir: Philosophical Writings*, M. A. Simons with M. Timmerman & M. Mader (eds), 153–8. Urbana, IL: University of Illinois Press.

Hume, D. 2000. *A Treatise of Human Nature*, D. F. Norton & M. J. Norton (eds). Oxford: Oxford University Press.

Husserl, E. 1967. *Cartesian Meditations: An Introduction to Phenomenology*, D. Cairns (trans.). The Hague: Martinus Nijhoff.

Husserl, E. 1970. *The Crisis of the European Sciences and Transcendental Phenomenology*. Evanston, IL: Northwestern University Press.

Husserl, E. 1982 [1913]. *Ideas Pertaining to a Pure Phenomenology and to a Phenomenological Philosophy, First Book*, F. Kersten (trans.). Dordrecht: Kluwer.

Husserl, E. 1989 [1928]. *Ideas Pertaining to a Pure Phenomenology and to a Phenomenological Philosophy, Second Book: Studies in the Phenomenology of Constitution*, R. Rojcewicz & A. Schuwer (trans.). Dordrecht: Kluwer.

Irigaray, L. 1993. *An Ethics of Sexual Difference*, C. Burke & G. C. Gill (trans.). Ithaca, NY: Cornell University Press.

James, W. 1950. *Principles of Psychology*. New York: Henry Holt.

Johnson, G. & M. B. Smith (eds) 1990. *Ontology and Alterity in Merleau-Ponty*. Evanston, IL: Northwestern University Press.

Kant, I. 1998. *Critique of Pure Reason*, P. Guyer & A. W. Wood (trans.). Cambridge: Cambridge University Press.

Kelly, S. D. 2005. "Seeing Things in Merleau-Ponty". In *The Cambridge Companion to Merleau-Ponty*, T. Carman & M. Hansen (eds), 74–110. Cambridge: Cambridge University Press.

Köhler, W. 1947. *Gestalt Psychology: An Introduction to New Concepts in Modern Psychology*. New York: Liveright.

Köhler, W. 1976 [1925]. *The Mentality of Apes*, E. Winter (trans.). New York: Liveright.

Kruks, S. 1981. *The Political Philosophy of Merleau-Ponty*. Brighton: Harvester.

Kruks, S. 1990. *Situation and Human Existence: Freedom, Subjectivity, and Society*. London: Unwin Hyman.

Kruks, S. 2001. *Retrieving Experience: Subjectivity and Recognition in Feminist Politics*. Ithaca, NY: Cornell University Press.

Lacan, J. 1977. *Ecrits: A Selection*, A. Sheridan (trans.). London: Tavistock

Langer, M. 2003. "Beauvoir and Merleau-Ponty on Ambiguity". In *The Cambridge Companion to Simone de Beauvoir*, C. Card (ed.), 87–106. Cambridge: Cambridge University Press.

Lawlor, L. 1998. "The End of Phenomenology: Expressionism in Deleuze and Merleau-Ponty", *Continental Philosophy Review* 31(1), 15–34.

Lawlor, L. 2006. *The Implications of Immanence: Toward a New Concept of Life*. New York: Fordham University Press.

Leder, D. 1990. *The Absent Body*. Chicago, IL: University of Chicago Press.

Leder, D. 1992. "A Tale of Two Bodies: The Cartesian Corpse and the Lived Body". In *The Body in Medical Thought and Practice*, D. Leder (ed.), 17–35. Dordrecht: Kluwer.

Lefort, C. 2005. "Thinking Politics". In *The Cambridge Companion to Merleau-Ponty*, T. Carman & M. Hansen (eds), 352–79. Cambridge: Cambridge University Press.

Levin, D. M. 1997. "Tracework: Myself and Others in the Moral Phenomenology of Merleau-Ponty and Levinas", *International Journal of Philosophical Studies* 6(3), 345–92.

Levinas, E. 1969 [1961]. *Totality and Infinity*, A. Lingis (trans.). Pittsburgh, PA: Duquesne University Press.

Levinas, E. 1978. *Existence and Existants*, A. Lingis (trans.). The Hague: Martinus Nijhoff.

Levinas, E. 1987. *Collected Philosophical Papers*, A. Lingis (trans.). Dortdrecht: Martinus Nijhoff.

Levinas, E. 1993. "On Intersubjectivity: Notes on Merleau-Ponty" and "On Sensibility". In *Outside the Subject*, M. B. Smith (trans.), 96–103; 107–15. Stanford, CA: Stanford University Press.

Levinas, E. 1996 [1964]. "Meaning and Sense", A. Lingis (trans.). In *Basic Philosophical Writings*, A. Peperzakm, S. Critchley & R. Bernasconi (eds), 33–64. Bloomington, IN: Indiana University Press.

Levinas, E. 1998 [1974]. *Otherwise than Being*, A. Lingis (trans.). Pittsburgh, PA: Duquesne University Press.

Lingis, A. 1994. *Foreign Bodies*. New York: Routledge.

Lingis, A. 2000. *Dangerous Emotions*. Berkeley, CA: University of California Press.

Low, D. 2000. *Merleau-Ponty's Last Vision: A Proposal for the Completion of "The Visible and the Invisible"*. Evanston, IL: Northwestern University Press.

Luckman, T. 1978. *Phenomenology and Sociology*. Harmondsworth: Penguin.

Madison, G. B. 1981. *The Phenomenology of Merleau-Ponty: A Search for the Limits of Consciousness*. Athens, OH: Ohio University Press.

Madison, G. B. 1988. *The Hermeneutics of Postmodernity: Figures and Themes*. Bloomington, IN: Indiana University Press.

Madison, G. 1991. "Merleau-Ponty's Destruction of Logocentrism". In *Merleau-Ponty Vivant*, M. Dillon (ed.), 117–52. Albany, NY: SUNY Press.

Malebranche, N. 1997. *The Search After Truth*, T. M. Lennon & P. J. Olscamp (eds). Cambridge: Cambridge University Press.

Marbach, E. 1993. *Mental Representation and Consciousness*. Dordrecht: Kluwer.

Marbach, E. 2007. "No Heterophenomenology without Autophenomenology: Variations on a Theme of Mine", *Phenomenology and the Cognitive Sciences* 6, 1–2.

May, R., E. Angel & H. F. Ellenberger (eds) 1958. *Existence: A New Dimension in Psychiatry and Psychology*. New York: Basic Books.

Mazis, G. 1993. *Emotion and Embodiment: Fragile Ontology*. New York: Peter Lang.

Miller, J. 1979. *History and Human Existence: From Marx to Merleau-Ponty*. Berkeley, CA: University of California Press.

Murphy, A. 2006. "Language in the Flesh: The Politics of Discourse in Merleau-Ponty, Levinas, and Irigaray". In *Feminist Interpretations of Merleau-Ponty*, D. Olkowski & G. Weiss (eds), 257–71. University Park, PA: Pennsylvania State University Press.

Olkowski, D. & J. Morley (eds) 1999. *Merleau-Ponty, Interiority and Exteriority, Psychic Life, and the World*. Albany, NY: SUNY Press.

Olkowski, D. & G. Weiss (eds) 2006. *Feminist Interpretations of Merleau-Ponty*. University Park, PA: Pennsylvania State University Press.

O'Neill, J. 1970. *Perception, Expression and History: The Social Phenomenology of Merleau-Ponty*. Evanston, IL: Northwestern University Press.

O'Neill, J. 1972. *Sociology as a Skin Trade*. London: Heinemann.

O'Neill, J. 1989. *The Communicative Body*. Evanston: Northwestern University Press.

Phillipson, M. 1972. "Phenomenological Philosophy and Sociology". In *New Directions in Sociological Theory*, P. Filmer, M. Phillipson, D. Silverman & D. Walsh (eds), 119–63. London: Macmillan.

Portmann, A. 1967. *Animal Forms and Patterns: A Study of the Appearances of Animals*, H. Czech (trans.). New York: Schocken.

Psathas, G. 1973. *Phenomenological Sociology*. New York: Wiley.

Purtilo, R. & A. Haddad 2002. *Health Professional and Patient Interaction*, 6th edn. Philadelphia, PA: W. B. Saunders.

Reynolds, J. 2004. *Merleau-Ponty and Derrida: Intertwining Embodiment and Alterity*. Athens, OH: Ohio University Press.

Risser, J. 1993. "Communication and the Prose of the World: The Question of Language in Merleau-Ponty and Gadamer". In *Merleau-Ponty in Contemporary Perspective*, Patrick Burke & Jan Van der Veken (eds), 131–44. Dordrecht: Kluwer.

Rizzolatti, G., L. Fadiga, V. Gallese & L. Fogassi 1996. "Premotor Cortex and the Recognition of Motor Actions", *Cognitive Brain Research* 3, 131–41.

Roche, M. 1973. *Phenomenology, Language and the Social Sciences*. London: Routledge & Kegan Paul.

Rothfield, P. 2005. "Attending to Difference, Phenomenology and Bioethics". In *Ethics of the Body: Postconventional Challenges*, M. Shildrick & R. Mykitiuk (eds), 29–48. Cambridge, MA: MIT Press.

Roy, J. M., J. Petitot, B. Pachoud & F. Varela 2000. "Beyond the Gap: An Intro-duction to Naturalizing Phenomenology". In *Naturalizing Phenomenology: Issues in Contemporary Phenomenology and Cognitive Science*, J. Petitot *et al.* (eds), 1–80. Stanford, CA: Stanford University Press.

Russon, J. 2003. *Human Experience: Philosophy, Neurosis, and the Elements of Everyday Life*. Albany, NY: SUNY Press.

Ryle, G. 1949. *The Concept of Mind*. New York: Barnes & Noble.

Sacks, O. 1985. *The Man Who Mistook His Wife for a Hat*. London: Pan.

Sartre, J.-P. 1971. *The Emotions: Outline of a Theory*, B. Frechtman (trans.). New York: Philosophical Library.

Sartre, J.-P. 1976. *No Exit and Three Other Plays*, S. Gilbert (trans.). New York: Vintage.

Sartre, J.-P. 1993 [1943]. *Being and Nothingness, An Essay in Phenomenological Ontology*, H. Barnes (trans.). London: Routledge.

Scheler, M. 1973. *Formalism in Ethics and Non-Formal Ethics of Values*, M. S. Frings & R. L. Funk (trans.). Evanston, IL: Northwestern University Press.

Schmidt, J. 1985. *Maurice Merleau-Ponty: Between Phenomenology and Struc-turalism*. London: Macmillan.

Schrift, A. 2001. "Judith Butler: Une Nouvelle Existentialiste?" *Philosophy Today* 12, 12–23.

Schütz, A. 1973. *The Structures of the Life-World (Strukturen der Lebenswelt)*, by Alfred Schütz & Thomas Luckmann, R. M. Zaner & H. T. Engelhardt Jr (trans.). Evanston, IL: Northwestern University Press.

Shildrick, M. 2004. "Queering Performativity: Disability after Deleuze", *SCAN: Journal of Media Arts* 1(3), n. p.

Silverman, H. J. 1994. *Textualities: Between Hermeneutics and Deconstruction*. London: Routledge.

Silverman, H. J. 1997. *Inscriptions: After Phenomenology and Structuralism*. Evanston, IL: Northwestern University Press.

Simons, M. A. 1999. *Beauvoir and* The Second Sex: *Feminism, Race, and the Origins of Existentialism*. Lanham, MD: Rowman & Littlefield.

Smart, B. 1976. *Sociology, Phenomenology and Marxian Analysis*. London: Routledge & Kegan Paul.

Sobchack, V. 2005. "Choreography for One, Two and Three Legs (A Phenom-enological Meditation in Movements)", *Topoi* 24(1), 55–66.

Spurling, H. 2003. *The Girl from the Fiction Department: A Portrait of Sonia Orwell*. Harmondsworth: Penguin.

Spurling, L. 1977. *Phenomenology and the Social World*. London: Routledge & Kegan Paul.

Stawarska, B. 2006. "From the Body Proper to Flesh: Merleau-Ponty on Intersubjectivity". In *Feminist Interpretations of Maurice Merleau-Ponty*, D. Olkowski & G. Weiss (eds), 91–106. University Park, PA: Pennsylvania State University Press.

Stewart, J. (ed.) 1998. *The Debate between Sartre and Merleau-Ponty*. Evanston, IL: Northwestern University Press.

Stoller, S. 2000. "Reflections on Feminist Merleau-Ponty Skepticism", *Hypatia: A Journal of Feminist Philosophy* 15(1), 175–82.

Stratton, G. 1896. "Some Preliminary Experiments on Vision Without the Inversion of the Retinal Image", *Psychological Review* 3, 611–17.

Stratton, G. 1897. "Vision without Inversion of the Retinal Image", *Psychological Review* **4**, 341–60, 463–81.

Sullivan, S. 1997. "Domination and Dialogue in Merleau-Ponty's *Phenomenology of Perception*", *Hypatia: A Journal of Feminist Philosophy* **12**(1), 1–19.

Taylor, C. 2005. "Merleau-Ponty and the Epistemological Picture". In *Cambridge Companion to Merleau-Ponty*, T. Carman & M. Hansen (eds), 26–49. Cambridge: Cambridge University Press.

Thomas, S. P. 2005. "Through the Lens of Merleau-Ponty: Advancing the Phenomenological Approach to Nursing Research", *Nursing Philosophy* **6**(1), 63–76.

Thompson, E. (ed.) 2001. *Between Ourselves: Second-person Issues in the Study of Consciousness*. Charlottesville, VA: Imprint Academic.

Toadvine, T. 2002. "Merleau-Ponty's Reading of Husserl: A Chronological Overview". In *Merleau-Ponty's Reading of Husserl*, T. Toadvine & L. Embree (eds), 227–86. Dordrecht: Kluwer.

Toombs, K. 1992. *The Meaning of Illness: A Phenomenological Account of the Different Perspectives of Physician and Patient*. Dordrecht: Kluwer.

Toombs, K. 1999. "What Does It Mean to Be Somebody? Phenomenological Reflections and Ethical Quandaries". In *Persons and Their Bodies, Rights, Responsibilities and Relationships*, M. J. Cherry (ed.), 73–94. Dordrecht: Kluwer.

Varela, F. 1996. "Neurophenomenology", *Journal of Consciousness Studies* **3**, 330–50.

Varela, F., E. Thompson & E. Rosch 1991. *The Embodied Mind*. Cambridge, MA: MIT Press.

Vasseleu, C. 1998. *Textures of Light: Vision and Touch in Irigaray, Levinas, and Merleau-Ponty*. London: Routledge.

von Uexküll, J. 1909. *Umwelt und Innerwelt der Tiere* [The Environment and the Inner World of Animals]. Berlin: Springer.

von Uexküll, J. 1932. *Streifzuege durch die Umwelten von Tieren und Menschen: Ein Bilderbuch unsichtbarer Welten* [Wanderings through the Environs of Animals and Humans: A Picturebook of Invisible Worlds]. Berlin: Springer.

von Uexküll, J. 1957. "A Stroll through the Worlds of Animals and Men: A Picture Book of Invisible Worlds". In *Instinctive Behavior: The Development of a Modern Concept*, Claire H. Schiller (ed. and trans.), 5–80. New York: International Universities Press.

von Uexküll, T. (ed.) 1992. "Special Issue: Jakob von Uexküll's 'A stroll through the worlds of animals and men'", *Semiotica* **89**(4), 279–391.

Waldenfels, B. 1981. "Perception and Structure in Merleau-Ponty". In *Merleau-Ponty: Perception, Structure, Language*, J. Sallis (ed.), 21–38. Atlantic Highlands, NJ: Humanities Press.

Waldenfals, B. 2000. "The Paradox of Expression". In *Chiasms: Merleau-Ponty's Notion of Flesh*, F. Evans & L. Lawlor (eds), 89–102. Albany, NY: SUNY Press.

Weate, J. 2001. "Fanon, Merleau-Ponty and the Difference of Phenomenology". In *Race*, R. Bernasconi (ed.), 169–83. Oxford: Blackwell.

Weber, M. 1978. *Economy and Society*. Berkeley, CA: University of California Press.

Weiss, G. 1995. "Ambiguity, Absurdity, and Reversibility: Responses to Indeterminacy", *Journal of the British Society of Phenomenology* **26**(1), 43–51.

Weiss, G. 1999. *Body Images: Embodiment as Intercorporeality*. New York: Routledge.

Weiss, G. 2002. "The Anonymous Intentions of Transactional Bodies", *Hypatia: A Journal of Feminist Philosophy* 17(4), 187–200.

Whiteside, K. 1988. *Merleau-Ponty and the Foundation of an Existential Politics*. Princeton, NJ: Princeton University Press.

Willis, J. 1999. "Dying in Country, Implications of Culture in the Delivery of Palliative Care in Indigenous Australian Communities", *Anthropology and Medicine* 6(3), 423–35.

Young, I. M. 2005. *On Female Body Experience: "Throwing Like a Girl" and Other Essays*. Oxford: Oxford University Press.

Zahavi, D. 1996. "Husserl's Intersubjective Transformation of Transcendental Philosophy", *Journal of the British Society of Phenomenology* 27(3), 228–45.

Zaner, R. 1988. *Ethics and the Clinical Encounter*. Englewood Cliffs, NJ: Prentice Hall.

Index